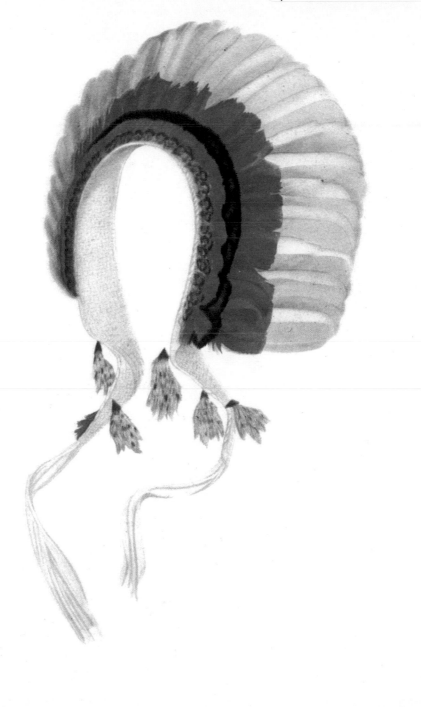

ICR STUDIES: 2

General Editor: Theodore L. Stoddard

INDIANS OF BRAZIL

IN THE

TWENTIETH CENTURY

INDIANS OF BRAZIL

IN THE

TWENTIETH CENTURY

Contributions by Gertrude Dole, Dale W. Kietzman, Darcy Ribeiro, Eduardo Galvão, and Herbert Baldus

Edited and Translated by Janice H. Hopper

Published by the Institute for Cross-Cultural Research

4000 Albemarle Street, N.W., Washington, D.C. 20016

Also published by the Institute for Cross-Cultural Research:
ICR Studies: 1, *Religion and Politics in Haiti.* (1966)

Library of Congress Catalog Card Number: 67-14551

Manufactured in the United States of America by
The Goetz Company, Washington, D.C.

This publication should be cited as *Indians of Brazil in the Twentieth Century,*
ICR Studies 2, Washington, D.C.: Institute for Cross-Cultural Research, 1967.

FOREWORD

Many societies throughout the world are being decimated by rapid and sometimes catastrophic change—war, disease, migration, and acculturation. To the extent that these processes are a matter of humanitarian concern, they may be modified or controlled by policies and actions that are developed on the basis of relevant, practical research. On the other hand, wide-ranging, basic ethnographic research must be undertaken before the data disappears. For both humanitarian and scientific reasons, therefore, the need for careful studies of rapidly changing and threatened cultures is urgent.

One of the most critical areas in the world is the Amazon basin. Brazil encompasses the major part of this area, and the Institute hopes the publication of this book will promote an increasing awareness of the critical problems to be studied there.

A large measure of basic linguistic research in Brazil is being undertaken by the staff of the Summer Institute of Linguistics. It is a pleasure to acknowledge the cooperation of SIL, and particularly the work of its field director in Rio de Janeiro, Dr. Dale W. Kietzman. His efforts speak for themselves in the first paper.

Although Dr. Kietzman's contribution might have been published separately, it seemed desirable to complement his paper with related studies from the Brazilian literature which were not available in English. Dr. Janice H. Hopper selected, translated, and edited these contributions. For a discussion of the problems she encountered and the guidelines she used, the reader is directed to her preface.

The preparation of this volume has benefited from the critical advice of several scholars, including Charles Wagley, Emilio Willems, Berta Ribeiro, and Gertrude Dole. Wolf Jesco von Puttkamer and William H. Crocker have permitted us to reproduce a number of their photographs. Drs. Darcy and Berta Ribeiro have consented to have several color illustrations reproduced from their handsome book on the feather art of the Kaapor Indians.

The Institute is also indebted to Harcourt, Brace & World, Inc., publishers of Alfred Kroeber's *Anthropology,* for permission to reproduce the map on page 171 ; and to the Human Relations Area Files Press and Professor George P. Murdock for permission to reproduce the map on page 178 .

This book was produced under the editorial supervision of Georgia Rhoades with the assistance of Winifred Wuterich, Angelika Jackson, and Valerie Auserehl.

The Institute for Cross-Cultural Research is an independent, nonprofit, educational organization committed to the support and publication of descriptive and theoretical studies of human problems in the developing world. The Institute welcomes suggestions for studies and publications which will promote international understanding of these problems.

Theodore L. Stoddard
Director
January 1967

THE AUTHORS

GERTRUDE E. DOLE is presently Visiting Assistant Professor at Vassar College. She brings to her teaching a background of field work in archaeology and ethnography and continuing specialization in Brazilian ethnology.

Dr. Dole completed all requirements including thesis for her doctorate at the University of Michigan in February 1957. As an undergraduate and graduate student she was the recipient of several scholarships and fellowships. The most relevant of these for the present volume is the Henry L. and Grace Doherty Foundation fellowship for field work in Brazil among the Kuikuru Indians of Mato Grosso in 1953-54. During this same year (in May 1954) she also surveyed the ethnographic collections of Tropical Forest Indians in the Museu Nacional of Rio de Janeiro. More recently (1960-61) she has made an ethnographic study of the Amahuaca Indians of eastern Peru.

Successively held appointments as a Lecturer in Anthropology at the New School for Social Research (summer 1958); Columbia University (1958-60; 1961-62); and New York University (1961-64) preceded Dr. Dole's present assignment. During 1964-65 she served New York University as an Adjunct Assistant Professor.

In collaboration with Robert Carneiro, Dole edited *Essays in the Science of Culture in Honor of Leslie A. White* (1960). She has published a number of articles in professional journals; the following suggest the range of her interest in and knowledge of the Kuikuru culture: "A Mechanism for Mobilizing Labor among the Kuikuru of Central Brazil" (1958); "Ownership and Exchange among the Kuikuru Indians of Mato Grosso" (1959); "La Cultura de los Indios Kuikuru del Brasil Central" (1959); "Techniques of Preparing Manioc Flour as a Key to Culture History in Tropical America" (1960); "Shamanism and Political Control among the Kuikuru" (1964); "A Preliminary Consideration of the Prehistory of the Upper Xingu Basin" (1964); "Anarchy without Chaos: Alternatives to Political Authority among the Kuikuru" (in press).

DALE W. KIETZMAN is Director of the Extension Department of the Wycliffe Bible Translators, Incorporated, and its affiliate, the Summer Institute of Linguistics. In preparing the original paper around which this volume was planned, Kietzman drew heavily upon his field experience as the initiator of the Summer Institute of Linguistics' work in Brazil.

Kietzman's life with the Summer Institute of Linguistics began in July 1946, after he had taken his B.A. at Wheaton College. His educational background includes two summers at the Summer Institute of Linguistics, University of Oklahoma (1946 and 1951), a Master of Arts degree in Anthropology from Northwestern University (1952), and graduate work in Latin American Studies at Stanford University as an NDEA fellow (1961-1962).

Kietzman's field experience started with his orientation assignment with the Summer Institute of Linguistics in Mexico (October 1946 to April 1947). His next assignment (1947-1951) took him among the Amahuaca Indians of Peru as a Bible translator. Administrative experience in Mexico (1952-1953), Chicago (1953-1956), and Brazil (1956-1961 and 1963-1966) overlapped with summer teaching at the Summer Institute of Linguistics (1952-1956).

Until June of 1966, Kietzman served the Summer Institute as Director of the Brazil field. His work and contacts have contributed information on the Indian tribes of Brazil that is as current as possible in a fluid and complex situation.

DARCY RIBEIRO is currently Professor of Anthropology of the Faculty of the Humanities, University of Montevideo. He also directs a seminar on university structure sponsored by the Comissão de Cultura da Universidad de República Oriental do Uruguai. These activities represent continuing devotion to two of the major interests of his professional life—socio-cultural studies and educational planning. His books and articles reflect a third major interest: the past, present, and future of the Indians of contemporary Brazil.

A 1946 graduate of the University of São Paulo, Brazil, Ribeiro received his degree in sociology and politics with a specialization in anthropology. Field research among the Indians of Central Brazil and the Amazon area occupied the first ten years of his professional life. Toward the end of this period (1953) he organized the Museu do Índio; at the close of the decade (1956) he was appointed to the anthropology faculty of the University of São Paulo.

Demonstrated concern with educational planning led to Ribeiro's nomination in 1957 as Director of Social Research of the Ministry of Education. Here he planned and carried out a broad program of socio-cultural research on regional variations in Brazilian society and their implications for educational policymaking. Beginning in 1958, he participated actively with other scholars in the campaign for legislative reform of Brazilian education. A substantial contributor to the planning for Brazil's first modern university, the University of Brasilia, Ribeiro became its first Rector in 1961. His tenure in that post was interrupted in 1962 when he was named Minister of Education and Culture of the Goulart government; he returned briefly to the rectorship in 1963.

As Minister of Education and Culture, Ribeiro established the first five year plan for the eradication of illiteracy, the restructuring and democratization of middle level education, and the establishment of a base for university reform. He served the Goulart government as head of the Casa Civil of the Presidency of the Republic until March 31, 1964.

A Política Indigenista Brasileira (1962) and *Arte Plumária dos Índios Kaapor* [with Berta G. Ribeiro] (1957) are among Ribeiro's contributions to the literature of Brazilian ethnology. A general study of Brazil and the Americas and a study of the process of Indian assimilation are in preparation.

EDUARDO GALVÃO is Director of the Division of Anthropology of the Museu Paraense Emílio Goeldi in Belém, Pará. A Columbia University Ph.D. (1952), Galvão is known to United States scholars for his field work among the Tenetehara Indians of Brazil in collaboration with Charles Wagley. Grants from the Institute of International Education, the Viking Fund (now the Wenner-Gren Foundation), the Department of Anthropology of Columbia University, and the National Research Council supported his graduate study. He maintains a rigorous field work schedule, publishing in Portuguese and more rarely in German or English.

Galvão was one of the student members of the Museu Nacional staff who accompanied Wagley on his first field trip among the Tenetehara (November 1941 - March 1942). Later (February-May 1946) Galvão, Nelson Teixeira, who also had been on the first trip, and a physical anthropologist, Pedro Lima, returned to the Tenetehara to check earlier observations and obtain additional data. Then, as now, Galvão's focus was on processes of change. The Wagley-Galvão monograph, *The Tenetehara Indians of Brazil: A Culture in Transition,* has been brought out in English (1949) and in Portuguese (1955).

Active involvement in museum work, field research, and education has characterized Galvão's career. From 1939 to 1947 he was on the Museu Nacional staff, initially as an unsalaried student. Having completed his graduate work at Columbia University, he returned to the Museu Nacional under contract (1950-1952). From 1925 to 1955 he was Chief of the Section of Orientation and Assistance of the Serviço de Proteção dos Índios of the Ministry of Agriculture. In 1955 he became acting director of the Division of Anthropology of the Museu Emílio Goeldi. Appointed Director of the Division in 1961, he has occupied this post without interruption except during the brief existence of the University of Brasilia. Galvão's appointment to the faculty of the University of Brasilia, which terminated in the spring of 1964, was a continuation of his consistent participation in the training of anthropologists. There is rarely a year in which Galvão's program does not include lecturing, educational consulting, and from one to six months of field work.

Galvão's thesis, *The Religion of an Amazon Community— A Study in Culture Change* (1952), brought out in Portuguese under the title *Santos e Visagems: um estudo da vida religiosa de Ita, Amazonas* (1955), was the first published study of the processes in the formation and integration of religion in *caboclo* culture. Galvão is a frequent contributor to anthropological journals.

HERBERT BALDUS, Director of the Museu Paulista, São Paulo, Editor of the *Revista do Museu Paulista,* and Honorary Fellow of the Royal Anthropological Institute of Great Britain and Ireland, needs no introduction among ethnographers, His colleagues on both sides of the Atlantic recently presented him with a commemorative volume, *Beiträge zur Völkerkunde Südamerikas, Festgabe für Herbert Baldus zum 65,* honoring him on his sixty-fifth birthday. His active career embraces teaching, field work, publishing, editing, and museum administration and organization.

Baldus was born in Wiesbaden, Germany, in 1899; he became a naturalized Brazilian citizen in 1941. He has a doctorate in philosophy from the University of Berlin, where he studied ethnology with Richard Thurnwald and American ethnology with K. Th. Preuss and Walter Lehmann. During his teaching career he has held the chair of Brazilian Ethnology of the School of Sociology and Politics of São Paulo and the chair of General and Brazilian Ethnography of the Faculty of Philosophy, Sciences, and Letters of Rio Claro.

In 1946 Baldus was asked by the Government of the State of São Paulo to organize the ethnographic collections of the Museu Paulista. A year later he was named Chief of the Ethnology Section of the museum; later he became its Director. Since 1947 he also has edited its journal, the *Revista do Museu Paulista*.

During field trips in 1923, 1927, 1928, 1933, 1934, 1946, 1947, and 1952, Baldus has studied the Indians of Paraguay and of the Brazilian States of São Paulo, Paraná, Rio Grande do Sul, Mato Grosso, Goiás, and Pará. Since 1927 he has published numerous articles in professional journals and in collective volumes in the Americas and in Europe. Among his books are the following: *Indianerstudien im nordöstlichen Chaco* (1931); *Ensaios de Etnologia Brasileira* (1937); *Dicionário de Etnologia e Sociologia* (1939) [in collaboration with Emílio Willems]; *Bibliografia Crítica da Etnologia Brasileira* (1954); and *Die Jaguarzwillinge* (1958).

CONTENTS

MAPS

LISTS

TABLES

ILLUSTRATIONS

Photographs 1-22   Courtesy of Wolf Jesco, Foto Jesco, Caixa Postal 567, Brasilia, D.F., Brasil.

Photographs 23-29   Canela Indians, Courtesy of William H. Crocker, Smithsonian Institution.

The color illustrations have been reproduced through the courtesy of Darcy and Berta G. Ribeiro from their book ARTE PLUMARIA DOS INDIOS KAAPOR, published in Rio de Janeiro in 1957. The objects are a headdress (endpapers), lip ornaments (pp. xxx and 76), a necklace (p. 166), and hair ornaments (p. 206), made by the Urubús-Kaapor.

The line drawings have been derived from a variety of sources and are not intended to represent a specific culture area.

PREFACE

by Gertrude E. Dole

Vassar College

This volume presents a classification of Brazilian Indians according to culture areas. The concept of culture area was introduced one hundred years ago by Adolph Bastian, then curator of the Royal Ethnographic Museum of Berlin, to facilitate the cataloging of cultural materials. Later the human geographer Ratzel adopted the concept to describe the cultures of the world (Boas 1930:105). Ratzel assigned all of the aboriginal cultures of Brazil to a single area, the Südost Indianer (Ratzel 1885-88). Meanwhile Boas, who had assisted Bastian in Berlin, brought the concept of culture area to the United States and taught it to his students. By 1896 O.T. Mason had divided the cultures of Brazil into three areas: the Andean Atlantic Slope, Mato Grosso and Central Brazil, and East Brazil (Mason 1896).

Since the turn of the century at least 15 different classifications of Brazilian Indians have appeared, but for many years the classifications remained very crude and little advance was made in analyzing differences within the three large areas outlined by Mason. With the accumulation of ethnographic accounts, however, many regional differences became apparent, and the maps that showed only one, two, or three divisions were no longer adequate. The first to stress these regional differences was David Stout, who outlined a number of enclaves in each of two major areas (Stout 1937).

As Stout himself acknowledged, his divisions are not strictly culture areas; rather they are culture *types* which occupy only parts of the major geographic areas outlined. This arrangement was an attempt to solve a problem which continues to plague students of culture areas today; that is, the lack of complete correspondence between culture type and geographic area. As used by some ethnologists the culture area concept "defines the coincidence in trait complex distribution" (Wissler 1923:58); it is used by others to "describe the typical common characteristics of culturally related tribes" (Boas 1930:105). Hence the concept is primarily a tool for classifying and describing cultural phenomena; the correspondence of a "trait complex" or "common characteristics" with a geographic area, although implied, is regarded as secondary to cultural homogeneity as a criterion. Actually the correspondence of a single geographic area with a single culture type is an ideal arrangement that is attained only after contiguous interacting societies have remained undisturbed over a long period. In fact it frequently happens that very different cultures are found as enclaves in a geographic area; and conversely some peoples who have cultures of the same type are widely separated. For these reasons a map of culture areas cannot be a completely accurate representation of both culture types and areas at the same time.

The lack of correlation between culture type and area requires a compromise between the use of geographic and cultural criteria in classifying data. Scholars who have mapped the culture areas of Brazil have tended to make the compromise in one of two ways: some have represented the boundaries as generalized or indeterminate; others have resorted to the use of enclaves, which represent cultural distributions more accurately. Stout's device of outlining enclaves was retained in the maps of both Cooper (1942) and Steward (1946-59, vol. 3:884, vol. 5:670).

Although the occurrence of cultural differences in a geographic area is troublesome to those engaged in classification, these very differences may ultimately be the most valuable aspect of the culture area concept, because they call our attention to problems to be solved. Some of the problems that arise from cultural differences in geographic areas in Brazil are the presence in the refuge area of the Upper Xingú of peoples representing four different language families almost surrounded by Gé speakers; the existence of hunters such as the primitive Xetá among Guaraní cultivators; and the movement of a Kajabí group (and more recently some of the Northern Kaiapó) away from their congeners and into the Upper Xingú area.

The culture area concept has been used primarily in the study of synchronic problems, such as the functional correlation of traits in a culture area. But the distribution of traits and even culture types does not remain static. Cultures change by evolving, and Indian groups are constantly being acculturated by one another or by the national culture. Moreover, whole societies have moved from one area to another under the pressure of advancing groups. Hence the picture of regularities is continually being disturbed by the development of new traits, migration, diffusion, or the loss of traits. Drastic changes occurred in Brazil between the 15th and 20th centuries. Some of the greatest of these might be mentioned here: large and dense Indian populations that had the most advanced cultures in the Brazilian territory disappeared completely from the shores of the Amazon; the size of Arawak-speaking populations in the extreme northwestern region was greatly reduced, and their cultures declined from a high (Circumcaribbean) level of complexity to the Tropical Forest level; people with a similar culture along the lower Tapajós disappeared and were replaced by people with a culture of the Tropical Forest level; many of the peoples with Tropical Forest cultures on the eastern coast disappeared, some of them migrating inland; and various other peoples on the coast and in the eastern highlands who had cultures of a less advanced Tropical Forest type have either disappeared entirely or have migrated westward, some of them apparently losing Tropical Forest traits so that modern ethnologists have regarded their cultures as "marginal." I am convinced that with some modification the culture area concept can be used to throw light on the nature and causes of these changes.

Admittedly very little can be learned about change from a single map of the distribution of culture types. For this purpose we need to know the distribution of peoples and culture types at successive periods. All the area schemes that have preceded the one presented in this volume have utilized information dating back to 1500 together with data of the 20th century. As Galvão points out, these classifications give static composite pictures that represent no particular period. Galvão's suggestion that classifications should now be drawn up to represent culture areas at various periods seems to me to be a very important one. The first step in that direction has been taken by the authors of the present volume in limiting their surveys to the data of this century. Perhaps three other historic periods should be represented: the 16th century period of discovery and colonization of the east coast; the 17th and 18th century period of colonization of the interior; and the 19th century up to the rubber boom.

A compilation of several maps for successive periods might reveal cultural continuities similar to the co-traditions of archeological data. It is clear from historical accounts, however, that in some parts of Brazil cultures have been displaced to such an extent that complete breaks occur in the local cultural traditions. Hence a system of co-traditions alone might not be adequate to represent cultural distributions in all areas. But a series of maps of the culture areas, together with information about the peoples and cultures in each area, would indicate how complete the breaks were. They also would indicate which groups had migrated, which had been acculturated, and perhaps even where evolution or major adjustments to the environment had taken place.

Galvão has hinted that it might be productive to map cultural distributions for precolumbian periods also. It would be very interesting to investigate, for example, the evidence for a tradition that developed from a hunting to a pottery-making horticultural level in eastern Brazil in the area now occupied by the Kaiapó. To show precolumbian distributions, of course, archeological data are needed. Until recently there have not been sufficient data on the prehistory of Amazonia to indicate much about either distributions or changes in cultures. But evidence is mounting to indicate, for example, that potters such as the historic Tupian peoples had arrived only recently in the east and south of Brazil; that ceramic traditions of a type similar to that of historic Tupians had existed on the northwestern tributaries of the Amazon; that the movement of peoples along the Amazon was extensive; and that several peoples with different ceramic traditions had entered the Upper Xingú area in recent centuries.

A particular kind of culture change is the evolution of more complex cultures from simpler ones, as for instance the evolution of the horticultural type from hunting. In this connection, a problem that is currently of great concern to South Americanists is the need for reassessing the evolutionary position of cultures that have been referred to as Marginal, and the possibility that historic changes have occurred in the culture type of some of the Marginal peoples. To study development and to determine the significance of "Marginals" to the development of Tropical Forest Culture, the areal distribution of culture types alone is not sufficient. We need also the concept of level, or degree of cultural complexity, which is implicit in most schemes of culture areas in Brazil.

The distinction between the Marginal as a hunting type and the Tropical Forest as a horticultural type is actually a distinction in cultural level which stems from Ratzel's classification of cultures. Ratzel had observed that the cultures of many peoples he found in marginal regions of land masses were simpler ("more backward") than those of the cultivators. Cooper and Steward took over the term Marginal to refer to the hunting culture type. When data were being compiled for the *Handbook of South American Indians* (Steward 1946-59), it was still commonly believed that many peoples in Brazil lacked horticulture aboriginally. For this reason both Cooper and Steward classed them as Marginals, extending the term to apply to simple cultures not only in marginal areas of land but also in the tropical forest, where they are currently referred to as "Internal Marginals." [1]

But it has by no means been clearly established that the "Marginals" in Brazil were all merely hunters. In fact it has become increasingly apparent in the past few years, both from a review of the earliest data available and from recent investigation of some of the "Marginals" living today, that many of them, including the Gé speakers of eastern Brazil, did have cultivated plants aboriginally. Moreover their cultures bear significant similarities to the Tropical Forest type and differ fundamentally from that of Marginal hunters and gatherers such as the Fuegians of southern South America. It is important to determine how many of these peoples had cultivated food plants aboriginally, and why some of them abandoned cultivation. It would be of interest also to establish how many actually had borrowed their cultivated plants and other Tropical Forest traits from their neighbors, as is so often alleged.

Of course, the fact that some peoples cultivated food plants does not mean that they had a typical Tropical Forest culture, which according to Steward is more advanced in a number of material traits, including a "developed" horticulture (1946-59, vol. 3:883). To accommodate such cultivators as the Eastern Timbira and Kaiapó, Galvão has suggested the introduction of an intermediate class between Steward's Tropical Forest and Marginal Types. The addition of this class would facilitate the study of such questions as the distribution of native horticulture in the tropical forest and the functional relation of horticulture to the widely different types of social organization that are found among Brazilian Indians.

To facilitate the study of development and related changes I would suggest that Galvão's proposed intermediate class (perhaps "Incipient Cultivators") be recognized as a relatively primitive subtype of Tropical Forest culture, thereby placing the cultivation practiced by Gé speakers, for example, in an evolutionary position between hunting and "developed" horticulture. Having made explicit the developmental status of this relatively primitive horticultural type, we would then be in a position to inquire into the effects of depopulation due to warfare, migration, and disease in historic times, in lowering the level of complexity of either subsistence technology or social organization. This approach would help considerably in explaining such anomalies as the existence of some large groups such as the Bororo who have a relatively stable and complex social organization but who now live largely by hunting, while others such as the Kuikuru have a "developed" type of horticulture but a simple, relatively unstructured cognatic kinship organization and little political control.

The authors of the present volume are the first to present estimates of population size and information on the degree of contact with civilization, information that will be indispensable to students of socio-cultural change in Brazil.[2] In Ribeiro's valuable essay on the processes and results of acculturation and assimilation he has shown that extensive depopulation and loss of native cultures occurred in the first half of this century, in spite of the protective influence of the Indian Service. Another of his most important contributions is his discussion of the *different types* of contact effected by different types of acculturative agents, with resulting differences in rates of extinction of native cultures.

Ribeiro has been intensely interested in the fate of the indigenous people. He concerns himself with the attitudes of the people in contact, their experience, reduction in their numbers, their social condition, and how they can be protected from exploitation and misery. But he also is interested in them from a cultural point of view, and makes some valuable suggestions for future research. One of these concerns the acculturation that occurs in areas of intertribal contact, in which shared traits are derived not from civilization but from different native cultures. This interesting phenomenon had been noted by Galvão (1953) among the peoples of the Upper Xingú region, where tribes of four different language groups have been acculturating one another.

This type of acculturation is important to the understanding of the development of culture areas. It often has been asserted that the occurrence of a single culture type in a geographic area is brought about by diffusion from a "primary center," or "culture climax." But the cultural homogeneity of the Upper Xingú, the Rio Negro-Vaupés area, and others pointed out by both Ribeiro and Galvão, cannot be traced to a primary center or culture climax. Rather, it is the result of mutual borrowing of traits among the various societies with different cultures that have been brought together by expansion or migration. We can assume that such a leveling of cultural differences had been at work among peoples of the tropical forest long before the coming of Europeans and that it is one of the principal factors responsible for areas of relatively homogeneous culture.

Galvão's extensive research in acculturation has led him to stress its importance in changing the ethnographic map of Brazil, and the necessity of distinguishing between the arrangements of culture types at different periods. Using data from his own investigations, he has shown that along the Rio Negro, where there once were only native cultures, there now is a continuum of change as the native cultures proceed through the *caboclo,* or rural Brazilian folk culture, into urban civilization (Galvão 1959). Taking account of such changes, he gives us a very different picture of the culture areas from that of any of his predecessors. His is the first map to represent the complete absence of Indian cultures along the Amazon and in a vast region of the eastern highlands. These are regions in which aboriginal populations have been either exterminated or assimilated into the national society.

Another feature of Galvão's classification represents cultural relations within areas. His subdivision of culture areas into subareas, which to some extent follows Steward's scheme, outlines major areas of cultural similarity and then identifies regional units that differ in minor respects within the major areas. This device expresses relative degrees of cultural similarity. Thus the inclusion of the Bororo as a subarea of the Tocantíns-Xingú area expresses the fundamental similarities of Bororo culture to those of other Gé speakers who occupy much of central Brazil, without implying the complete homogeneity of cultures over this extensive region.

Using Galvão's classification, Kietzman has outlined both the areas and subareas somewhat more precisely. He also locates and describes a considerable number of additional groups not mentioned by either Galvão or Ribeiro, and goes beyond these two in giving more complete information than was available to either of the former on population size, linguistic affiliation, and conditions of contact. His data and areal maps provide a basis for comparison with Greenberg's linguistic classification of South American languages (Greenberg 1960). Such a comparison should yield valuable results for those who are interested in the culture history of Brazil.

Ribeiro's listing, as he himself insists, is exploratory, based on the incomplete data available to him in 1957. He urged that more research be done and has personally encouraged investigations by the Summer Institute of Linguistics and other missions; the Brazilian Indian Service has facilitated their work among the Indians. Kietzman's survey is a welcome result of this international cooperation among scholars. The added precision of his survey has been made possible by the availability of extensive and detailed information collected in the past few years by missionary-linguists, ethnographers, and agents of the Indian Service. A comparison of Ribeiro's data for population size, degree of contact, and location with Kietzman's, compiled 10 years later, provides the most reliable information available for a study of demographic changes, movements of people, and changes in the distribution of cultures over the past decade.

But the information is not complete even yet. In Brazil, perhaps more than in any other part of the world, there remain relatively unknown groups with native cultures still to be investigated. Moreover, some groups are in the process of changing their geographic location or their cultural affiliation, and thereby disturbing the boundaries of culture areas. Kietzman's use of broken lines to express the uncertain and overlapping boundaries of these groups is a helpful innovation.

Much of the information in this publication is oriented toward facilitating contact with Indians by field workers. All the authors give information on location, population size, degree of contact, and linguistic affiliation of indigenous groups. How many ethnographers have combed the literature to find just such information when selecting a group to study! The information about the location of potentially hostile groups should be of special interest to field workers, whether they be ethnographers, missionaries, or Indian Agents.

The usefulness of this publication is by no means limited to field workers, however. The precise information on locations, areal boundaries, and linguistic affiliations, as well as the data on population size and conditions of acculturation—all this information is more adequate than any that has been available previously. It provides ethnologists with a basis for more scientifically valid studies of cultural change among Brazilian Indians.

It is to be hoped either that this volume may someday be expanded to include all the aboriginal peoples of South America, or that similar surveys of other areas will be published while there are still Indian cultures to be studied.

FOOTNOTES

1. It should be noted that through this modified usage the term has come to mean simple cultures *wherever* they are found, and not merely those in marginal geographic regions.

2. See also the exhaustive and richly illustrated catalog of tribes published in 1962 by the Brazilian Indian Service (Malcher 1964).

REFERENCES

BOAS, Franz

1930   "Anthropology." *Encyclopaedia of the Social Sciences* 2, 73-110.

COOPER, John M.

1942   "Areal and Temporal Aspects of Aboriginal South American Culture." *Primitive Man* 15, 1-38.

GALVÃO, Eduardo

1953   "Cultura e Sistema de Parentesco das Tribos do Alto Rio Xingú." *Boletim do Museu Nacional*, Nova Série. Antropologia 14. Rio de Janeiro.

1959   "Acculturação Indígena no Rio Negro." *Boletim do Museu Paraense Emílio Goeldi* 7. Belém.

MALCHER, José M. Gama

1964   *Índios.* Rio de Janeiro: Ministerio da Agricultura.

MASON, O. T.

1896   *Influences of Environment upon Human Industries or Arts.* Smithsonian Institution, Annual Report for 1894-5. Washington, D. C. 639-665.

RATZEL, Friedrich

1885-88 *Völkerkunde.* 3 Vols. Leipsig and Wien: [publisher unknown].

STEWARD, Julian H., Ed.

1946-59 *Handbook of South American Indians.* 7 Vols. (Bureau of American Ethnology, Bulletin 143). Washington, D. C.: U.S. Government Printing Office.

STOUT, David B.

1937   "Culture Types and Culture Areas in South America." *Michigan Academy of Science, Arts and Letters, Papers* 23, 73-86.

WISSLER, Clark

1923   *Man and Culture.* New York: Thomas Y. Crowell Company.

INDIANS AND CULTURE AREAS
OF
TWENTIETH CENTURY BRAZIL

by Dale W. Kietzman

Summer Institute of Linguistics

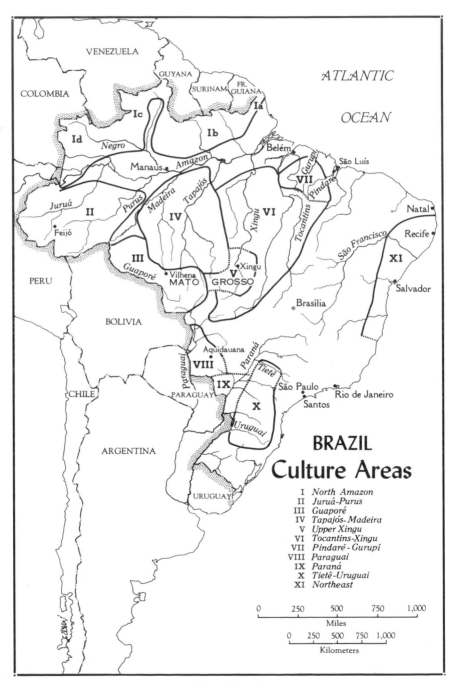

BRAZIL
Culture Areas

    I   *North Amazon*
   II   *Juruá-Purus*
  III   *Guaporé*
   IV   *Tapajós-Madeira*
    V   *Upper Xingu*
   VI   *Tocantins-Xingu*
  VII   *Pindaré - Gurupí*
 VIII   *Paraguai*
   IX   *Paraná*
    X   *Tietê-Uruguai*
   XI   *Northeast*

0   250   500   750   1,000
                Miles
0   250   500   750 1,000
              Kilometers

Map No. 1

INDIANS AND CULTURE AREAS OF TWENTIETH CENTURY BRAZIL

by *Dale W. Kietzman*

INTRODUCTION

The following catalog of Brazilian Indian tribes known to exist at the present time was organized in this form for the Institute for Cross-Cultural Research. Most survey attempts have included data from older sources without accurately distinguishing the time layers involved. Such lists are more comprehensive for certain research purposes, but they are confusing for the investigator hoping to begin current field study.

The initial organization of our data collection followed the model established by Ribeiro (1957). To his basic data was added all reliable information on existing tribes coming to our attention. The primary source of this updated information has been our colleagues of the Summer Institute of Linguistics, who are now carrying on linguistic field research in 36 tribes in Brazil under an agreement with the National Museum of Rio de Janeiro. In addition, we have had excellent rapport with other sources, including government Indian agents, the National Council for the Protection of Indians, anthropologists, and missionaries.

A satisfactory comparative linguistic classification of Brazilian languages is still to be devised. For many tribes no linguistic information is available. Suggested linguistic affinities are given even when more accurate data are lacking; they are based either on past consensus, on scattered words that may have been recorded, or on the opinion of neighboring Indian tribes. There is no attempt, therefore, to apply a definitive linguistic label in any case.

By the same token no new culture area scheme is offered here. The basic outline is that suggested by Galvão (1960). In placing all existing tribes into his system, some modifications, and possibly unwarranted violence, may have ensued.

We have attempted to follow the convention of the Brazilian Anthropological Association in the use and spelling of tribal names. Where small groups have coalesced and are known by a single name to neighboring Brazilians, that name has been used. This departs from the usual practice of using the self-designation of the tribe.

A listing of this sort has many imperfections. The tribal situation in Brazil is extremely fluid. The value of this catalog is for those now doing field work, and as a somewhat fuzzy snapshot of this moment in Indian time.

Dale W. Kietzman
Extension Director
Summer Institute of Linguistics
Santa Ana, California

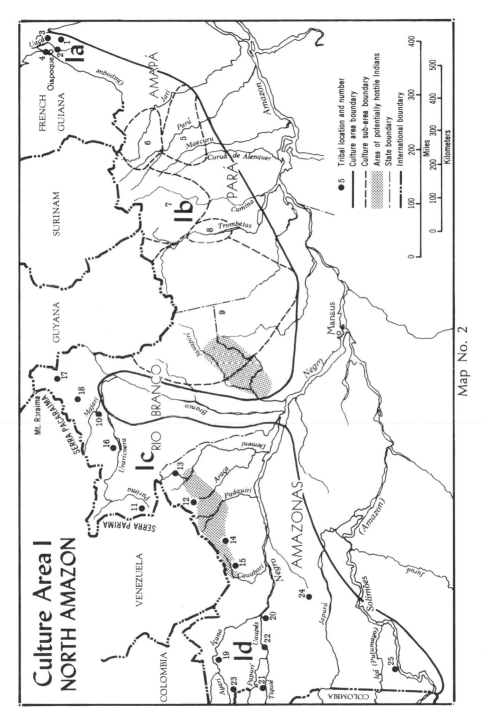

Map No. 2

CULTURE AREA I: NORTH AMAZON

This culture area includes all Indian areas in Brazil north of the mainstream of the Amazon. For convenience it will be described in a series of sub-areas. But the entire area has been characterized by a large degree of intertribal acculturation; as a result there is a certain cultural homogeneity. The size of Indian settlements is uniformly small. A village of more than 60 to 80 persons is exceptional. The Indians retain a high degree of mobility. These factors, combined with a general lack of information on the area, make description difficult.

Brazilian penetration is greatest in Amapá, at the eastern end of the area, and along the Rio Negro—Rio Branco system. Elsewhere permanent population centers are scarce, and Indian groups above the fall line are relatively undisturbed. With the exception of some groups in northern Pará in the region of the Jauaperí River, and in the area north of the Rio Negro from the Demeni to the Cauaborí River, all groups receive outsiders on a friendly basis.

The information on the Rio Branco and Savannah areas is based primarily on a private communication dated May 18, 1966, from W. Neill Hawkins of Unevangelized Fields Mission.

a. Amapá

The Amapá Territory has been an area of intense acculturation. Most Indian groups have long since disappeared from the scene. Four distinct groups can be described. All four are highly acculturated, retaining only a fraction of the aboriginal culture; and all are bilingual, if indeed they retain any of their native language.

1. *Palikúr*. An Aruak tribe of 450 Indians in Brazil, and a reported 200 in French Guiana. The Brazilian section is divided into two villages located on the Urucauá River, a tributary of the Uaçá, reached through the town of Oiapoque.

2. *Karipúna*. A group of 400 reputedly Tupi Indians who now speak only Creole and Portuguese. They are located in a single village group on the Caripi River, tributary of the Uaçá, where they are aided by the SPI Pôsto Luiz Horta. [SPI: Serviço de Proteçáo aos Índios.—Ed.]

3. *Galibí-Marwôrno*. Between 500 and 600 on the Rio Uaçá, who use the name Galibí, but have forgotten the language. The Indians are aided by the SPI.

4. *Galibí*. A village of 62 Indians speaking this Karib language is located on the Brazilian side of the Oiapoque River. The group has come over to Brazil within the past decade. There are reports of a general southward movement of the 2,000 or more Indians of this tribe still living in French Guiana. The Indians are well integrated into local society. Many of them speak French, Portuguese, and Creole, as well as Galibí, but they nonetheless maintain tribal identity and discipline.

b. North Pará

The sub-area includes not only all of the State of Pará, but also the eastern portion of Amazonas and Roraima (Rio Branco) to the mainstream of the Rio Branco. All Indian groups are located north of the fall line, and are relatively isolated. The area is best known by Protásio Frikel (1958) who has provided a summary of the tribal situation. Frikel estimates a total population of 7,000 Indians in the area; at the same time he names a total of 144 tribal groups; the language of the overwhelming majority either belongs to the Karib family or is unclassified.

This atomization of tribal groups is characteristic of the culture area. In addition, the local groups are so small that the area defies precise description. The map drawn by Ed Koehn of the Summer Institute of Linguistics locates 100 Apalaí Indians along a limited section of the Parú River. The ten dwelling locations are not always occupied at the same time because the Indians move freely from place to place. Frikel's figures and the map well illustrate the situation.

Frikel suggests that the Karib groups can be divided into five dialect areas:

5. *Apalaí* (Aparaí). A total of 200-300 Indians living north of the equator along the Parú de Leste, Jari, Maecuru and Curuá de Alenquer Rivers. Some sections of the tribe still have not made contact.

6. *Urukuyána*. With the *Wayana* group, a total of 300-400 Indians located on the headwaters of the Jari, Parú de Leste, Itani, and Paruma Rivers.

7. *Pianokotó-Tiriyó*. A score of closely related dialect groups, the majority in peaceful contact; a total of 1,200 Indians. They are located on the upper and eastern tributaries of the Trombetas River, and extend into Surinam.

8. *Waríkyana* or *Arikiéna*. A cluster of 10 dialect groups, totaling about 300 Indians, close to the central Trombetas River.

9. *Parukotó-Charúma*. The largest group of dialects, encompassing 1,500 individuals all located to the west of the Trombetas River, their territory including some of the tributaries of that river, and extending into the State of Amazonas. The *Hixkaryána* tribe, on which linguistic studies have begun to appear, is a member of this group. The dialect area extends northward into Guyana (formerly British Guiana) and the Territory of Roraima (Rio Branco) where it is represented by the *Waiwai* tribe.

c. Rio Branco

An area of forest and savannahs north of the Rio Negro, including the area to the west of the Rio Branco to the Cauabori River. To date there has been little systematic exploration, and there are no reliable ethnological reports from this area. Estimates place the population at 4,000: the northern Waiká groups, located along the upper reaches of the Uraricoera River and spilling over into Venezuela, are the most numerous. The Indians appear to be seminomadic, with relatively little agriculture.

10. *Xirianá*. This name is used as a self-designation by perhaps 250 Indians, living on the Mucajaí River, at the Cachoeira dos Índios,

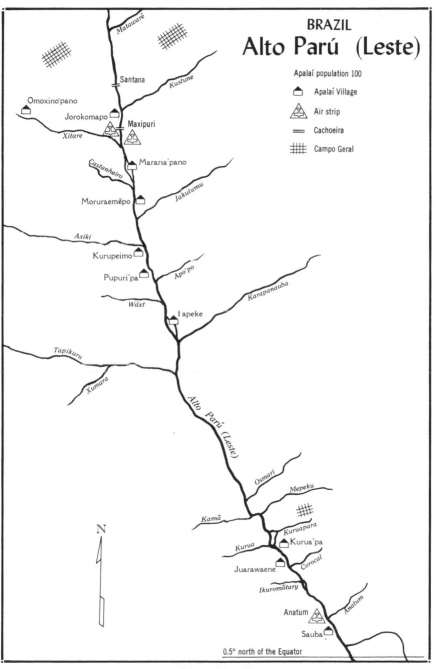

BRAZIL
Alto Parú (Leste)

Apalaí population 100

⌂ Apalaí Village

△ Air strip

= Cachoeira

▦ Campo Geral

Matawarè

Santana

Kustune

Omoxino'pano

Jorokomapo

Maxipuri

Xitare

Mararia'pano

Castanheiro

Moruraemēpo

Jakulumu

Axiki

Kurupeimo

Pupuri'pa

Apo'po

Wäxt

Karapanauba

Iapeke

Tapikuru

Xumara

Alto Parú (Leste)

Osmari

Mepeku

Kamā

Kuruapara

Kurua

Kurua'pa

Juarawaene

Corocal

Ikuromōtary

Anatum

Anatum

Sauba

N

0.5° north of the Equator

Map No. 3

along the Uraricaá River, in the region of the R. Ericó, and along the upper R. Paragua in Venezuela. The name Xiriana is used in reference to other Indians, their close neighbors, by Indians in the headwaters of the Tootobi and the Auaris.

11. *Waiká*. This term is used as a self-designation by two small groups, one on the Uraricoera at about 63° 10′ W longitude, and one in the upper basin of the R. Ajarami. The latter group shows more divergence from the other Xirianan languages than any of the other languages studied. All Xirianan groups west of 63 degrees refer to themselves collectively as *yanomam* "people," or some dialectical variant of this term, although almost all use local designations for each village. Speech is at least 90% mutually intelligible among most of the groups living between 63 and 64 degrees west longitude, all the way from the Uraricoera on the north to the Tootobi on the south.

An important sub-group in this Central Waiká language area is the *Parahúri*, living along the Parima River, from about 03° 00′ N to about 03° 45′ N. There is little divergence from Central Waiká language, but ten or more villages refer to themselves as Parahúri.

12. *Pakidái*. Several local groups of Xiriana speech, found on the Demeni, Araça, and Padauiri Rivers.

13. *Aiwatéri*. A Xiriana group on the Mapulau and Tootobi Rivers, tributaries of the Demeni.

14. *Guaharíbo*. This term is used extensively, but not by Xirianans, as far as can be determined. The name probably refers to Indians called *Xamatari* not by themselves but by other Xirianans, but living in the Serra Parima between 02° 30′ N and 03° 30′ N, and across into Venezuela. Their language diverges considerably from Central Waiká, the divergence increasing as one travels west. Some travelers have applied the name Guaharíbo to Indians of a different language in the Xirianan group, living along the entire length of the Auaris and the Araça Rivers, and probably north and south into Venezuela. Don Borgman of the Unevangelized Fields Mission, who works with the latter, calls the language *Sanymá* which is a dialectical variant of the term *yanomam* given above.

15. *Mandawáka*. A supposedly Aruak group on the upper Cauabori River. Other groups are also occasionally reported in the area and identified, without presentation of either linguistic or cultural data, as Aruak.

16. *Mayongóng*. This term is used exclusively in Brazil to refer to the

only village of the comparatively large Maquiritáre tribe (Karib) existing at present in Brazil. There are about 80 persons in this village,
located on the upper Auaris.

d. Savannah

An area of savannahs to the east of the Rio Branco system extending
into Guyana, occupied by two major groups.

17. *Taulipáng* and *Makuxí*. The Taulipáng are a Karib tribe estimated
to exceed 1,000 population, with many villages on the mountain sides
approaching Roraima and Pacaraima. This tribe is closely related to
the *Makuxí*, which number somewhere between 3,000 and 5,000 and
live in villages scattered throughout the savannah and mountainous
region 03° 00′ N to 04° 45′ N in Brazil, and stretching into Guyana,
through the savannahs and southern Pacaraima Mountains as far east
as the Rupununi River.

18. *Wapitxâna*. An Aruak tribe located in many villages, with an estimated population of some 4,000, with perhaps 200 or 300 in Brazil
in the savannahs east of Boa Vista, and one small group on the Majari
River, the remainder living in the southern savannah of Guyana.

e. Rio Negro

The core of the sub-area is represented by the Indian groups found
along the Içana and Uaupés Rivers. Two main groups are present:
the Baníwa and the Tukána. There has been a great deal of intertribal
acculturation among the tribes or local groups of these two ethnic
divisions. In addition, these people have held in subjection and largely
assimilated many of the bands of Makú Indians thought to be the
original inhabitants of the area. There has been a great deal of commercial movement along the main waterways of the area, although
there are not many permanent Brazilian settlements. There has been
intense missionary activity both on the Brazilian side and among the
same groups in Colombia. Here, as among the Karib groups to the
west, villages are small and mobility is the rule. The total population
is estimated at 3,500 but it is difficult to assign specific populations
to villages and sub-tribes.

19. *Baníwa*. The principal tribe on the Içana River. The speakers of
this Aruak language can be divided into two groups, the *Káru* on the
lower Içana, and the *Karupáka* on the upper.

20. *Tariána*. A tribe on the lower Uaupés that originally spoke a

Baníwa language, but that now for the most part has adopted the Tukána tongue. The population, including a vassal group which maintains its social identity, although not a distinct language, is above 500.

21. *Tukána*. A series of small groups, including the *Pokangá* and *Tuyúca*, living on the Tiquié and Papurí Rivers. Tukána has generally been classified in a distinct language family grouping.

22. *Wanâna*. A second Tukána language group, found along the Uaupés River below the mouth of the Tiquié. The *Waikíno* and *Desâna* tribes are included within this dialect grouping.

23. *Kobéwa*. Several small local groups, sometimes referred to as clans, living between the Uaupés and the headwaters of the Ayari, a tributary of the Içana. There is reason to believe that these groups may have been Baníwa that were acculturated both culturally and linguistically to the Tukána.

24. *Makú*. Also referred to as Makunabödö. The Indians are scattered in local bands of not more than a score of individuals in the vast jungle and lake area between the Uaupés and the Japurá Rivers. Some groups probably have been absorbed by the larger tribes to the north. Present identifiable population is probably less than 300. Some groups in the area of the Waiká Indians have also been referred to as Makú, but there is no linguistic evidence to confirm a relationship.

f. Putumayo

25. *Tukúna* (Ticúna). An exceptionally large tribe located between the lower courses of the Solimões (Amazon) and the Içá (Putumayo) Rivers, including sections of Peru, Colombia, and Brazil. Official SPI figures place the population in Brazil at not over 1,500, but Summer Institute of Linguistics personnel who have traveled extensively in the tribal area suggest a total population which may reach above 10,000, approximately half of which is in Brazil. The section of the tribe located in Peru is much more acculturated and is experiencing economic progress. There is intertribal movement across the international frontier. The SPI maintains Pôsto Ticunas at Santa Rita (25). The linguistic affiliation of Tukúna has not yet been determined.

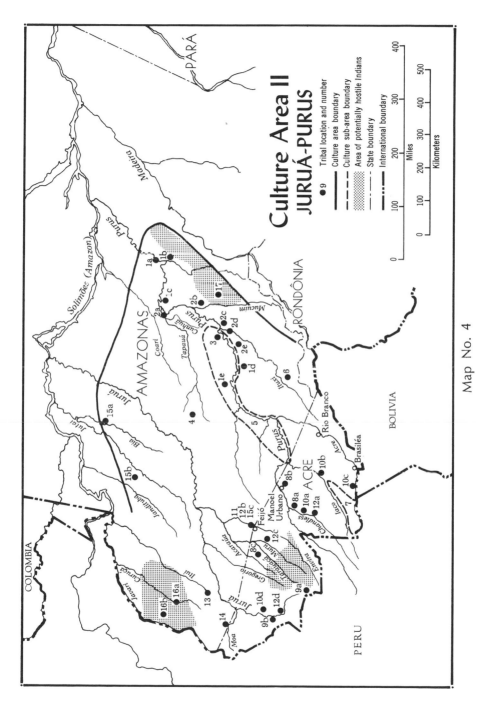

Culture Area II
JURUÁ-PURUS

● 9   Tribal location and number
──── Culture area boundary
─·─·─ Culture sub-area boundary
░░░░ Area of potentially hostile Indians
─·─·─ State boundary
─··─ International boundary

Map No. 4

CULTURE AREA II: JURUÁ-PURUS

The area includes the valleys of all rivers flowing into the Amazon from the south, from the Purus River to the Javari, which divides Brazil from Peru. This was the area most affected by the rubber boom at the end of the last century and the beginning of this one. Consequently the tribes that survived the period of the rubber boom are badly fragmented and scattered. Villages are small and quite frequently one section of a tribe is not aware of the continuing existence of other sections of the tribe. Two major linguistic groups are represented, the Aruak (tribes 1 to 9) and the Pano (tribes 10 to 14). There also are a few unrelated tribes. Tribes located along the mainstreams are generally well integrated into the local economy, while those on headwaters are often very isolated and even out of contact with Brazilians.

1. *Apurinã*. An Aruak tribe, quite acculturated, but perpetuating some religious beliefs that often result in acts of hostility toward surrounding communities. Five local groups with a total population of 230 have been contacted, all near the shores of the middle Purus (a-e).

2. *Paumarí.* An Aruak tribe distinguished by its adaptation to a roving life along the rivers. Families often live on raft houses, although permanent village sites are also maintained. Five principal locations have been identified, with a combined population of about 250 (a-e).

3. *Jaruára.* An Aruak tribe totaling about 120 Indians, located in two closely linked villages. All tribal members are involved in service to local *patrões.* The language represents a dialect of Jamamadí (below).

4. *Daní.* An Aruak tribe occupying a cluster of four villages on the headwaters of the Tapauá-Cunhuã River. The population of this relatively isolated group can not be less than 320.

5. *Jamamadí.* The largest Aruak tribe in this area, numbering about 450. To date 10 locations have been found, all on the west side of the Purus River but stretching from the southern tributaries of the Tapauá to the mouth of the Iaco River. The tribe is divided into several local dialects, or possibly clans, each calling itself by a different name. This has caused considerable confusion in older reports concerning these Indians.

6. *Kaxararí.* Perhaps 50 persons of this Aruak tribe are working for a rubber collector on the headwaters of the Ituxi River, at the mouth of the Remansinho.

7. *Manitenéri.* This is the same as the Peruvian *Piro* tribe. These Aruak Indians are scattered in very small groups in an area of open forests between the upper Iaco and Acre Rivers; most of the 150 individuals reported are located well back from the main rivers.

8. *Kulína.* A total of 350 individuals of this Aruak tribe have been counted in five villages, three on the Chandless River (a), and two others at Manoel Urbano on the Purus (b) and on the Acarauá River well to the west (c). There appears to be considerable movement to and from other locations in the direction of Peru, which would seem to involve a larger population than now reported.

9. *Kámpa.* A tribe of about 115 members at two locations on the headwaters of the Juruá River. They appear to be related in culture and language to the Aruak *Campa* tribe of Peru, and may represent a section of that tribe that was displaced during the rubber boom.

10. *Jamináwa.* The most widely scattered of the Brazilian Pano tribes with the 220 individuals distributed in 11 small villages in four principal areas: along the lower Chandless River (a), along the lower Iaco River (b), along the Acre River just above the town of Brasiléa (c), and on the River Juruá where there is an isolated group of 20 on a

rubber plantation (d). All sections of the tribe are in permanent contact with local Brazilian communities.

11. *Tamanáua.* A small group of Panoan Indians using this name, but locally called Kanamarí, is located just outside of Feijó. The latter name could link this group with a reportedly larger group of Panoan Indians said to live on the middle Gregorio River, and called locally either Katukína or Kanamarí.

12. *Kaxináua.* Just over 100 of these Panoan Indians were identified at four different points (a-d) across the Acre, with the largest group on the Muru River (c).

13. *Marûbo.* The most isolated of the Panoan tribes in contact with civilization, it has also maintained the largest population group, over 400 individuals, in a single location. Within a limited area on the headwaters of the Itui River there are some five or six closely knit village groups which recognize village and tribal leaders.

14. *Poyanáwa.* About 50 survivors of this Panoan tribe, which numbered above 500 when contacted in 1908, live on a rubber plantation on the upper Moa River. A number of Panoan tribes have been reported by other sources, and our own reports show unidentified Indian groups on the headwaters of Envira, Muru, Tarauacá, and Gregorio Rivers. Various names are given locally for these Indians, but no linguistic data is available as a basis for identification. In addition, such known Panoan tribes as the Amahuáka and Kapanáwa, occasionally reported in this area, may represent only incursions of these tribes from across the Peruvian border.

15. *Katukína.* The tribe is located in three widely scattered villages, one on the Rio Bia (a) with 100 Indians, a second on the Jandituba with 25 (b), and the third at Feijó (c), with approximately 150. The language has not yet been classified.

16. *Máya.* Two villages have been identified in aerial surveys, one on the Rio Curuçá (a), and the second on the Javari (b). The size of the villages would indicate a population of several hundred. The warlike nature of this tribe has induced the withdrawal of all Brazilians from the area. In earlier peaceful contacts this tribe was sometimes identified as being identical with the Mayoruna reported in Peru and identified there, on other than linguistic grounds, as Panoan.

17. *Júma.* A local group of 12 adults has been contacted on the tributaries of the Mucuim River. The full extent of the tribe is not known. Since it has been the object of extermination raids mounted by local rubber workers the population cannot be great. Preliminary data indicate that this group speaks a Tupi language.

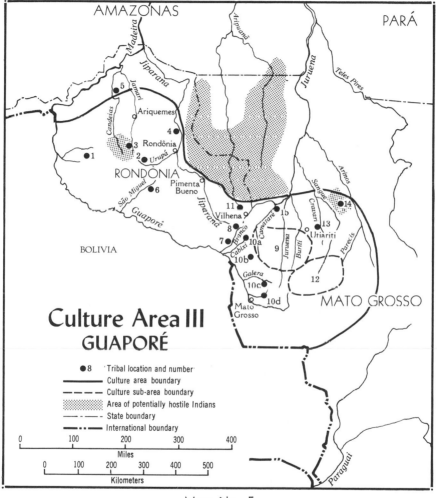

Culture Area III
GUAPORÉ

● 8   ·Tribal location and number·
─────   Culture area boundary
─ ─ ─   Culture sub-area boundary
▓▓▓▓   Area of potentially hostile Indians
─·─·─   State boundary
─··─··─ International boundary

Map No. 5

CULTURE AREA III: GUAPORÉ

Since the beginning of the century the area between the Guaporé and Jiparaná Rivers has been thoroughly penetrated by bands in search of rubber. Although even today the permanent Brazilian population is very small, the tribal picture has been seriously disrupted. An estimated 70% of the tribes has become extinct during the past half century. Dense jungle cover along the rivers gives way to scrub growth on the uplands. The tribal groups living in this area apparently were always relatively small, and intertribal relationships were characterized by hostility.

1. *Pakaas Novas.* A Txapakura tribe pacified only about 10 years ago. The population has been considerably reduced since that time, and now probably totals approximately 300.

2. *Urupá.* A second Txapakura tribe with a much longer history of contact. The main group, numbering possibly 150 Indians, is scattered along the upper Rio Urupá; a few have been transferred to the Rio Jamari by the SPI.

3. *Karipúna.* A reputedly Pano tribe still roams the area between the upper Candeias River and the Ig. [*Igarapé*] Santa Cruz, near the town of Ariquemes. If the name given is correct, portions of this tribe were settled on SPI posts in the past, but have since become extinct. The size of the surviving group is unknown.

4. *Arara.* Indians referred to by this name are located on the Jiparaná, at the mouth of the Agua Azul River. Some are now working near the town of Rondônia. The same name is applied to uncontacted groups across the Jiparaná to the east, but there is no evidence that they represent the same tribe. Total Arara in contact with Brazilians: about 40.

5. *Karitiâna.* There are 45 Indians of a reputed Tupi tribe now living on the lower Candeias River, and working for Brazilians in the area.

6. *Puruborá.* Another reputedly Tupi tribe living in the headwaters of the São Miguel River. The tribe, numbering under 100, is in permanent contact with an SPI sub-post.

7. *Tuparí.* Fewer than 50 Indians of a reputedly Tupi tribe are located in the dense jungles of the right bank of the lower Rio Branco.

8. *Arikapú* or *Maxukí.* About 50 Indians on the headwaters of the Rio Branco, near Vilhena, and in continuous contact. The language family is uncertain.

9. *Nambikuára.* Between 200 and 250 survivors of this formerly strong nation roam a territory between the Camararé and Buriti Rivers, and to the south of the towns of Utiariti and Nambikuára. Five local groups are known, but each occupies several village sites during various seasons, and there is considerable visiting between local groups.

10. A series of Nambikuára-related groups are found west of highway BR29, and occasionally appear along the Guaporé River.

Penetration into this area is possible only at three points; therefore precise information is still lacking. Four groups can be distinguished, but these may prove to be minor subdivisions of a single tribe. There are three villages of *Mamaindé* (a) Indians within 14 miles of the highway, in the watershed of the Cabixi River. Indians called *Manairisú* (b) by the Nambikuára are located about 30 miles to the south, but have not been contacted by investigators. Several villages along the Galera River are occupied by Indians called *Galera* (c); their language is known to be very similar to Nambikuára. There are 90 Indians living on the Sararé River, who are referred to variously as

Sararé or *Kabixí* (d). During the dry season they often appear along the Guaporé River below the town of Vila Bela (Mato Grosso). The *Sararé* or *Kabixí* may be simply a part of the Galera group. The total population is unknown; it may total 1,000 for the four groups we have mentioned.

11. *Sabones.* A few scattered remnants of this Nambikuára-related tribe are to be found in Vilhena, at the SPI Pôsto Espiro, and working at a rubber post northwest of Vilhena called Marco Rondon. There is a total of perhaps 30 individuals.

12. *Paresí.* A known population of 230 Indians live in 15 or more locations within 50 miles north and south of highway BR29, between the town of Parecis and the crossing of the Juruena River. While this Aruak tribe maintains normal commercial relations with local Brazilians, it nevertheless conserves much of its native language and culture.

13. *Irántxe.* An Aruak tribe sometimes called a subgroup of the Paresí by virtue of similarities in culture although the two groups are quite different linguistically. About 45 survivors still live outside of Utiariti, in the direction of the Cravari River.

14. *Beiço de Pau.* An uncontacted tribe of unknown linguistic affiliation, living between the Arinos and Sangue Rivers. They have resisted recent attempts at contact.

15. *Cinta Larga.* An uncontacted group with a very warlike reputation, reported in most of the area east of the Jiparaná, from Vilhena northward to the level of Pimenta Bueno. One large village of possibly 100 inhabitants, located at the junction of the Camararé, Iquê, and 12 de Outubro Rivers has been sighted from the air. A short vocabulary obtained from an Indian girl said to come from this area suggests a Tupi relationship.

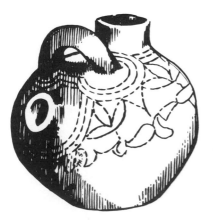

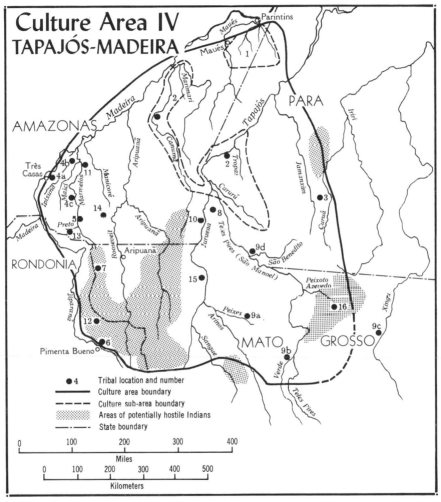

Map No. 6

CULTURE AREA IV: TAPAJÓS-MADEIRA

This is an area of forest interrupted by grasslands, comprising the valley of the Tapajós and the territory between the valley and the Madeira River. The area has been heavily infiltrated by Brazilians in search of rubber and gold. Indians along the north and west sides of the territory are acculturated and in continuous contact with Brazilians. Indians along the south and southeast edges continue to be relatively isolated from contact, although only one or two groups have been left completely untouched.

The bulk of the groups in this area are reputedly Tupi tribes. Many of these (4-9) are presumed to be remnants of the historic Kawahib tribe located by Curt Nimuendajú in the area around the confluence of the Teles Pires and Juruena Rivers. But this is a group which was dislocated by the expansion of the Mundurukú, the most aggressive tribe of the Middle Amazon in the 18th century. The unrelated languages found along the southern fringe of the area may represent an older layer of occupation, predating the arrival of the Tupi tribes.

1. *Mawé*. Also called *Sataré* in some areas of the tribe. Heavily acculturated and influenced by both Catholic and Adventist missionary activity, the tribe is located in at least 11 different village or river clusters between 56° 15′ W and 57° 35′ W and 2° 45′ S and 3° 55′ S. The known villages are on the Rio Andirá, the Maraú, Mirití, Maués-Açu, Mariaquá, Gurumatuba, Mamurú, Uaicurapá and Aryã Rivers, in the lake and paraná system just south of the Amazon, between the supply towns of Parintins and Maués. The population is probably in excess of 2,000, although the largest village, located on the Rio Mirití, has only 100 people. On the Rio Andirá, for instance, apart from the two villages, a total of 300 Indians scattered along both banks has been counted.

2. *Mundurukú*. The center of this probably Tupi tribe is now located between the Tropas and Cururú Rivers, immediately to the east of the Tapajós. A Franciscan mission and a post of the SPI are located on the Cururú River, and serve the 450 Indians living along the river and, to a much lesser extent, the approximately 700 Indians living on the grasslands between the two rivers. These groups still use their native language almost exclusively. Of the various Mundurukú groups that pushed out from this center in all directions during the last 200 years, only one significant group has survived, the 240 Mundurukú on the Canumã River, extending from its mouth to the headwaters. An additional 100 Indians are to be found over on the Marimari River. Most of the native language and culture has been lost.

3. *Kuruáya*. An isolated group reported to be similar to the Mundurukú or to the Kayapó. The grasslands Mundurukú refer to the group as being located between the Jamanxim and Curuá Rivers; traders report an uncontacted group along the banks of the Curuá.

4. *Parintintín*. Possibly originally the largest Kawahib subgroup, the tribe is now reduced to a maximum of 150 members. There are three villages, one near Três Casas on the Madeira River (4a), a second on the Ipixuna River (4b), and a third on the Rio Nove de Janeiro (4c) about six days travel up the Marmelos River.

5. *Tenharím* or *Bôca Preta*. A tribe of 70 Indians speaking a Tupi-Kawahib dialect almost identical with the Parintintín, located on the Marmelos River at 8° 5′ S latitude. The tribe also has fields on the Rio Preto a bit farther south.

6. A cluster of several small Kawahib tribes along the Jiparaná River, representing the southernmost penetration of this group. There are

about 50 Indians each of the *Paranawát, Wiraféd,* and *Tukunaféd* tribes, somewhat intermixed and living along the small tributaries Riosinho, Leitão, Muqui, and Cacoal. They are in permanent contact with Brazilians, and generally are employed on ranches and rubber camps in the area. The groups can be reached through the town of Pimenta Bueno.

7. Tupi-Kawahib groups called the *Itogapúk* and *Bôca Negra* are located in the relatively isolated area between the Jiparaná and Roosevelt Rivers and in the extreme headwaters of the Marmelos. These groups are undoubtedly roaming in the area, so that the population may not be in excess of 100, even though they have been contacted or maintained villages for a time at rather scattered points.

8. *Tapayúna.* An isolated group said to be Tupi-Kawahib, located in the delta area at the junction of the Tapajós and Teles Pires Rivers. They have been reported as far south along the Juruena River as the mouth of the Sangue.

9. *Kayabí.* A rather large tribe, probably numbering in excess of 1,000, sometimes classified as Kawahib, but probably not as closely related to groups 4—8 as they are to each other. A series of four villages are located on the Rio dos Peixes (9a), from 25 to 90 miles from the mouth. A group, possibly decimated in recent years, is located near the former site of an SPI post near the mouth of the Rio Verde (9b). Some of these Indians have migrated to village sites in the Xingu valley, also mentioned under Culture Area V (9c). Many Kayabí are said to be living on the São Benedito River, and just below its junction with the São Manoel (9d). Although they seem to occupy a large territory, the groups of Kayabí contacted total only between 500-600. The Xingu group is very acculturated; those on the Rio dos Peixes are quite peaceful, but seldom contacted; the other groups still are somewhat hostile in contact situations.

10. *Apiaká.* The last definitely Tupi tribe to be listed in this area. The tribe was once reported to be extinct, but several families have been encountered on the middle Tapajós (10a); living among the Mundurukú along a limited stretch of the Canumã River (10b); and reportedly along the lower Juruena (10c). All individuals seem to be quite assimilated. Mundurukú or Portuguese is generally spoken in preference to their own language.

11. *Mura-Pirahã.* A group of about 150 Indians speaking a very unusual tonal language seemingly unrelated to any other thus far encountered. The main group of about 80 Indians is scattered along

the Marmelos and Maici Rivers, relatively close to the junction. Other smaller groups are found on the Manicoré and Capanã Rivers to the northeast of the principal location.

12. *Suruí* and *Gavião*. Between two and three hundred Indians living on the right bank of the Jiparaná, between the Lourdes and the Riachuelo, call themselves Gavião. They claim that the Suruí, who roam the area eastward to the Roosevelt, and also northward toward Aripuanã, speak the same language, although there is little contact between the two groups.

13. *Morerébi* and *Diarrói*. Two groups on which no linguistic information is available, living on the Rio Preto, upper tributary of the Marmelos. Each tribe is reported to number less than 100. There is very infrequent travel into the area occupied by these tribes.

14. *Orelha de Pau* or *Numbiaí*. A peaceful group of 50 Indians living in the high country between the Marmelos and the Aripuanã Rivers. No linguistic information is available.

15. *Aripaktsá*. A tribe speaking a language as yet unclassified. The only contact is at a point on the Juruena River about 120 miles downriver from the mouth of the Arinos, which is the only trade route into the area. At most, there are about 100 Indians now living on the Juruena. But the existence of villages inland to the west has been confirmed by the reports of Indians and of occasional hunting parties from the interior. The center of the tribe probably lies along the high ground between the Juruena and the Aripuanã.

16. *Ipewí*. The existence of this group is confirmed by the Kayabí, and villages have been sighted from the air along the upper course of the Peixoto Azevedo River. The Tupi name is given to the tribe by the Kayabí, and therefore is not useful in making a guess at classification.

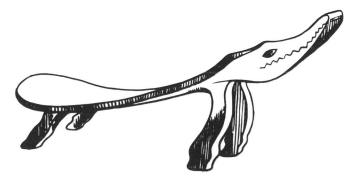

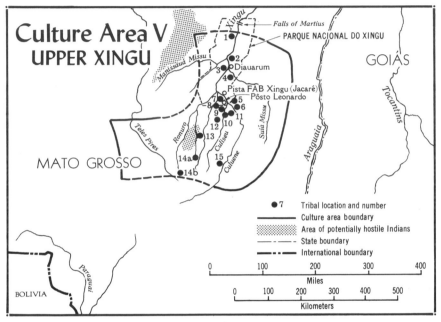

Map No. 7

CULTURE AREA V: UPPER XINGU

Geographically the region is defined as the headwaters of the Xingu River above the Falls of Martius. It is an area of gallery forests and lakes, with extensive grasslands on the high ground between rivers. The area is notable for the fact that Indians of widely differing linguistic backgrounds have adopted a quite homogeneous cultural pattern and have become interdependent through trade and an annual cycle of games and other social interchanges. The majority of the Upper Xingu Valley is now under federal control as the Parque Nacional do Xingu, to which the protection of flora and fauna has been entrusted, along with the supervision of contact with the Indian groups and the provision of social and medical assistance for them. Park headquarters are at Pôsto Leonardo (D), with a continuously manned subpost at Diauarum (A). The SPI also maintains Pôsto Vasconcellos. In addition, the Brazilian air force has an emergency strip, with a small permanent crew, at Pista FAB Xingu (B), also called Jacaré on some maps. At each of these locations there usually can be found a collection of Indians from various tribes, present on a semi-permanent basis, but belonging to one or another of the tribes listed below. Entrance into the Park is dependent upon authorization by Park officials.

1. *Txukahamẽi.* A branch of the Kayapó nation centered to the north, on the middle course of the Xingu, but mentioned here since this group, which entered the Park area about five years ago, is definitely attempting to be integrated into the intertribal patterns of the Park. There are about 200 Indians in a single village.

2. *Jurúna.* A Tupi tribe located six hours downstream by outboard from Diauarum. The population of 60 individuals is scattered on both banks of the river.

3. *Kayabí.* Another group that has only recently—i.e., within the past twenty years—moved into the Xingu area, coming from the west, where the bulk of the tribe remains. The tribe is also mentioned, therefore, under Culture Area IV. About 120 members of this Tupi-Kawahib group live in four closely clustered villages near Diauarum.

4. *Suyá.* About 70 Indians of a Jê tribe, somewhat different linguistically from the Kayapó groups, live in a single village about two hours upstream by outboard from Diauarum. The tribe, once reputed to be very fierce, has been pacified to the point of apparently losing the "will to live," undoubtedly in consequence of the extremely rapid reduction in population it has experienced during the past ten years.

5. *Matipuhy* and *Nahukuá.* Two Karib tribes originally located a bit further south of the present village. Because the population of both groups has declined, they now have combined forces in a single village. The total population of the tribe is just over 50.

6. *Kalapálo.* Another Karib tribe that now has just under 50 survivors. They also recently have moved to a point closer to the administrative center of the Park for greater protection and assistance.

7. *Kamayurá.* A single village of 110 Indians speaking a Tupi language, located on the shores of Lake Ipavu, about two hours walking distance from Pôsto Leonardo.

8. *Waurá.* A single village of about 70 Indians of an Aruak tribe located on the Batovi River 15 minutes by air from Pôsto Leonardo.

9. *Yawalapití.* An Aruak tribe of 22 Indians in a small village about a 10 minute walk from Pôsto Leonardo.

10. *Mehináku.* Another Aruak group that has moved closer to the administrative center of the Park in recent years. In 1962 this tribe had a population of 68 individuals.

11. *Kuikúro.* A Karib tribe of over 100 individuals which within the last three years has moved into the National Park from a point farther south.

12. *Awéti.* A village of 26 Indians of a Tupi tribe.

13. *Txikão.* A tribe which has resisted all efforts at contact during the past several decades. During 1964 Park officials made contact with a group which appeared to speak a Karib language. There are possibly two villages with a total of not more than 100 individuals.

14. *Bakairí.* A Karib tribe, quite thoroughly assimilated to the local Brazilian culture, but still retaining the native language. There are three villages, each with an SPI post. Pôsto Simões Lopes has a population of about 120 Bakairí (14b). Pôsto Rio Nôvo, on the same Indian reserve but several hours distant on horseback, aids the 50 Indians of Tuiuiu village. The third village of about 60 Indians is located on the Pôsto Batovi (14a), which was created to attract the Xavánte tribe; the Bakairí families were moved there as workers on the new post.

15. *Agavotokuéng.* A tribe known to the Indians of the Park, but not yet seen by Park officials. It is said to be "like" the Yawalapití. Based on similar but less definite reports of the Indians, Park officials believe a tribe called the Uaiarú exists to the east of the Agavotokuéng, and that two unknown and possibly differentiated tribes live to the northwest of the Park.

Trumái. A tribe of undetermined linguistic affiliation, definitely a member of this same Upper Xingu culture area, but with fewer than 20 survivors and no village. The survivors are to be found living with the Suyá (4) and at the Pista FAB Xingu (B); individuals are occasionally encountered at other points.

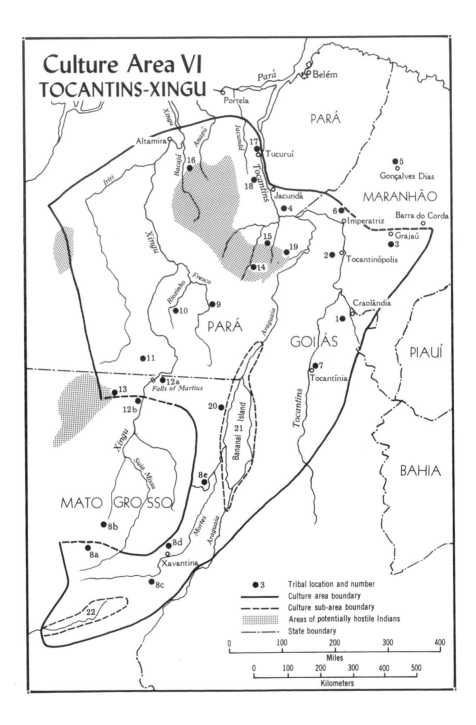

Culture Area VI
TOCANTINS-XINGU

● 3   Tribal location and number
──────   Culture area boundary
── ── ──   Culture sub-area boundary
░░░░░░   Areas of potentially hostile Indians
─ · ─ · ─   State boundary

0   100   200   300   400
Miles

0   100   200   300   400   500
Kilometers

CULTURE AREA VI: TOCANTINS-XINGU

The geographical area takes in all of the middle and lower Xingu valley, and the entire Tocantins River system, including an intrusion southwestward that follows the course of the Rio das Mortes. The majority of the tribes in this area belong to the Jê family. The unifying characteristic of the culture area, however, is a relatively uniform type of social and village organization. Most of the area is quite open country with occasional gallery forests; the exception is the heavily forested lower Xingu valley. It is assumed the Kayapó groups were pushed into the valley by the expansion of cattle raising and the consequent slow immigration of Brazilians from the less desirable areas of the northeast. The Jê tribes of the area are generally classified into three groups on the basis of supposed linguistic differentiation: Timbíra (1-6) in the Tocantins valley, Kayapó (9-14) in the Xingu valley, and Akuê (7-8) along the southern edge of the area.

1. *Krahô.* A tribe of about 425 Indians speaking a Timbíra-Jê language. There are four villages on the Craolândia Indian reservation. The Indians maintain permanent contact with the Brazilian population, but continue to be quite conservative in matters of language and culture.

2. *Apinayé.* Two villages of this Timbíra-Jê tribe, totaling about 210 Indians, are located immediately west of the town of Tocantinópolis, less than an hour away by motor vehicle. Contact with Brazilians is intense and the Indians are integrated into the regional economic pattern.

3. *Canela.* Considered one of the most conservative of the Timbíra tribes, the Canela have recently been severely attacked by local Brazilians. The contemporary situation is somewhat confused. Many of the Canela have abandoned their villages and are camping around the SPI posts in Grajaú and Barra do Corda, Maranhão, as the only possible protection against further attack. The villages, both of which are south of Grajaú, had a combined population of 400 a few years ago. From current reports it seems probable that these sites have been completely abandoned, and that less than 200 Indians have found refuge at the posts.

4. *Gavião.* Located in a jungle area east of the Tocantins, between Mãe Maria and Jacundá, this tribe also has suffered a great population loss and consequent social disorganization as a result of contact. The population of this Timbíra group is not known, but probably totals only a few hundred.

5. *Krem-yê.* A group of Timbíra that has ceased to exist as a tribal entity. Families are scattered well to the north of the former center of the tribe; a number of individuals are living on the SPI Pôsto Gonçalves Dias.

6. *Krikatí.* A Timbíra tribe living north of the town of Imperatriz within the fringe of the jungles. Population probably does not exceed 100, and tribal life is quite disorganized in consequence of rapid depopulation.

7. *Xerénte.* One of the two remaining Akuê-Jê tribes, a total of 260 individuals live in or near the SPI Pôsto Tocantínia.

8. *Xavánte*. A much larger and more conservative Akuê group than the Xerénte, the Xavánte resisted contact efforts until about 20 years ago, when several sections of the tribe accepted help from the SPI and the Salesian mission. In most cases contact is still very strictly controlled, so that acculturation has been minimal. Recent estimates of the population placed the total at 1,660 located in five villages: Pôsto Simões Lopez (a), Pôsto Batovi (b), São Marcos (c), Xavantina (d), and Suiá-Missu (e).

9. *Gorotíre*. The first of the Kayapó-Jê tribes to be pacified; since 1936 it has also been the base for most contact work with other Kayapó groups in the Xingu valley. About 200 individuals who have little contact with Brazilians, except through the SPI Pôsto Gorotíre and the Protestant mission working in the Xingu.

10. *Kubén-Kran-Kegn*. Between 300 and 400 Kayapó Indians living above the Cachoeira Fumaça on the Riozinho. Contact is still largely limited to the SPI and missionaries.

11. *Kubén-Kragnotíre*. A smaller group of Kayapó Indians living on the headwaters of the Iriri River; possibly 150.

12. *Mentuktíre* and *Txukahaméi*. A rather large Kayapó tribe living along the mainstream of the Xingu. The main group lives below the Van Martius Falls and is still without regular contact (12a). This group may number 300 to 400. The Txukahaméi subgroup has come within the influence of the Parque Xingu and now maintains permanent contact (12b); they are also listed, therefore, under Culture Area V.

13. *Dioré*. A Kayapó tribe possibly numbering more than 500, which still maintains hostile relations with Brazilians who are encroaching from the east.

14. *Xikrín*. A second Kayapó tribe in this same area. The Xikrín have accepted contact with the SPI, but continue to have some conflict with Brazilians gathering nuts in the tribal area. The tribe also is suffering the effects of disease introduced through contact. There are possibly fewer than 200 individuals at this time.

15. *Kréen-Akaróre*. A tribe known only by the Indians of the area, with population and language affiliation unknown. This may be the same as the Ipewí tribe reported in Culture Area IV.

16. *Arara*. Non-Kayapó groups called by this name have had both peaceful and warlike contact with Brazilians along the northern edge of the Xingu region. They are most frequently reported along the

Anapú, Bacajá, and Jacundá Rivers, and near the towns of Altamira and Portela, which they occasionally visit to beg and steal. There is reason to believe that at least some of these Arara groups are Karib, although others may well be sections of the Tupi tribes immediately to the southeast.

17. *Asuriní.* There are 35 of these Tupi Indians living on Pôsto Trocará, 15 miles downstream from Tucuruí. There are also uncontacted members of the tribe who occasionally appear at the post. Total population cannot exceed 60 on the Tocantins side. Asuriní are occasionally reported on the Xingu, but there has been no opportunity to confirm the linguistic affiliation of these latter groups.

18. *Parakanân.* A small tribe (definite population unknown) living in the jungles well back from the Tocantins River. They occasionally appear at Tucuruí. The language apparently is Tupi, but somewhat different from Asuriní judging from comments of the Asuriní.

19. *Mudjetíre.* A small, supposedly Tupi tribe, called by this name by the Kayapó, living on the Sororosinho River. The Mudjetíre are not in permanent contact with either Indians or Whites.

20. *Tapirapé.* Fewer than 50 survivors of this Tupi tribe now live in a single village on the SPI Pôsto Heloisa Alberto Torres.

21. *Karajá.* A tribe that has adapted its way of life to a roving existence along the beaches of the Araguaia River, particularly around the island of Bananal and immediately to the north of the island. There are 865 known Karajá divided into 13 village groups. Each village group has a "high water" location, but spends the dry season in smaller bands moving up and down the river. The *Javaé* constitute a subsection of the Karajá tribe, speaking a dialect only slightly different from Karajá. The 250 Indians who speak the Javaé dialect occupy the eastern side of the island. There are a few survivors of the *Xambioá* dialect group now intermingled with Karajá families in the extreme northern part of the tribal area. To date the Karajá language is unclassified.

22. *Borôro.* A formerly large tribe now reduced to a population between 700 and 800. A few large villages continue to survive around SPI posts, but the tribe has suffered heavily from the intensive penetration of Brazilians into the area, and is rapidly disintegrating. A few families may be found as outcasts and beggars on the fringes of various towns in the area. The language is not yet definitely linked with any larger group, but Borôro culture shows remarkable similarity with that of the Jê groups.

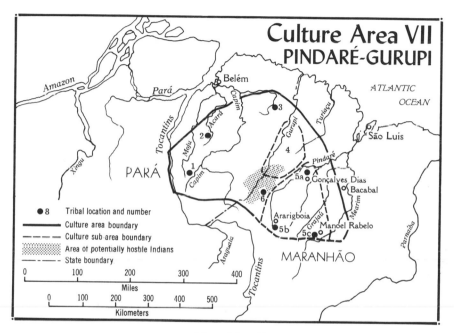

Culture Area VII
PINDARÉ-GURUPI

Map No. 9

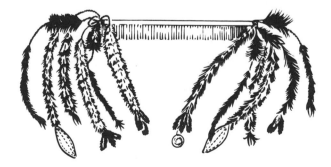

CULTURE AREA VII: PINDARÉ-GURUPÍ

A group of Tupi tribes located in an area of forests characterized particularly by vast groves of *babaçu* and other palms, the fruit of which has attracted an influx of Brazilians in recent decades. The southern part of this territory, occupied primarily by the Guajajára tribe, has been particularly affected. The Urubús and the Guajá are largely outside of contact. Although the first three groups are in relatively isolated areas, they have been decimated by contacts with the expanding population in the Belém area.

1. *Amanayé*. A group of under 50 Tupi Indians on the headwaters of the Capim and Moju Rivers.

2. *Turiwára*. Scattered families living with Tembé Indians on the Acará River, and on the Cairari, a tributary of the west bank of the Moju River. There may be fewer than 50 survivors in this tribe as well.

3. *Tembé*. A total of possibly 200 Tembé Indians, completely integrated into the local Brazilian population, are scattered between the Gurupi River and the Acará River in the state of Pará. Several families are grouped around the site of a former SPI post, the point marked on the map.

4. *Urubús-Kaapor*. A tribe pacified in the past three decades, with some sections still withdrawn from contact. Approximately 1,000 Indians are scattered in 15 or more villages along the upper Gurupi, and in the general area between the Gurupi and the Pindaré, including the headwaters of the Turiaçu. They are assisted by the SPI Pôstos Pedro Dantas and Felipe Camarão.

5. *Guajajára*. Approximately 2,600 Indians are scattered in at least 35 villages in a huge triangle marked off roughly by the SPI Pôsto Gonçalves Dias on the north (A), and by Pôsto Ararigboia (B) and Pôsto Manoel Rabelo (C) on the south. The center of population is toward the southern end of the triangle, and the least integrated sections of the tribe are along the west leg.

6. *Guajá*. Small groups of Indians, possibly totaling above 300 individuals, occupy the forests between the upper Gurupi and Pindaré Rivers, to the south of the area of the Urubús-Kaapor. Hostile relations are maintained with the Urubús, and occasionally a Guajá Indian is found as a prisoner in an Urubús village. There is no permanent contact.

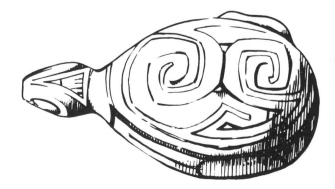

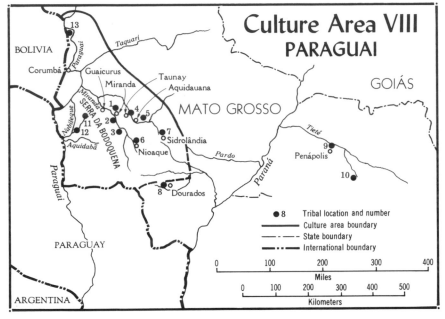

Map No. 10

CULTURE AREA VIII: PARAGUAI

Tribes now in this area originated in the Chaco area to the west. The Terêna were originally subject to the Kadiwéu, a branch of the Caballero Indians that once dominated the Chaco. The Guató, apparently of the same origins, are nevertheless quite different culturally. The latter are a river people, whereas the former are sedentary agricultural peoples located on open grassy plains.

Terêna. A major group with a population estimated by the SPI as between 5,000 and 6,000. They live in large villages both on and off Indian land, retain their own language, and recognize Indian leadership. Nevertheless they are well assimilated into the economic life and material culture of the surrounding Brazilian population. Many young people now are leaving the tribal villages and seeking advancement elsewhere. The largest concentration, 1,200 Indians, is on the SPI Pôsto Cachoeirinha (1), located eight miles northeast of Miranda, Mato Grosso. To the south and east of Miranda, and within three miles of the city, are the villages of Passarinho, Moreira, and União (2). Thirty-five miles to the south is Pôsto Lalima (3), where a few individuals, survivors of the related *Kinikinão* and *Layána* tribes, generally intermarried with Terena, may still be found. Pôstos Taunay and Ipegue and the village of Bananal, with a combined population in excess of 1,000 (4) are located just north of and within walking distance of the railroad station of Taunay. The small village of Limão Verde (5) is located at some distance northeast of Aquidauana. South of the rail line, which has been a major attraction for the Terêna, there are sizeable groups of Indians at Pôsto Capitão Vitorino (6) in the *município* of Nioaque, at the Pôsto Buriti in Sidrolândia (7), and at the Pôsto Francisco Horta (8) just four miles from Dourados. The SPI has moved several dozen families to other posts, primarily as employees. These are now permanently located on Pôsto Icatu in Penápolis (9) and on Pôsto Curt Nimuendajú in Avaí (10), both in the state of São Paulo; and on Pôsto Presidente Alves de Barros (11), the principal Kadiwéu post west of Terêna territory in Mato Grosso.

Kadiwéu. Less than 200 Indians live rather primitively on a huge reserve that occupies most of the territory between the Serra da Bodoquena and the Nabileque and Aquidabã Rivers. They are assisted by Pôsto Presidente Alves de Barros (11), which can be reached in one hard day on horseback from the railroad station Guaicurus, and the SPI cattle ranch Nalique (12).

Guató. Several families, probably not more than 30 individuals, intermarried with Brazilians. The Guató still remember some of the native language. They live in the lake district (13) north of Corumbá, the easiest point of access.

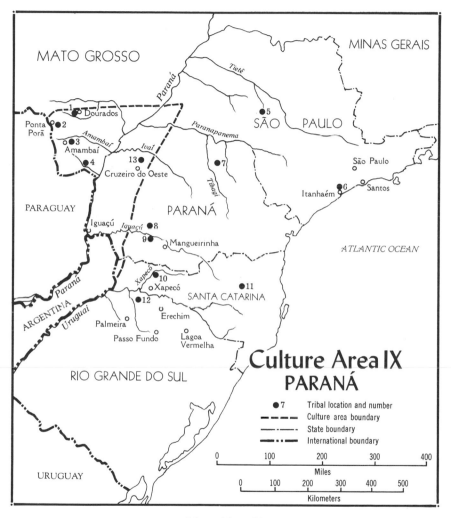

Map No. 11

CULTURE AREA IX: PARANÁ

Located in a geographical area transversed by the Paraná River, the Guarani groups that make up the culture area are now intermingled both with the Brazilian population and with the Terêna Indians on the west and the Kaingáng groups on the east, all of which have been described elsewhere. The differentiation commonly made among Kaiwá, Mbuá, and Nandéva is based on linguistic evidence. Today, however, it is sometimes difficult to sort these groups out, for "messianic" migrations have carried small groups eastward as far as the Atlantic, and migratory movements initiated by the SPI administration also have complicated the picture. We include the Xetá in this group, even though they are not Guarani, for they do speak a Tupi language and would seem to be related to similar wild groups reported from the Paraguay side of the Paraná River. Thus they represent aboriginal groups which possibly were not contacted by the missions that originally opened this area.

Kaiwá. The Kaiwá are the most compact and least assimilated of the Guarani groups, with a population approaching 3,000. The northern limit of the tribe is marked by a cluster of villages all within a few miles of Pôsto Francisco Horta (1), just north of Dourados, Mato Grosso. There also are sizeable villages on Pôsto José Bonifacio (2) at Ponta Porã, around Pôsto Benjamim Constant (3) four miles from Amambaí, and at Pôrto Lindo (4), all in the extreme south of the State of Mato Grosso.

Nandéva. Also called Apopokúva. At the turn of the century the Nandéva dialect was concentrated along the Paraná River above Iguaçú. Nandéva speakers have been scattered widely by the religious movements referred to above. Today there are probably fewer than 500 Indians, with no large villages. Groups are to be found at Pôsto Francisco Horta (1), and at Pôrto Lindo (4) in Mato Grosso; at Pôsto Curt Nimuendajú (5) near Avaí, and at Itariri, Itanhaém, and Pôsto José de Anchieta (6), south of Santos in the state of São Paulo; and on Pôsto Barão de Antonina (7), in Paraná.

Mbuá. Also referred to as *Kainguá.* This group is possibly as large as the *Kaiwá,* but is dispersed across the four southern states in small communities and scattered family groups. Some members are found near Itanhaém, São Paulo (6), at Pôsto Rio das Cobras (8) and Pôsto Mangueirinha (9), in the southern part of Paraná; at Pôsto Xapecó (10) and Pôsto Duque de Caxias (11) in Santa Catarina; and at Pôsto Guarita (12) in Rio Grande do Sul. These also probably are the Guarani reported to be living at the shelters (*tôldos*) maintained by the state government at Palmeira, Erechim, Lagoa Vermelha, and Passo Fundo, in Rio Grande do Sul.

Xetá. A small nomadic group of possibly fewer than 100 Indians living in the open, sandy forests of the Ivaí valley, in the *município* of Cruzeiro do Oeste (13), Paraná. They were contacted briefly early in the century; since 1955 they have been contacted periodically by faculty members of the University of Paraná.

Map No. 12

CULTURE AREA X: TIETÊ-URUGUAI

A cluster of Kaingáng (Jê) groups located in the region between the upper Uruguai valley and the Tietê River in São Paulo. The area was originally covered by vast forests, and is now one of intense agricultural development carried out largely by first and second generation European immigrants.

Kaingáng, the major group with a total population well in excess of

3,000, is located entirely on SPI posts and reserves. Within the limits of SPI supervision and protection, all groups are well integrated into the local economy, but uniformly preserve Kaingáng as the native language and continue to observe many religious and some social practices of the aboriginal culture. There is a remarkable linguistic homogeneity observed today, with only a very gradual dialectical shading from north to south, which leads some specialists to separate the São Paulo Kaingáng from those farther south.

The local groups, varying in numbers from 100 to 500, are located as follows:

Pôsto	Município	State
1. Icatú	Penápolis	São Paulo
2. Vanuire	Tupã	São Paulo
3. Laranjinha	Bandeirantes	Paraná
4. Barão de Antonina	Arariporanga	Paraná
5. Apucaranã	Londrina	Paraná
6. Queimadas	Reserva	Paraná
7. Ivaí	Pitanga	Paraná
8. Rio das Cobras	Iguaçú	Paraná
9. Boa Vista	Iguaçú	Paraná
10. Fioravante Esperança	Palmas	Paraná
11. Mangueirinha	Mangueirinha	Paraná
12. José Maria de Paula	Guarapuava	Paraná
13. Xapecó	Xapecó	Santa Catarina
14. Cacique Doble	Lagoa Vermelha	Rio Grande do Sul
15. Ligeiro	Getúlio Vargas	Rio Grande do Sul
16. Nonoái	Sarandi	Rio Grande do Sul
17. Guarita	Palmeiras	Rio Grande do Sul

In addition to the SPI posts listed above, the Rio Grande do Sul State Land Inspectorate maintains shelters (tôldos) for Kaingáng Indians at six points in the extreme north of the state. There is no information available with reference to a permanent population at these shelters.

Xokléng, a less tractable group of Indians, somewhat more separated from the main group linguistically than the dialect divisions suggested for the Kaingáng above. The Xokléng were not pacified until 1914, but have suffered heavily in the process of being integrated into the local Brazilian society. About 200 survivors are located at Pôsto Duque de Caxias (18), município de Ibirama, Santa Catarina, and a few dozen more are intermingled with the Kaingáng at Pôsto Laranjinha (3).

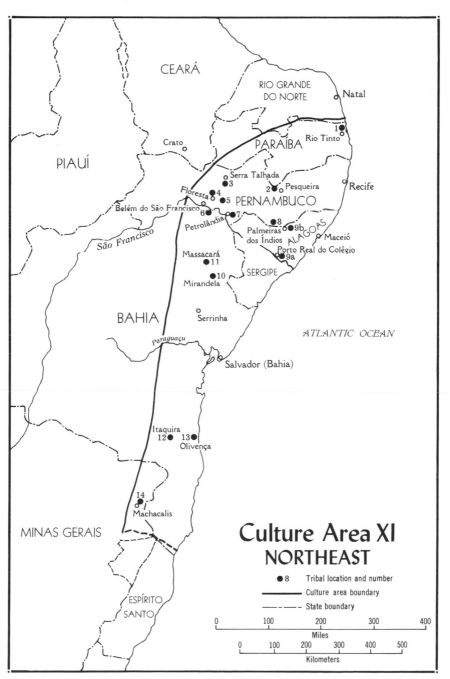

CEARÁ

RIO GRANDE
DO NORTE   o Natal

1 o

PARAÍBA   Rio Tinto o

Crato o

PIAUÍ

Serra Talhada o
3
Floresta o o 4
Belém do São Francisco   o 5   PERNAMBUCO
6   7
Petrolândia   8
Palmeiras o o 9b
dos Índios   ALAGOAS   o Maceió
Porto Real do Colégio
Massacará   9a
11
10   SERGIPE
Mirandela

São Francisco

2 o o   Pesqueira   o Recife

BAHIA   o Serrinha

Paraguaçu

ATLANTIC OCEAN

o Salvador (Bahia)

Itaquira
12 o   13 o
Olivença

14
o
Machacalis

MINAS GERAIS

Culture Area XI
NORTHEAST

o 8   Tribal location and number
———   Culture area boundary
—·—·—   State boundary

ESPÍRITO
SANTO

0   100   200   300   400
Miles
0   100   200   300   400   500
Kilometers

Map No. 13

CULTURE AREA XI: NORTHEAST

Tribes located between the Atlantic coast and the São Francisco River, and immediately to the north of the lower course of that river. These tribes are of uncertain but presumably diverse linguistic and cultural background. All are well integrated into the local economic and social scene, and have lost most traces of their aboriginal language and culture. There are two outstanding exceptions to this rule: the Fulniô and the Maxakalí.

1. *Potiguára.* A Tupi tribe with a current population probably in excess of 1,000. Villages are scattered along the coast. The village of São Francisco is the most isolated and probably the most conservative. A series of ten elementary schools is administered by the SPI from Pôsto Nísia Brasileira, 25 miles from the city of Rio Tinto, Paraíba.

2. *Xukurú*. A group of 1,500 integrated Indians living on the Serra Urubá, 10 miles from Pesqueira, Pernambuco. An outcast group of 40-50 individuals lives at Brazinho, beyond the SPI Pôsto São José which serves this area. The Indians use many Xukurú words in a Portuguese context.

3. *Kambiwá*. About 200 families are scattered throughout central Pernambuco; the largest concentration, consisting of about 20 families, is at São Serafim, near Serra Talhada. All Kambiwá were driven from the Serra Negra in the recent past by incoming settlers. They never have regrouped and generally are living in very poor circumstances.

4. *Uamué* or *Aticum*. During the rainy season 1,500 Indians live and work within an area 4 by 20 miles on the Serra d'Uma, near Floresta, Pernambuco. During the dry season they disperse throughout central Pernambuco, generally finding day labor on fazendas. Leading men of this group exercise religious leadership among both Indians and non-Indians of the area.

5. *Pankarará*. In 1952, 225 Indians were reported as located on the Serras de Cacaria e Arapuá, about 40 miles northeast of Rodelas on the São Francisco River. They were under heavy pressure from landowners.

6. *Tuxá* or *Rodela*. 200 completely acculturated Indians, targets of strong anti-Indian sentiment, live at the SPI Pôsto Rodelas, 15 miles downstream from Belém do São Francisco, Pernambuco.

7. *Pankararú*. There are 2,200 Indians living on the 4 square miles of the SPI Pôsto Pancararus, 20 miles from Petrolândia, Pernambuco. The Indians recognize two groups, the Pankarú and the Pancaré, both said to be descendants of the Makarú nation.

8. *Fulniô*. Approximately 1,800 Indians live in and around the town of Aguas Belas, Pernambuco. Of these, 1,260 are located on the SPI Pôsto Dantas Barreto. The rest are in the town or in neighboring villages and fazendas. This is the most conservative tribe of Pernambuco, retaining the native language and maintaining many features of the aboriginal culture, especially in the area of religion.

9. A group which now calls itself the *Xukurú-Karirí* lives in the SPI Pôsto Padre Alfredo Damasco (9a) in Pôrto Real do Colégio (250-300 individuals) and at Pôsto Inspetor Ireneu (9b) in Palmeiras dos Índios (250 individuals), both in the state of Alagoas. It seems probable that these two groups represent the descendants of the Xukurú, Natú, and Xokó tribes, all reported to be existing as separate entities in this area

as late as 30 years ago. Their common tie at present would seem to be faith in leading *pagés* (medicine men) who have used the present tribal name to the exclusion of the others.

10. *Kiriri.* About 1,000 descendants of the Kiriri nation live around Mirandela, Bahia, where they are aided by the SPI Pôsto Kiriri.

11. *Kaimbé.* The 500 descendants of the Kaimbé tribe live at the Caimbé subpost of the SPI located in Massacará, about 25 miles from Mirandela. They have forgotten all traces of language or culture.

12. *Pataxó-Hahahãi.* Just 25 descendants, only two of whom are full-bloods, live at SPI Pôsto Caramuru, 2 miles from Itaquira, Bahia.

13. *Gueren.* Several thousand completely assimilated descendants of Gueren Indians are living in the region of Olivença, Bahia. Their ancestors were presumably the Gueren or Botocudo Indians aboriginal to this area.

14. *Maxakalí.* Just over 200 individuals of this very conservative and monolingual group live on SPI reserves, 25% at the Pôsto Eng. Mariano de Oliveira and 75% at Pradinho reserve. The two posts are just a few miles apart and approximately 20 miles from the town of Machacalis, Minas Gerais.

BRAZIL

Team Locations

SUMMER INSTITUTE
OF LINGUISTICS

5○   Team location and number

Map No. 14

1

Kaxináhua (Culture Area II) Two boys [Photo by Jesco]

2

Kampa (Culture Area II) Woman cutting manioc [Photo by Jesco]

3 *Kampa (Culture Area II) Women and dugout with manioc [Photo by Jesco]*

4 *Kampa (Culture Area II) [Photo by Jesco]*

Kampa (Culture Area II) [Photo by Jesco]

5

6 Marubo (Culture Area II)
[Photo by Jesco]

7 *Marubo (Culture Area II) [Photo by Jesco]*

8 *Mehinaku (Culture Area V) Village [Photo by Jesco]*

9 *Mehinaku (Culture Area V) Quarup ritual [Photo by Jesco]*

10 *Mehinaku (Culture Area V) Quarup ritual [Photo by Jesco]*

11 *Mehinaku (Culture Area V) Quarup flute players [Photo by Jesco]*

12 *Mehinaku (Culture Area V) Quarup flute players [Photo by Jesco]*

13 *Mehinaku (Culture Area V) Yavari rituals [Photo by Jesco]*

14 *Mehinaku (Culture Area V) Yavari ceremonies [Photo by Jesco*

15 *Mehinaku (Culture Area V) Kamaiure boys drilling a stone [Photo by Jesco]*

16 *Kuikuru (Culture Area V) Piqui fruit harvest [Photo by Jesco]*

17 *Kuikuru (Culture Area V) Father and son*
[Photo by Jesco]

18 *Txukahamẽi (Culture Area V or VI) [Photo by Jesco]*

19 *Txukahamẽi (Culture Area V or VI) Boys [Photo by Jesco]*

20 *Txukahamẽi (Culture Area V or VI) [Photo by Jesco]*

21 *Karajá (Culture Area VI) [Photo by Jesco]*

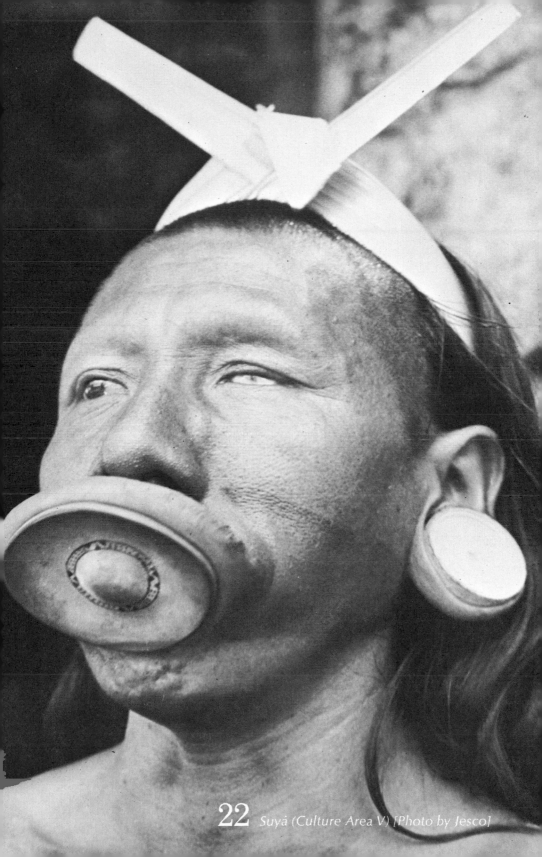

22 *Suyá (Culture Area V) [Photo by Jesco]*

23

Canela (Culture Area VI) The child's hair is being cut in preparation for presentation to the village elders. [Photo by William H. Crocker]

24

Canela (Culture Area VI) The man is holding a stack of hats worn by boys during an initiation ceremony. [Photo by William H. Crocker]

25

Canela (Culture Area VI) A sing-dance leader. The man is leading the social singing and dancing of a line of women facing him. He is partly covered with falcon down applied with tree resin diluted in coconut oil. [Photo by William H. Crocker]

26

Canela (Culture Area VI) The young man is standing beside a log used in log racing. [Photo by William H. Crocker]

27 Canela (Culture Area VI) The man is carrying a shock of rice inside a house. [Photo by William H. Crocker]

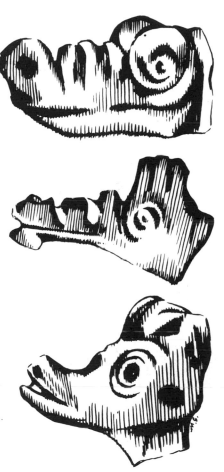

28

Left, opposite
Canela (Culture Area VI) One of
a pair of summer festival girls
representing a village moiety. She
remains out of her house during
the summer. When winter begins,
she is returned to her house and
the hollow log is placed out doors
to indicate that winter rules prevail.
[Photo by William H. Crocker]

29

Right, opposite
Canela (Culture Area VI) The girl
wears a wrap-around skirt; young
boys may wear aprons. [Photo by
William H. Crocker]

TRANSLATOR'S PREFACE

by Janice H. Hopper

Institute for Cross-Cultural Research

TRANSLATOR'S PREFACE

by Janice H. Hopper

Institute for Cross-Cultural Research

"Words travel, too." [1] Yet in these days of accelerating communication much of the growing body of Latin American anthropological literature is unavailable to students in the United States who cannot transcend the language barrier.

Three papers are translated here from the Portuguese of Brazil. Galvão's contribution to the culture area concept in application to Brazil and Baldus' bibliographic review for the years 1953-1960 have never before appeared in English. Only Part III of Ribeiro's culture contact paper has ever been made accessible to an English-speaking audience. The implications of these papers for anthropology and sociology generally lead us to hope that we have lent the authors' words wings to reach the English-speaking student, whatever his specialized interest.

Three major hazards confront the translator of social science materials. The first of these pitfalls derives from the absence of internationally standardized definitions of key social science concepts. The second renders literal translations hazardous: exact equivalencies between vocabularies are rare. The third problem stems from a lack of consensus on the spelling of the names of nonliterate Indian groups.

---

1. Fernando de Azevedo, *Brazilian Culture*. Translated by William Rex Crawford, New York: The Macmillan Company, 1950, p. 1.

Brief discussions will alert the reader to these hazards and explain why the translator has had to choose among less than fully satisfactory solutions.

For most of the key concepts in the social sciences there is no generally accepted formal definition even in the language in which the concept is most often used. Consider for example the definition of the archaeological concept *area co-tradition* in British and American usage.[2] Even more relevant for the precise translation of Darcy Ribeiro's paper in this volume is the concept of *detribalization*.[3] It is to be noted wryly that deculturation is not mentioned in the UNESCO dictionary. The Portuguese term used by Ribeiro is *decaracterização*. *Decharacterization* might appear a tempting equivalent, but no such English word exists. With Berta Ribeiro's perceptive collaboration we use *detribalization* or *deculturation* and spell out the definition of the concept on its first appearance in Darcy Ribeiro's essay.

The absence of exact equivalencies—or the failure of even the best bilingual dictionary to provide a full, rich social science vocabulary—places a premium on the translator's knowledge of the field and consciousness of shades of difference among synonyms. There are instances in which the argument for or against a given choice has scientific overtones; frequently, however, the defense must rest on insubstantial grounds. We might of course have insisted in advance of translation on a convention for the handling of a given word each and every time it appeared. That rigidity was rejected here on the grounds that any author is apt to use the same word with some inconsistency, and that context is the best test of intent.

The spelling of Indian names is the third area of choice among indifferent alternatives. One possibility was to follow the example set by the *Handbook of South American Indians*. In his introduction to volume I, Steward says:

> Spelling follows a simple orthography, which aims to be intelligible in English, Spanish, and Portuguese. Vowels have their Spanish values, and accents fall on the antepenult unless otherwise indicated. As *k* does not occur in Spanish and Portuguese, *c* has been substituted

---

2. See Julius Gould and William L. Kolb, Eds., *A Dictionary of the Social Sciences*, compiled by the United National Educational, Scientific, and Cultural Organization, New York: The Free Press of Glencoe, 1964, pp. 36-37.

3. Ibid., p. 195.

before *u, o,* and *a,* except in spelling which is too well
established to permit change. No attempt is made at
phonetic spelling. . . .[4]

To have adopted the *Handbook* spellings would have saved us
many a headache. We concluded, however, that the student and the
general reader who perused materials on the twentieth century Indians
of Brazil would encounter a variety of spellings and might therefore
profit from exposure to the range of possibilities now. We therefore
resolved to retain the spelling used by each author. Thus there should
be internal consistency in spelling within each of the papers in this
volume, including Kietzman's which is the paper of a linguist written
in English. But consistency in spelling among the four authors is
somewhat less than perfect.

For the benefit of the student we call attention to acceptable
differences in the spelling of the names of indigenous groups. The
following are used interchangeably in the Brazilian-Portuguese
literature:

the *u* and the *w*	e.g., Akuên (Akwê)
	Mauá (Mawé)
	Nahukuá (Nahukwá)
the *c* and the *k*	e.g., Aticum (Atikum)
	Caduveo (Kaduveo)
	Caingang (Kaingang)
	Cayapó (Kaiapó, Kayapó)
	Mundurucú (Mundurukú)
the *x, ch,* and *sh*	e.g., Xavante (Chavante, Shavante)
	Xerente (Sherente)
	Xokléng (Shokléng)
the *w* and the *v*	e.g., Wapidian (Vapidiana)
the *i* and the *y*	e.g., Iawalapití (Yawalapití)
	Oiampi (Oyampik)
	Suiá (Suyá)
the *b* and the *k*	e.g., Maxubi (Maxuki)
the *i* and the *j*	e.g., Iamanada (Jamanadí)
vae and *vahe*	e.g., Javaé (Javahé)

---

4. "Introduction." In *Handbook of South American Indians.* Julian H. Steward, Ed.,
   Vol. I "The Marginal Tribes" (Bureau of American Ethnology, Bulletin 143). Washington, D. C.: U. S. Government Printing Office, p. 7.

the *w* and the *g*   e.g., Waharibo (Guaharibo)
the *b* and the *v*   e.g., Kabixi (Kavixi)
the single and double *l*   e.g., Canela (Canella)

Dale Kietzman uses spellings consistent with his understanding of the convention of the Brazilian Anthropological Association. Ribeiro followed the same guidelines earlier. Galvão has not indicated what his standard was. Typographical errors in English and in Portuguese are not uncommon, although we did make an effort to catch all of them. Malcher, whose recent volume is among those cited in Appendix IV, sometimes has spellings all his own. We would suggest Kietzman as a reliable guide to most recent usage. Appendix I, Index of Indian Groups in Contemporary Brazil, cues the reader in on the most frequently encountered ways of referring to given groups.

My personal debt to Brazilians and to my countrymen is easily stated but hardly to be repaid. William Rex Crawford[5] and Samuel Putnam[6] have set high standards for Portuguese-to-English translation. In the 1940's General Rondon stimulated a North American neighbor's interest in the situation of the Brazilian Indian: he is remembered with respect and appreciation. Florestan Fernandes, T. Lynn Smith, Charles Wagley, Emilio Willems, Eduardo Galvão, Darcy Ribeiro, and David Maybury-Lewis are among those who personally or through their writing have contributed to my knowledge of and interest in the Brazilian Indian as a member of an ethnic minority.

More specifically in the preparation of these texts I am indebted to many knowledgeable individuals. Berta Ribeiro's feel for the English language and her painstaking reading of the translation of Darcy Ribeiro's paper contributed immeasurably to its readability and accuracy. Gertrude Dole, Charles Wagley, Emilio Willems, Herbert Baldus, and Dale Kietzman have been generous and constructive in their detailed comments. In compiling the bibliography I have drawn heavily on the work of both Herbert Baldus and William Crocker. The encouragement, criticism, and suggestions of my late husband, Rex D. Hopper, are reflected in the best of these pages.

---

5. Fernando de Azevedo, Op. cit.

6. Euclides da Cunha, *Rebellion in the Backlands*. Translated with Introduction and Notes by Samuel Putnam, Chicago: University of Chicago Press, 1944.

Valerie Auserehl meticulously proofed the lists of Indian groups, beseiging me with helpful questions. Her collaboration in the smoothing of awkward sentences also is appreciatively acknowledged, as is Winifred Wuterich's patient, accurate, and intelligent typing and proofing, and Georgia Rhoades' fine editorial hand.

As I review the hours of striving for a readable accurate English text, my consciousness of the assets of training in sociology and political science and of the liabilities of lack of formal training in anthropology is heightened. None of the many thoughtful contributors to the final form of the English version are, of course, in any wise responsible for the failings of the translator.

Janice H. Hopper
Institute for Cross-Cultural Research
Washington, D. C.   1966

INDIGENOUS CULTURES
AND
LANGUAGES OF BRAZIL

by Darcy Ribeiro

Facultad de Humanidades, Universidad de Montevideo

Translated by Janice H. Hopper from the Portuguese text: "Culturas e Linguas Indigenas do Brasil." (*Educação e Ciências Sociais,* Vol. 2, No. 6, Novembro de 1957, Rio de Janeiro)

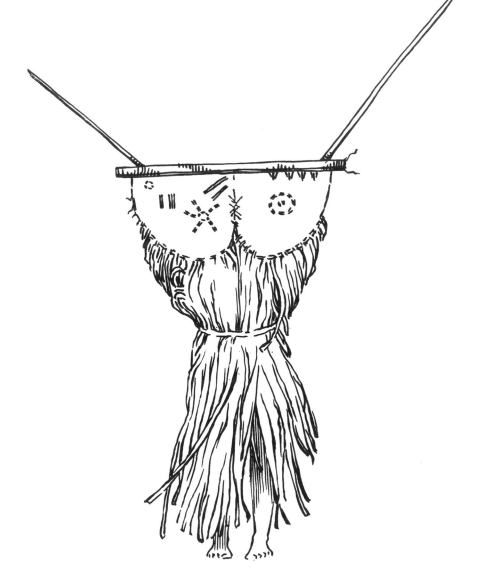

INDIGENOUS CULTURES AND LANGUAGES OF BRAZIL

by Darcy Ribeiro

I. INDIGENOUS BRAZIL IN THE 20TH CENTURY

This essay examines the behavior of indigenous Brazilian groups during the last fifty years, the manner and timing of their conservation or disappearance, and their detribalization or deculturation (*descaracterização*); that is, the extinction of their languages and cultures. Our aim is to formulate the most urgent tasks facing Brazilian ethnology and linguistics.

We shall try to achieve this goal by systematically comparing the situation in which Brazilian indigenous groups were found at the turn of the century with their situation today, examining both the extent of their integration into the national society and, correlatively, their preservation or loss of cultural and linguistic autonomy. Our basic task, therefore, is the elaboration of two reports on Brazilian indigenous groups. These reports have been organized on the basis of the degree of integration characteristic of each tribe in 1900 and 1957, the beginning and end of the period under analysis.

For this purpose our principal source is the archives of the Serviço de Proteção aos Índios [1] which since 1910 has been copiously documenting the life experiences of the Indians of Brazil. We shall refer also to Curt Nimuendajú's *Mapa Etno-Histórico* and its respective indices as a basic source, adopting his linguistic classifications and many of his findings on the location, existence, or disappearance of tribes. Our principal bibliographic source is the *Handbook of South American Indians;* it has been supplemented by a great many articles and books which provide firsthand information on tribal groups.[2] In many cases we shall profit, moreover, from our field experience, as well as from the direct knowledge of various colleagues and employees of the Serviço de Proteção aos Índios.

Regrettably, our sources on entire areas and for various groups are questionable and frequently contradictory. These deficiencies are most evident in relation to the regions of Juruá-Purus and Guaporé. Indeed, each source on Juruá-Purus appears to attribute the same tribal names almost arbitrarily to different tribes. The consequent confusion recalls Martius' old concept of *colluvies gentium*. Similar difficulties arise from the heterogeneity of information recorded at different points in time. Yet in some cases we had no choice but to use data in which there are discrepancies of ten or fifteen years or more.

One of our basic problems was that of defining the unit of data gathering: should the tribe be taken as a whole, or should we work with the better delineated tribal subdivisions, or even with local groups? Our experience in the early stages of the study confirmed the impracticality of rigorous adherence to a single criterion, however ideal that criterion may appear. Gaps in the ethnographic bibliography preclude precise discrimination of tribes from subtribes for all but a few Indian groups. On the other hand, there are instances during the half-century under study in which members of a tribe that is scattered over a vast area and divided into several subgroups nonetheless have had life experiences that are essentially the same. In still other cases, the life experience of each subgroup has differed, with the result that the several related subgroups cannot be treated as a unit.

Under such circumstances and given our sources and the limitations which the form and length of an article impose upon our work, we are obliged to consider each case in its complexity, or at least to the fullest possible extent. In the data-gathering process, therefore, we have been essentially mindful of the history of each tribe's relations with the national society. Where these relations were constant for the entire tribe, unnecessary subdivisions have been avoided; where they differed, each variation has been recorded. As a result, the 230 cases included in this study are indigenous groups whose life experience of relations with civilization has differed, rather than tribes or tribal subdivisions uniformly defined. Thus, for example, the Guarani, among whom a certain number of subgroups may be distinguished, have been treated as a single unit; it has been necessary to treat the Timbíra, the Kayapó, the Kaingáng, and others in terms of their several subgroups.

Given these unavoidable imprecisions, our work should be

regarded as an exploratory description to be corrected and refined in the light of criticism. Nonetheless, it will be apparent that the data used are sufficiently broad and representative to validate our generalizations.

Indigenous Brazil in 1900

The first canvas portrays indigenous Brazil in 1900; tribal groups which had survived until the turn of the century are classified by type of tribal contact with civilization.

The first column, headed *isolated*, lists tribes which still inhabit or depend for subsistence on lands in zones as yet unpenetrated by Brazilian society; these tribes only accidentally and rarely enter into contact with civilized peoples. Isolated tribes were either simply withdrawn or hostile; the latter category tended to include tribes whose locations near pioneer frontiers had exposed them to violence at the hands of the invaders. Some of these tribes through their own efforts had retained the land on which they lived and established the conditions for the maintenance of full cultural autonomy.

List I

Brazilian Indigenous Groups by Degree of Integration into the National Society as of 1900

Isolated	Intermittent Contact	Permanent Contact	Integrated
TUPI			
Amniapé	Amanayé	Apiaká	Guaraní
Arawíne	Emerilon	Guajajára	Karipúna
Aré (Xetá)	Jurúna	Mundurukú	Kokáma
Arikên	Kuruáya		Mawé
Aruà	Oyanpík		
Asuriní	Tembé		
Awetí	Turiwára		
Boca Negra	Xipáya		
Canoeiros (Avá)			
Guajá			
Guarategaja			
Ipotewát			
Itogapúk			

Isolated	Intermittent Contact	Permanent Contact	Integrated
Jabutiféd			
Kabixiâna			
Kamayurá			
Karitiâna	-		
Kayabí			
Kepkiriwát			
Makuráp			
Manitsawá			
Mialát			
Mondé			
Mudjetíre			
Parakanân			
Paranawát			
Parintintín			
Puruborá			
Rama-Rama			
Sanamaiká			
Takuatép			
Tapirapé			
Tukumanféd			
Tuparí			
Urubus-Kaapor			
Urumí			
Wiraféd			
ARUAK			
Agavotokueng	Hohodene	Katiâna	Kayuixána
Barawâna	Kanamarí	Kuníba	Kinikináo
Ipurinân	Karutâna	Manitenerí	Layâna
Irántxe	Kaxararí	Marawá	Pasé
Kulína	Koripako	Palikúr	Terêna
Kustenáo	Kujijenerí	Paresí	Wainumá
Mandawáka	Paumarí	Wapitxâna	
Maopityan	Tariâna		
Mehináku	Warekéna		
Waurá	Yamamadí		
Xiriâna	Yuberí		
Yabaâna			
Yawalapití			

Isolated	Intermittent Contact	Permanent Contact	Integrated
KARIB			
Aipatsê	Apalaí	Bakairí (Rio	Galibí
Araras	Bakairí	Paranatinga)	Makuxí
Atruahí	(Rio Batovi)	Pauxí	Palmelas
Bakairí	Ingarikó	Pauxiâna	
(Rio Curisevo)	Katawiân		
Kalapálo	Kaxuiâna		
Kuikúro	Purukotó		
Matipuhy	Sikiâna		
Mayongong	Taulipang		
Nahukuá	Wayâna		
Naravúte			
Parikotó			
Pianokotó			
Salumá			
Tirió			
Tsuva			
Waimirí			
Waiwai			
JÊ			
Dióre	Kayapó-Kradaú	Apâniekra	Kaingáng
Gaviões	Krahó	Apinayé	(Paraná)
Gorotíre	Krem-Yê	Kênkateye	Kaingáng
Kaingáng	(Cajuapara)	Krem-Yê	(Sta. Catarina)
(S. Paulo)	Ramkókamekra	(Bacabal)	Kaingáng
Kubén-Kran-		Krikatí	(R. G. do Sul)
Kegn		Timbíra	Kayapó do Sul
Kubén-		(Araparitiua)	
Kragnotíre		Txakamekra	
Mentuktire		Xerénte	
Suyá			
Xavante			
(Akuên)			
Xikrin			
Xokleng			
OTHERS			
Aiwaterí	Amahuáka	Botocudos	Fulniô

Isolated	Intermittent Contact	Permanent Contact	Integrated
Arikapú	Borôro	(Itambacuri)	Kamakân
Baenân	Desâna	Espinhos	Mirânia
Botocudos	Iawano	Guató	Natú
(Pancas)	Kanamarí	Kadiwéu	Pakarará
Botocudos	Kapanáwa	Karipúna	Pankararú
(Crenaque)	Karajá	Kuyanáwa	Potiguára
Guaharíbo	Katukína	Marakaná	Tuxá
Huarí	(Pano)	Marúbo	Uamué
Javutí	Katukína	Matanawí	Wakoná
Javaé	Kaxináwa	Maxakalí	Xokó
Kabixí	Kobéwa	Mayorúna	Xukurú
Kréen-Akaróre	Kurína	Mura	
Máku (Auarí)	Marináwa	Parawá	
Makunabödö	Nukuiní	Poyanáwa	
Nambikuára	Pakanáwa	Sakuya	
Ofaié	Pokanga	Torá	
Otí	Tukána	Yumá	
Pakaánovas	Tukúna	Yurí	
Pakidái	Tuxináwa		
Pataxó	Tuyuca		
Papayúna	Waikíno		
Trumái	Wanâna		
Txikão	Witóto		
Umotína	Xipináwa		
Urupá	Yamináwa		
Waiká			
Wayoró			
Xirianá			

Among the *isolates* in the year 1900 there were 105 tribes[3] or 45.6% of the total of 230. Of all the Brazilian tribes known in 1900, these were the most populous; their members were the most vigorous physically, and had best conserved their cultural inheritance. Some industrial objects such as metal instruments and adornments frequently were to be found in their villages; they also had animals and cultivated plants of foreign origin. By and large, these culture elements had been obtained through war or exchange with neighboring tribes; occasionally their acquisition rested on the pillage of products from pioneering nuclei.

The second column lists groups maintaining *intermittent contacts* with civilization. These Indians were living in regions already being swallowed up in Brazil's pioneering expansion. Ever since the pioneer intrusion, a criterion of civilized people—i.e., the value of the lands the Indians occupied or their own value as laborers in a market economy—has been the fundamental determinant of their destiny. Indians in *intermittent contact* continued to retain a certain cultural autonomy, making provision for their subsistence through traditional processes. But they already had acquired needs which could be satisfied only through economic relations with civilized peoples.

Frequently groups in *intermittent contact* had ambivalent attitudes toward civilized people. On the one hand, they were impelled by fear, a fundamental product of all the tribal experience that had taught them to expect only misfortune at the hands of the white man; on the other hand, they were entranced by superior cutting instruments and enthusiastic about equipment that was infinitely more efficient than theirs in its action on nature. Their activities of necessity became considerably diversified. They found themselves obliged to carry on their normal subsistence tasks and also either to devote an increasing amount of time to the production of surplus articles for exchange with the Whites, or to hire themselves out as a labor force. Their culture and their language were beginning to reflect these new experiences.

In this phase, contacts were almost always accidental and were restricted to such specialized groups as a rubber-collecting enterprise, or a mission, or a trader, or some other agency of civilization. Whatever the circumstances, the contact was limited to a nucleus or individual representing only a narrow, limited facet of the national society.

According to our data, there were 57 groups in the *intermittent* stage in 1900—24.7% of the total of 230. Judging by known cases, the decimating effects of epidemics of grippe, measles, and other morbid agents carried by civilized peoples would have reduced their population by at least half of what it was while they were still isolated. There had been thoroughgoing transformations in their way of life, changes attributable to ecological and biotic factors rather than to the process of acculturation.[4]

Tribes in *permanent contact* are found in the third column. In 1900 the tribes cited were maintaining direct and permanent com-

munication with numerous and differentiated representatives of civilization. A great part of the cultural autonomy of these groups had
been lost as they became completely dependent upon a supply of
metal, salt, medicine, cloth, and other such industrial products. Those
traditional customs compatible with their new situation were preserved, although at the same time profoundly modified by the
cumulative effects of the ecological, economic, and cultural constraints of this stage of their integration. The number of individuals
able to express themselves in Portuguese had soared, amplifying
their channels of communication with the national society. Their
population had continued to decrease. In some instances, population
decline had reached proportions so high as to render the ancient
social organization inoperative; in consequence, a series of original
institutions had disappeared completely.

Participation in the national economy had disorganized tribal
subsistence systems. The old patterns of cooperation were broken;
the Indian's dependence upon the agents of the national society was
increasing at every turn. And, unlike the tribal Indian, the individual
living in *permanent contact* was dependent upon the national society
as an individual rather than as a group member. Freed from the
ancient system of social control by the breakdown of tribal sanctions,
the group was headed for disintegration. As this process unfolded,
a movement for cultural reorganization began. The intensity of the
movement varied by tribe and by the circumstances of contact. Some
groups tried to flee contact and to reorganize their lives on the old,
already impracticable bases. Others became involved in revivalistic
movements. In 1900 there were 39 indigenous groups—16.9% of
the total of 230—in these conditions of *permanent contact*.

Under the heading *integrated,* the last column of List I sum-
marizes the situation of those groups which had survived the pressures
discussed above and entered the twentieth century as islands in the
midst of the national populace. At the turn of the century their
economic role was that of a reserve labor force or of specialized
producers of certain marketable commodities. They were an un-
wanted minority, restricted to segments of the lands they had formerly held or cast out of territory rightfully theirs and forced to roam
from place to place. Twenty-nine tribes (12.6% of the total) were
in these straits; of all the survivors, these integrated tribes were en-
during the most precarious conditions of life in the greatest dependence and misery. Between these contemporary Indians and their
isolated ancestors—in some cases members of the preceding genera-

tion—there was an enormous gap. Even a hazy reconstruction of their ancient tribal culture by simple direct observation or by recall was beyond them. Many of the groups at this stage of contact had forgotten their own language. They had become, therefore, virtually indistinguishable from the rural Brazilians among whom they lived. Equally Mestizo, wearing the same clothing—although perhaps the Indians' was a little more ragged—and eating the same food as their Brazilian neighbors, they could have passed unperceived had they themselves not been certain of their identity as a people and loyal to their ethnic background. Their attachment to their ethnic identity resembles that of the more acculturated Jew or gypsy. These tribes had run the gamut of acculturation. But some imponderable obstacle blocked their assimilation; there was a final step that they were unable to take.

Some groups, e.g., the *Pankararú* of Pernambuco or the *Potiguára* of Paraíba, developed rituals in the effort to reinforce their solidarity. These rituals persist in the present, for the contemporary practitioners cherish them as an inheritance from their ancestors.

Half a Century Later

List II reflects the present situation of the same groups of which we have been speaking, whether they have remained *isolated*, entered into *intermittent* or *permanent contact*, been *integrated*, or, finally, are now *extinct*, i.e., have disappeared as differentiated tribal groups during this half-century.

List II

Brazilian Indigenous Groups by Degree of Integration into the National Society as of 1957

Isolated	Intermittent Contact	Permanent Contact	Integrated	Extinct
TUPI				
Asuriní	Aré (Xetá)	Jurúna	Amanayé	Amniapé
Boca Negra	Awetí	Mundurukú	Guajajára	Apiaká
Canoeiros	Kamayurá	Paranawát	Guaraní	Arawíne
(Avá)	Kayabí	Parintintín	Karipúna	Arikên
Guajá	Puruborá	Tapirapé	Mawé	Aruà
Mudjetíre	Urubus-	Tukumanféd	Tembé	Emerilon
Parakanân	Kaapor	Tuparí		Guarategaja
		Wiraféd		Ipotewát

Isolated	Intermittent Contact	Permanent Contact	Integrated	Extinct
				Itogapúk
				Jabutiféd
				Kabixiâna
				Karitiâna
				Kepkiriwát
				Kokáma
				Kuruáya
				Makuráp
				Manitsawâ
				Mialát
				Mondé
				Oyanpík
				Rama-Rama
				Sanamaiká
				Takuatép
				Turiwára
				Urumí
				Xipáya

ARUAK

Isolated	Intermittent Contact	Permanent Contact	Integrated	Extinct
Agavoto-kueng	Mehináku	Hohodene	Kanamarí	Katiâna
Barawâna	Waurá	Ipurinân	Palikúr	Kaxararí
Mandawáka	Yawalapití	Irántxe	Paresí	Kayuixâna
Maopityan		Karutâna	Tariâna	Kinikináo
Xiriâna		Koripako	Terêna	Kujijenerí
Yabaâna		Kulína	Wapitxâna	Kuníba
		Paumarí		Kustenáo
		Yamamadí		Layâna
				Manitenerí
				Marawá
				Pasé
				Wainumá
				Warekéna
				Yuberí

KARIB

Isolated	Intermittent Contact	Permanent Contact	Integrated	Extinct
Atruahí	Apalaí	Ingarikó	Bakairí (Rio	Aipatsê
Mayongong	Kalapálo	Taulipang	Paranatinga)	Araras

Isolated	Intermittent Contact	Permanent Contact	Integrated	Extinct
Parikotó	Katawiân	Wayâna	Galibí	Bakairí
Tirió	Kaxuiâna		Makuxí	(Rio Batovi)
Waimirí	Kuikúro			Bakairí (Rio
	Matipuhy			Curisevo)
	Nahukuá			Naravúte
	Pianokotó			Palmelas
	Salumá			Pauxí
	Sikiâna			Pauxiâna
	Waiwai			Purukotó
				Tsuva

JÊ				
Dióre	Kubén-Kran-	Gorotíre	Apinayé	Apâniekra
Gaviões	Kegn	Krahó	Kaingáng	Kayapó-
Kubén-	Xavante	Ramkóka-	(S. Paulo)	Kradaú
Kragnotíre	(Akuên)	mekra	Kaingáng	Kayapó do Sul
Mentuktire	Xikrin		(Paraná)	Kênkateye
Suyá			Kaingáng (Sta.	Krem-Yê
			Catarina)	(Bacabal)
			Kaingáng (R.	Krem-Yê
			G. do Sul)	(Cajuapara)
			Xerénte	Krikatí
			Xokleng	Timbíra
				(Araparitiua)
				Txakamekra

OTHERS				
Aiwaterí	Javaé	Amahuáka	Fulniô	Baenân
Guaharíbo	Nambikuára	Arikapú	Kapanáwa	Botocudos
Kabixí	Trumái	Borôro	Kaxináwa	(Itambacuri)
Kréen-	Xiriâna	Desâna	Marináwa	Botocudos
Akaróre		Iawano	Mura	(Crenaque)
Máku		Kadiwéu	Pakarará	Botocudos
(R. Auarí)		Karaiá	Pankararú	Espinhos
Makunabödö		Katukína	Potiguára	(Pancas)
Pakaánovas		Katukína	Tuxá	Guató
Pakidái		(Pano)	Tuxináwa	Huarí

Isolated	Intermittent Contact	Permanent Contact	Integrated	Extinct
Tapayúna		Kobéwa	Uamué	Jabutí
Txikão		Marúbo	Umotína	Kamakân
Waiká		Maxakalí	Wakoná	(Hahahaí)
		Nukuiní	Xipináwa	Kanamarí
		Pakanáwa	Xokó	Karipúna
		Pokanga	Xukurú	Kurína
		Tukána		Kuyanáwa
		Tukúna		Marakaná
		Tuyuca		Matanawí
		Urupá		Mayorúna
		Waikíno		Mirânia
		Wanâna		Natú
		Witóto		Ofaié
		Yamináwa		Otí
				Parawá
				Pataxó
				Poyanáwa
				Sakuya
				Torá
				Wayoró
				Yumá
				Yurí

The same categories of contact lend themselves to a delineation of the situation of Indian groups either half a century earlier or that much later. These classes or classifications represent, in reality, the successive and necessary stages of the process of integration of tribal groups into the national society.

The essential differences, from 1900 to our times, in the conditions of life synthesized in each of these categories reflect the presence of a new factor, the protective intervention exercised by the Serviço de Proteção aos Índios. By virtue of this interference, the process of contact, integration, or extinction no longer operates spontaneously, as it did in the past; on the contrary, it is in large measure artificially controlled. For this reason, the contemporary condition of *isolation,* or of *intermittent* or *permanent contact,* or of *integration* does not correspond precisely to the stage earlier designated in the same terms.

Thus, for example, the condition of *intermittent contact* maintained artificially by the SPI on the Xingu in order to assure the Indians a rate of change slow enough not to threaten their survival, differs from *intermittent contact* as achieved and experienced freely by an indigenous group with any nucleus of the national society. Thanks to the type of intervention in the various stages of integration practiced by the SPI, thousands of Indians can survive who would otherwise be extinct, victims of various socially disorganizing influences.

In essence, however, as List II indicates, in the now shrunken but still vast unexplored areas of Brazil · there are *isolated* groups and groups in *intermittent* or *permanent contact* or *integrated* status. Variations in contact situation reflect the degree to which the national society has penetrated each area.

A comparison of the two lists shows that the number of isolated groups was reduced from 105 (45.6%) in 1900, to 33 (23%) in 1957. Those maintaining *intermittent contacts* dropped from 57 (24.7%) to 27 (18.8%), while the number in *permanent contact* rose from 39 (16.9%) to 45 (31.4%) and the number *integrated* rose from 29 (12.6%) to 38 (26.5%). The last column of List II, referring to *extinct* groups, shows that of the 230 tribes reported, 87 or 37.8%, have disappeared during the last fifty years.

The first observation to which these data give rise is that we are facing not only a drastic reduction in the number of tribes, but also a profound modification in the survivors. While in 1900 the largest percentage of tribes was *isolated* (45.5%), and the smallest, *integrated* (12.6%), in our times the numbers are almost inverted, the proportion *integrated* (26.5%) being greater than that *isolated* (23%).

Partial computations, as for example in Table I, permit the refinement of this analysis. We see that the 105 *isolated* tribes of 1900 were distributed as follows in 1957: 33 remained *isolated,* 23 had entered into *intermittent contact,* and 13 were in *permanent contact,* 3 had been *integrated,* and 33 were *extinct.* An examination of the list of tribes by category (Table II) in the context of the history of the frontiers of economic expansion shows that the preservation of a group in the condition of *isolation* or its entry into *intermittent* or *permanent contact* depends essentially on the dynamics of the national society. Thus the proportion of groups in each of the various categories of integration expresses the rapidity and power with which the areas they occupied were opened up, rather than the resistances or receptivities of the indigenous culture to acculturation.

Table I

Number of Contemporary Indigenous Groups by Degree of Integration into the National Society Compared with the Distribution of these Groups in 1900

Degree of Integration	Totals 1900	1957				
		Isolated	Inter-mittent Contact	Perma-nent Contact	Inte-grated	Extinct
Isolated	105	33	23	13	3	33
Intermittent Contact	57	—	4	29	10	14
Permanent Contact	39	—	—	3	8	28
Integrated	29	—	—	—	17	12
Totals 1957	230	33	27	45	38	87

The 33 groups continuing in isolation today comprise only 23% of the total number of groups, in contrast to the 45.6% found in isolation in 1900. The majority of the isolated Indians—that is, 60%—now lives in unexplored areas; the remaining 40% is settled in regions already penetrated by agents of civilization, with whom many of these groups are engaged in bloody conflict. None of these groups has preserved its original culture. Their present way of life is explicable only in terms of the contingency of the life of flights, forays, and battles which has been imposed upon them and has profoundly affected the form and functioning of their institutions. It is improbable that a single group which has been entirely exempt from the influence of civilization survives today, for even those not yet touched by the Brazilian national society are experiencing its influence indirectly through interaction with displaced tribes that have been thrown in their midst, and through bacteria, viruses, and artifacts that have been passed from tribe to tribe until the last refuge of the isolated group has been reached.

The 23 groups which have made the transition from *isolation* to the condition of *intermittent contact* with the national society live in areas of recent occupation or areas that are economically marginal and therefore rarely entered. The majority has been pacified by the

SPI[5] and assured by that agency of reservations for their permanent residence in relative freedom from the pressures to which they would be subjected were they to establish direct and free contacts with agents of the national society. The greenhouse conditions of reservation life do not prevent drastic reductions in group size, but they do permit the survival and preservation of the cultural autonomy of some groups, as, for example, the nine tribes of the Upper Xingu region[6] and others whose docility would otherwise lead to their prompt envelopment and liquidation.

Of the 105 tribes that were *isolated* in 1900, thirteen, all considerably decimated, are now found in *permanent contact*. The situation of most of these tribes clearly demonstrates the difficulties of survival. There are only three cases of groups whose status has changed from that of *isolated* to that of *integrated:* the groups involved are the *Umotína* of Mato Grosso, *Kaingáng* of São Paulo, and *Xokleng* of Santa Catarina. All three have in common their experience of the rapid occupation—motivated by special regional economic attractions—of their living areas. Protective intervention explains their survival. Although the protective program has been unable to prevent their substantial depopulation,[7] it did enable them to retain their ethnic identity while undergoing the dramatic experience of the leap from the tribal condition to the status of civilized Indians.

Finally, by examination of the first series of Table I, we have established the fact that 33 groups progressed from *isolation* to *extinction* in fifty years. So rapid has been the disintegration of these tribes that it is worth noting whether they passed rapidly through the stages of intermittent and permanent contact and integration, or did not live through these stages at all. The proportion is meaningful, representing as it does 31.4% of a total of 105. It is the more significant because if we exclude the groups which have remained isolated— since the majority of the latter have not yet encountered civilization— the number of tribes that have become extinct is almost the same as the number of tribes reported as having passed through the two conditions of contact and achieved integration (39 groups). In other words, the data signify that almost half of the tribes who have come face to face with our civilization have disappeared within less than fifty years thereafter, and at times even more rapidly.

Examining now the column referring to groups in *intermittent contact* on the same Table I, we see that of 57 groups found in *intermittent contact* in 1900 only four have remained at this stage, these being the Karib groups of the unexploited zones of Brazilian Guiana. Twenty-nine have come to maintain permanent contacts, and ten are now integrated tribes, that is, entirely dependent upon the national society and in a state of profound linguistic and cultural deculturation. Finally, 14 groups have become extinct—that is, the proportion of eclipse is approximately the same as it was among groups reported as isolated at the start of the same period.

Of the 39 groups that were found in *permanent contact* in 1900, three have remained in this category and eight have been integrated, while 28 or 71.7% have disappeared. The proportion now extinct indicates that the number of groups liquidated at the stage of *permanent contact*—before integration—is extremely high. Correlated with the finding that 41.3% of the 29 tribes that had been *integrated* as of 1900 were extinct as of 1957, these data suggest that passing from *permanent contact* to *integration* increases the chances of survival. Effectively, *integration* as conceptualized in this study appears in certain cases to be a precarious but feasible form of accommodation. That is, *integration* appears to afford some ethnic groups an opportunity to survive and to participate in the national society as segments of the society differentiated only by their indigenous origins. The condition for such survival is a measure of adaptation to the requirements enabling tribal peoples to live with civilized peoples. Specifically, tribal peoples adapt by developing greater resistance to disease and divesting themselves of their linguistic and cultural uniqueness.

The Faces of Civilization

So far we have been treating the national society as if it were a constant in the process of integration. In reality, we are dealing with one of the basic variables that requires examination. The capacity of the national society to determine the fate of the Indians varies with the forms that the former may assume. The national society presents strikingly diverse faces to the Indians as it assumes the shape of an extractive, pastoral, or agricultural economy in their confrontations. Each segment of the economy is motivated by unlike interests in the exploitation of the environment; each is organized in terms of its own structural principles; and each imposes its distinctive constraints on the tribal groups it confronts.

The extractive economy mobilizes individuals detached from their communities of origin and consequently unfettered by the traditional forms of social control, to catapult them into unexplored territories. The recruits are organized in mobile bands to penetrate the forests in search of scattered, commercially valuable natural products. In face to face encounters with indigenous groups, these men tend to expel the Indians from their lands by force. Alternatively, if the situation permits, the extractors try to place the Indians in their service, compulsorily enlisting the men to help locate new reserves of forest products and for the work of rowers, bearers, and so on, and the women as mistresses and producers of foods. This type of economy imposes a vast spatial dispersion of population. Men engaged in expanding this economic frontier generally collide with the Indians at widely separated locations; it is possible, therefore, for a warring tribe to continue in conflict for many years, impeding the occupation of its territory at great cost to both sides.

Within this basic framework tribal groups live through the stages of *intermittent* and *permanent contact* and of *integration* in conditions conducive to a prompt disorganization of family life, the rupture of tribal unity, and finally a specific form of participation in the economy and institutions of the national society.

The frontiers of pastoral economy are formed by populations supported by the natural environment—populations composed of family groups who advance across unexplored areas in search of new pastures for their herds. Essentially, their actions toward the Indian are motivated by the necessities of clearing the fields of their human inhabitants to turn them over to the cattle, and of preventing the Indian from substituting attacks upon the herds for the hunting of which he has been deprived. In such circumstances, the interaction of the Indian and the settler frequently assumes forms of bloody conflict and rarely gives way to direct living together, or to intermarriage and miscegenation as in the first-mentioned case.

Expanding agricultural frontiers generally involve both larger human masses and much more powerful equipment than are characteristic of the expanding extractive economy. Agricultural pioneers see the Indian as merely an obstacle to their expansion, and they resort to conflict to take possession of the lands he occupies and thus extend the area in use for agricultural production.

Rapidly and drastically transforming the landscape, the frontiers of agricultural expansion create new ecological conditions in which the adaptive tribal system becomes inoperative. Within a few years, the Indians find themselves obliged to adopt new forms of eking out subsistence and surrounded by a relatively dense population to whose ways of life they must accommodate if they are to survive.

In Table II the data on the degree of integration of indigenous groups from 1900 to 1957 were distributed by type of economy prevalent today in the areas which they occupied or still occupy. To a certain extent, this arrangement permits us to verify the way in which the behavior of indigenous groups confronted with agricultural, pastoral, or extractive frontiers differs from the behavior of similar groups in regions that are still unexplored.

Table II

Impact on Brazilian Indigenous Groups of Confrontation with the Several Fronts of Economic Expansion of the National Society, 1900-1957

| Degrees of Integration | Areas of the Economy | | | | | | | | TOTALS | |
| | Agricultural | | Pastoral | | Extractive | | Unexplored | | | |
	1900	1957	1900	1957	1900	1957	1900	1957	1900	1957
Isolated	6	—	6	—	50	13	43	20	105	33
Intermittent Contact	—	—	5	2	47	6	5	19	57	27
Permanent Contact	2	—	14	9	23	36	—	—	39	45
Integrated . .	2	4	18	19	9	15	—	—	29	38
Extinct	—	6	—	13	—	59	—	9	—	87
Totals	10		43		129		48		230	

As a preliminary, we must remark that these categories are not pure economic variants; rather, they are also successive stages of the penetration of civilization and consequently correspond to varying degrees of intensity of interaction. Thus, the extractive fronts are frequently recent and exploratory penetrations which will be followed by a definitive occupation on an agricultural base. In Brazil the establishment of agriculture rarely assumes the form of a frontier of expansion into unexplored areas; as a rule, Brazilian agriculture develops in regions previously exploited by gatherers of forest products. The pastoral economy, operating generally on the plains or in the natural savannahs that do not attract an extractive economy, always assumes the form of a pioneering frontier advancing upon indigenous groups to launch the bases of an economy that will retain the same character when consolidated.

As already indicated, the extractive front mobilizing scattered populations over vast areas is equated with a much lower level of interaction than that linked to the pastoral and agricultural frontiers. Table II reflects these facts in the much higher percentage of groups found in the areas of extractive economy (48.9%), a concentration which cannot be interpreted as signifying the greater capacity of these Indians to coexist with nationals on these fronts. It must, rather, be seen as a reflection of the circumstance that these are zones of more recent occupation and that their Brazilian population is more widely dispersed. In contrast, the finding that only 2.8% of the tribes are in areas of agricultural economy reflects the essential character of these areas as zones of more ancient occupation in which, before the twentieth century, other indigenous groups experienced the same problems now characteristic of other areas.

Far from invalidating the significance of the percentages of groups which have ceased to exist in the several areas under scrutiny, these qualifying variables merely make it imperative to interpret the statistical data in the light of the historical information which clarifies its true meaning.

Predictably, the percentage of tribes becoming extinct between 1900 and 1957 (18.7%), is lowest in unexplored or economically marginal regions. The proportion increases to 30.2% in zones of pastoral economy; in areas of extractive economy it rises to 45.7%, reflecting both the violence with which the groups of tappers of standard and substandard latex, and the nut collectors and other gatherers of forest products have come into conflict with the Indians, and the conditions of life that the former have imposed upon tribes with whom they have established pacific relations.

Little tribes, which soon after their first contacts with civilization—just before or shortly after 1900—succumbed to various epidemics, are the principal contributors to this high rate of group disappearance from the scene. In the area between the telegraphic line opened by the Rondon Commission from 1907 to 1913 and the course of the Guaporé River exclusively, about 18 tribes became extinct within a few years. All 18 had been virgin to contact before the twentieth century. Virulent epidemics alone cannot explain so high a rate of extinction. Various factors appear to have acted cumulatively, among them the docility with which some tribes spontaneously approached civilized men who came to them with the all-powerful attractions of metal instruments, porcelain beads, guns, and other marvels. After their first meeting with the officials of the Rondon Commission, many tribes, entranced by their prodigal welcome, sought contact with rubber collectors in the belief that the latter were the same people. The consequences were fatal; within a few years one tribe after another was exterminated, and those who survived suffered such substantial reductions in numbers [8] that today their ranks constitute infinitesimal fractions of the former population.

In the areas of agricultural economy, we come up with the highest proportion of extinct tribes, for 60% of the groups known in 1900 no longer exist. In every case we are dealing with tribes that had succeeded in surviving in isolation in the forest belts near the Atlantic coast, in the States of Minas, Espírito Santo, and Bahia, that remained unexplored until the twentieth century. We refer to the *Botocudos, Baenân, Pataxó,* and *Kamakân* who remained hostile until the first quarter of the century although reduced to small frightened bands and entirely deculturated by a century of bloody encounters with civilized men.

The establishment of peaceful relations following massive contacts, the outbreak of epidemics among susceptible Indian groups, and the transformation of their landscape of virgin forests into pasture zones or gigantic tobacco, cotton, cocoa, coffee, or other plantations, completed their extinction within a few years.

Considering, from the same Table II, the total number of groups continuing in isolation until our times, we find 20 in unexplored areas and 13 in zones of extractive economy. The latter are tribes living on the frontiers of civilization, where they now are experiencing the first impacts of our inexorable expansion: they still are resisting contact and maintaining their cultural and linguistic autonomy. Many of these tribes are involved in bloody conflicts which may lead to their extermination even before they have experienced the predictable stages of integration, or debilitate them so profoundly as to condemn them to extinction as they take their first steps toward incorporation into the national society. These are the *Xiriana* (Aruak), *Aiwaterí, Guaharíbo,* and *Pakidái* who live at the headwaters of the tributaries of the left bank of the Rio Negro in bloody conflict with extractors of latex *(balateiros),* and collectors of palm fibers *(piaçaba)* who are advancing upon their territory in a ferocious wave. They are also the *Atruahí* and *Waimirí* of the Jauaperi

River who, in their turn, confronting extractors of pau-rosa (wood of a tree of the Leguminosa family) and other gatherers, are trying every possible means of defending their independence and their control over their own territory. And they are the *Pakaánovas* of Guaporé in permanent battle with the waves of rubber collectors advancing upon their settlements. The *Pakaánovas* have only recently begun to establish direct relations with civilization, represented by another of its aspects: the pacification squads of the Serviço de Proteção aos Índios. And finally, they are the *Asuriní* and *Parakanân* groups, both Tupi, and the *Gaviões, Kubén-kragnotíre, Mentuktíre,* and *Dióre* of the Jê language, all inhabiting southern Pará which was the scene of the most violent expansion movement of the Brazilian society a few years ago. Here three frontiers of expansion, two extractive and one pastoral, are interwoven with each other. The first is formed by the rubber collectors who exploit the Xingu and the valleys of its middle tributaries, frequently working two by two, one to collect latex, the other to cover his companion against *Kayapó* attacks. These conflicts are so ancient that these Indians appear to be specialists in the life of flight, attack, and counterattack which has been forced upon them by colonization. After the bitter experience of their handicaps in battles in which they were armed only with clubs *(tacapes),* bows and arrows against firearms, they took possession of some carbines and practiced shooting. Today one of the motivations to conflict is the acquisition of new arms and munitions. Their knowledge of the region and the advantages of their specialized adaptation contribute to their great mobility; it is possible for small groups to cover enormous distances in their flights and to guard a vast territory, blocking or impeding the exploitation of the rubber trees that exist on their land and are coveted by the representatives of civilization.

Another frontier is formed by the nut collectors *(castanheiros)* who exploit the marginal forests of the Itacaiunas River, where they come face to face with two other Kayapó groups *(Xikrín* and *Dióre),* and the right bank of the Tocantins, where they collide with the *Gaviões.* The latter are the last remaining Timbíra groups to conserve full cultural and linguistic autonomy; they have remained intact because, after they had experienced the impact of civilization in the natural fields of their former territory in southern Maranhão, they penetrated the Amazon forest and found new fields where they were able to reconstitute their life on its old bases. They know what to expect from the Whites and up to the present have avoided en-

72532

counters except under special circumstances of their own making.

A third frontier, the pastoral, is advancing through the grass-lands of Conceição do Araguaia; it also is coming into conflict with the Kayapó.

Their autonomy notwithstanding, all these groups experience such profound changes in their ways of life that their contemporary cultures cannot be treated as if they were their original heritage. Thus it is apparent that even before direct and permanent contacts are established, the behavior of tribal groups is profoundly affected by civilization. And moreover, the fundamental determinant of the destiny of indigenous tribes, of the conservation or loss of their languages and cultures, is the national society or even the international economy. The quotation for rubber, nuts, and other products on the New York market, or the perspectives of peace or of war among the great powers, influence the ebb or flow of the waves of extractors of forest products, permitting the last remaining autonomous tribes to survive or condemning them to extermination.

Returning to Table II, we now focus on the groups which in 1900 were maintaining *intermittent contacts* with civilization. As we have seen, during this half-century, the number of these tribes has declined from 57 to 27. Of the five tribes originally found in areas of pastoral economy, two remain, the *Xavante* and the *Javaé*, united by the circumstance of having been first pacified in 1949 by the SPI. Their pacification has permitted the cattle raisers of Goiás to occupy extensive fields previously unused for fear of Xavante and Javaé attacks. Today these ranchers are advancing through the whole region, overrunning the *Karajá*, *Javaé*, *Tapirapé*, and *Avá (Canoeiros)*. In consequence, the life situation of these tribes will be undergoing drastic changes during coming years.

In the areas of extractive economy there were 47 groups, of which only 6 remain; of the other 41 groups, 27 have gone on to other stages of integration and 14 have vanished. Principal among these latter are the tribes of the region of Juruá-Purus which, during the last years of the past century, were faced with the most powerful expansion ever experienced by extractive industries in Brazil. We refer to the caucho, balata, and rubber extractors who went up the Juruá and Purus rivers as far as Acre, advancing upon tribal groups like an avalanche of destruction during the years of the highest commercial quotations for these products. The speed and the violence of this invasion is reflected in the fact that this recently occupied area is one of the least known both ethnologically and linguistically.

In the unexplored areas, the number of tribes in *intermittent contact* has risen from 5 in 1900, to 19 in our own days. Here is a clear indication that the conquest of the country will be complete within a few years. The last remaining Indian groups will then have lost the isolation and complete autonomy that they still enjoy at present.

In the column of groups in *permanent contact,* also on Table II, the rise in the number of tribes in the area of the extractive economy from 23 in 1900, to 36 in 1957 merits attention. The increase reflects the passage to this category of tribes that had survived the earlier stages of contact. The phenomenon shows up even more clearly in the column headed *integrated* (29 to 38), confirming our earlier observation that the chances of survival appear to increase as groups proceed from permanent contact to integration. The risks of extinction are far greater in the first stages of contact than in the last stage.

Table III

Brazilian Indigenous Groups by Linguistic Family with Respect to Degree of Integration into the National Society or Extinction, 1900 to 1957

Degree of Integration	Tupi		Aruak		Karib		Jê		Others		Totals	
	1900	1957	1900	1957	1900	1957	1900	1957	1900	1957	1900	1957
Isolated	37	6	13	6	17	5	11	5	27	11	105	33
Intermittent Contact	8	6	11	3	9	11	4	3	25	4	57	27
Permanent Contact	3	8	7	8	3	3	8	3	18	23	39	45
Integrated ..	4	6	6	6	3	3	4	7	12	16	29	38
Extinct	—	26	—	14	—	10	—	9	—	28	—	87
Totals	52		37		32		27		82		230	

Indigenous Cultures and Languages "in extremis"

Examination of the same data tabulated by linguistic family (Table III) enables us to grasp other uniformities in the process of integration.

The number of representatives of various linguistic families that have disappeared during the twentieth century is striking. The

Tupi, represented in 1900 by 52 groups, have been reduced to 26; the Aruak, who in 1900 numbered 37 groups, today number 23; the number of Karib groups has dropped from 32 to 22; the Jê, from 27 to 18. The 82 remaining groups in our sample declined to 54.

It is worthwhile to probe here the relative weight of cultural variations as determinants of the destiny of indigenous groups. Examination of the data permits us to conclude only that Tupi groups are more susceptible to disintegrating factors generated in the process of integration, for they have lost 50% of their representatives, a far higher proportion than the others. Perhaps the phenomenon is explicable in terms of cultural distance. For the Tupi are culturally very close to the civilized representatives of the frontiers of expansion with which they have come face to face. Brazilian society, particularly in its rural aspects, conserves a clearly Tupi cast. This is recognizable in the ways of guaranteeing subsistence and in various other aspects of the culture.

This resemblance, which in our times still surprises each rural dweller *(sertanejo)* who comes upon a Tupi group, extends from the ways of cultivating the land and of preparing and consuming food to the expressions used to designate objects and mutually acceptable conceptions of the supernatural. Under such circumstances, the more promptly channels of communication are established, the more accelerated the passage through the stages of integration. The accumulation of socially disorganizing effects under such conditions explains the greater speed with which these groups approached the bearers of civilization and were wiped out.

But the principal clarifications that Table III affords refer to the number of representatives of various linguistic families that have disappeared during the twentieth century. We have already examined the data globally, in terms of the four principal linguistic stocks. To these observations can be added the disappearance of the various representatives of the Pano linguistic stock (8 out of 18), *Txapakúra, Katukína, Tukána, Guaikurú,* and *Mura.*

Various unaffiliated languages once spoken in limited geographic areas have disappeared completely. In the majority of cases we are unacquainted with them, for we lack even documentation satisfactory for the formulation of merely classificatory propositions. Such is the case of the languages of the *Ofaié* [9] and *Guató* of southern Mato Grosso, of the *Otí* of São Paulo, of the *Maxubí* (Arikapú), *Wayoró* and *Huarí* of Guaporé, the *Botocudos* of Minas

Gerais, the *Baenân, Kamakân,* and *Pataxó* of Bahia, and the *Torá, Matanawí,* and probably the *Mirânia* of Amazonas.

Although our data permit us to determine the conservation or disappearance of languages only in terms of the survival or extinction of respective ethnic groups, certain inferences concerning the process of deculturation are possible. Language is one of the most persistent elements of culture; moreover, it necessarily reflects the life experiences of the group. Thus language diversification operates as a concomittant to the processes of integration and acculturation, at the very minimum to explain the new world of which the group is becoming a part. As these processes advance, the native tongue undergoes changes arising out of the circumstance that it is spoken by bilinguals and, in certain cases, can enter into competition with the new indigenous idiom or with Portuguese—but at long last it is abandoned.

The simple necessity of communicating with representatives of the national society leads some individuals perforce to master Portuguese. Intensification of contacts is accompanied by continuing increases in the number of bilinguals, so that as a general rule, by the time the stage of permanent contact is reached, all adult males are capable of expressing themselves in Portuguese. In integrated groups one observes a true competition between the two languages, tending to culminate in the abandonment of the maternal tongue when certain socially unfavorable factors intervene. We have observed this situation among the *Guaikurú* and *Terêna* Indians of Lalima in southern Mato Grosso, who, when they came to live together, were faced with difficulty in communicating because they spoke different languages, and had to adopt Portuguese as their common tongue. In these circumstances, the younger generation, including in part children of mixed Indian unions, never learned the languages of their parents. Similar phenomena must have been experienced by various other groups.

Thus in Northeastern Brazil we find the largest Indian population which speaks Portuguese exclusively. The *Pankararú, Xokó, Xukurú, Pakarará, Wakoná,* and *Uamué* exemplify the case in point. It appears that the same process is underway among the *Palikúr, Karipúna, Emerilon,* and *Galibí* of the Territory of Amapá. These Indians had adopted a French dialect—*criolle*—spoken in French Guiana, and now are switching to Portuguese.

Indian tribes have always lost their languages through the adoption of the idioms of conquering groups. This phenomenon, which, given the original conditions of interaction, should be a rare occurrence, appears to be stepped up by virtue of the interference of civilized nuclei. The increasing predominance of the Tukano language along the Rio Negro at the cost of Aruak and other languages is a case in point.

Even today in the same Rio Negro region we find remnants of diverse Indian groups who have lost their native languages by adopting a new aboriginal language introduced by the agents of civilization. Here we have in mind *lingua geral,* a variation of Tupi which was adopted and modified by the colonizer, and became the most frequently spoken language of Brazil during the first two centuries of colonization. By virtue of the great isolation in which the Rio Negro region has remained until recently, *lingua geral,* although completely displaced by Portuguese everywhere else in Brazil, has survived and even progressed here. The groups found on the advancing frontiers of this area that only now are entering into contact with civilization are learning *lingua geral* rather than Portuguese, because the former is the most current idiom of the pioneers and the basic form of communication among indigenous groups with whom they come in contact.

Extra-linguistic factors have acted as determinants in all these cases of the loss or obsolescence of tribal idioms. Where social pressures generated in the process of integration did not weigh heavily, the indigenous languages were preserved, undergoing only such modifications as adapted them to the new conditions of the life of the group. Thus, a majority of the integrated groups, including some who can count centuries of living jointly with civilized peoples and who have a perfect command of Portuguese, have continued to speak their native tongues.

Brazilian Indigenous Population

The formation of a practical concept of the Indian applicable to groups that have survived in the contemporary period is an indispensable prerequisite to the evaluation of the indigenous population, given their distance from their original cultural and social characteristics and from the stereotypes in terms of which they generally are described. In view of the impracticability of using the racial and cultural criteria commonly employed for this purpose, the task is hardly simple.

A purely racial criterion would include among the indigenous population millions of Brazilians who could not be so defined on the basis of their other social characteristics, for a glaringly indigenous phenotype predominates in the population of the vast regions of the Amazon, the Northeast, and the extreme South. So great is the mass of aboriginal traits incorporated into Brazilian life that a broad criterion of culture base, defining as indigenous the communities which have conserved culture elements of pre-Columbian origin, would include other millions of people. These facts only verify the invalidity of defining the Indian by strictly racial and cultural criteria in a country whose population has been formed by the mixture of Whites, Indians, and Negroes and whose culture has been enriched by the mingling of various heritages.

The indigenous population of contemporary Brazil is that segment of the population which presents problems of nonadaptation to Brazilian society in any of its several variations, motivated by the conservation of customs, habits, or mere loyalties that bind their members to a pre-Columbian tradition. Or, even more broadly: an Indian is any individual recognized as a member of a community of pre-Columbian origin who identifies himself as ethnically different from nationals and is considered indigenous by the Brazilian population with whom he comes in contact.

The imprecision and subjectivity of which these conceptualizations can be accused notwithstanding, they lend themselves well to our practical proposition of distinguishing the Indians from other Brazilians. Furthermore, they can be properly applied to the various conditions and modalities in which the former are found after four centuries of direct and indirect contacts with Whites and Negroes.

For example, little Dária, an almost blonde, blue-eyed girl child, daughter of an Indian woman and a transient White male, whom we met in an *Urubu-Kaapor* settlement, will be included among the Indians so defined. Dária spoke only the Tupi dialect of these Indians, had a world-view similar to that of any other child of her settlement, and was considered a member of the tribe by everyone, her exotic coloring notwithstanding. Similarly the sons of Luís Prêto, a dark Mulatto married to an Indian and living in the *Kadiwéu* settlement, would be included. Those boys not only were considered authentic *Kadiwéu* by the tribe, but also shared their fellow tribesmen's difficulties in establishing relations with strangers.

In point of fact, a definition based upon racial criteria would preclude our classifying either Dária or the sons of Luís Prêto as indigenous. These are individual and extreme examples. but much to the point. For entire indigenous groups are today highly mixed with Whites and Negroes, without having ceased nonetheless to be Indians from the standpoint of the difficulties they have in finding a place in the national economic structure, of their self-concept, and of the consensus of the Brazilian population with which they came into contact.

The definition we propose applies equally well to groups with the most diverse degrees of acculturation. It includes isolated tribes that never have come face to face with an agent of the national society, and that have conserved their traditional culture. It covers the detribalized groups that differ little or not at all from their rural neighbors linguistically and in their ways of life, and are Indians only because they so consider themselves and are so regarded.

The most authoritative estimates of the Brazilian indigenous population vary greatly, but there is a constant tendency to accept progressively lower totals. One of the most ambitious estimates, dated 1922 and attributed to Luís Bueno Horta Barbosa, former director of the Serviço de Proteção aos Índios, put the indigenous population at 1,250,000. Among the many subsequent estimates is Julian Steward's,[10] which is based upon a vast ethnological documentation: Steward estimated a reduction in the indigenous Brazilian population from 1,100,000 in 1500 to 500,000 in 1940. Our own calculation [11] of 150,000 Indians, based on an official inquiry undertaken by the SPI and completed in collaboration with Eduardo Galvão in 1953, was overly optimistic.

In 1940 and again in 1950 the national census included questions which, had they been accompanied by special instructions, would have permitted a realistic estimate of the indigenous population. We refer to the items concerning color (White, Black, Mulatto, Indian) and *persons present over five years of age who do not habitually speak Portuguese in the home.* Lamentably, the opportunity was lost, as much through the lack of uniform criteria for the use of the census takers as through failure to take the census in the most remote areas where the major concentrations of indigenous groups are located. Thus, the total of 45,019 Indians, sum of the persons defined as indigenous by color in the 1950 census,[12] does not correspond to the reality. Examining the respective tables, we have discovered that in various cases not one Indian is registered in municipalities where we know with absolute certainty that there are substantial groups; in other cases numbers far too low for accuracy are reported. The same discrepancies are evident in totals by state and territory; for example,

543 Indians are reported in Pará, 14 in Amapá, 8 in Guaporé, and 16 in Acre.

The glaring discrepancies of even the most authoritative estimates encourage us to try an indirect evaluation. Despite predictable imprecisions, we are confident that our results will more closely approximate reality; at the least, the revised estimates will serve as a working instrument until valid data are available.

When we have information that merits confidence, we have consistently included population data in the attached report of indigenous tribes. As even these data frequently vary by double or more, we have decided to use the following class intervals: groups of under 50 people, of 50 to 100, of 100 to 250, of 250 to 500, of 500 to 1,000, of 1,000 to 1,500, of 1,500 to 2,000, and of over 2,000. The sum total permits us to evaluate the minimum and the maximum indigenous population estimates admissible in the light of documented sources on contemporary Brazil.

Proceeding as indicated, we have succeeded in obtaining data for 109 of the 142 groups presently in existence. The remaining 33 were reported under the rubric "population unknown." As among these latter there are predominantly isolated groups (21 of 33) with an average of over 1,000 persons per group, we judge that in a general computation of the population there would be no exaggeration in attributing to the isolated groups an average of 500 persons per group. The sum total of the estimated population of the 109 groups for which we have figures, plus the estimated average population of the 33 isolated groups, puts the present indigenous Brazilian population at a minimum of 68,100 individuals or a maximum of 99,700. The valid total ought to be somewhere between these two figures, give or take 10%.

The substitution of such dissimilar estimates for earlier and widely discrepant figures, or even the simple and more certain confession of our ignorance in this respect may be but little help. However, the available documentation offers no basis for greater precision. For this reason, we are encouraged to proceed in the effort to determine, however crudely, the regional distribution of the present Brazilian indigenous population by linguistic stocks and by degree of integration.

Returning to the scrutiny of the 109 groups for which we can make direct population estimates, we observe that 51 groups have fewer than 250 persons; 21 have between 250 and 500; 18 between

Table IV

Brazilian Indigenous Population, 1957, by Size of Group and Degree of Integration

Class Size	Isolated			Intermittent			Permanent			Integrated			Total		
		Population			Population			Population			Population			Population	
	groups	Min.	Max.	groups	Min.	Max.	groups	Min.	Max.	groups	Min.	Max.	groups	Min.	Max.
under 50....	—	—	—	4	200	200	5	250	250	1	50	50	10	500	500
50-100	1	50	100	3	150	300	7	350	700	1	50	100	12	600	1,200
100-250	2	200	500	7	700	1,750	12	1,300	3,250	9	800	2,000	30	3,000	7,500
250-500	2	500	1,000	5	1,250	2,500	6	1,750	3,500	8	2,000	4,000	21	5,500	11,000
500-1000 ...	4	2,000	4,000	3	1,500	3,000	8	4,500	9,000	3	1,500	3,000	18	9,500	19,000
1000-2000 ..	1	1,500	2,000	—	—	—	3	3,000	4,500	9	10,000	14,500	13	14,500	21,000
over 2000...	2	7,000	8,000	1	2,000	3,000	—	—	—	3	9,000	12,000	6	18,000	23,000
Unknown ..	21	(10,500)	(10,500)	4	(2,000)	(2,000)	4	(2,000)	(2,000)	4	(2,000)	(2,000)	33	(16,500)	(16,500)
TOTALS	33	21,750	26,100	27	7,800	12,750	45	13,150	23,200	38	25,400	37,650	143	68,100	99,700

500 and 1,000; 19 over 1,000. Of the latter, only six have populations exceeding 2,000 and perhaps only one attains 5,000.

Thus the multiplicity of groups is as much an established characteristic of the present state of the Brazilian indigenous population as is the scarcity of human beings. While groups of fewer than 250 persons, comprising 36% of the total groups, represent 6% to 9% of the population, groups exceeding 1,000 comprise only 13% of the total, including from 53% to 63% of the population.

From Table IV, showing the admissible maximum and minimum indigenous population by class size and degree of integration, it is seen that the 33 *isolated* groups comprise 24% of the total number of groups, including a minimum of 21,750 and a maximum of 26,100 people, or respectively, 31 and 26% of the population. The 27 groups in *intermittent contact,* comprising 10% of the total of groups, total a minimum of 7,800 and a maximum of 12,750 people, or respectively, 11.4% and 12.7% of the indigenous population. The 45 groups in permanent contact that represent 31% of the total groups have a minimum population of 13,150 and a maximum of 23,200, or respectively, 14.3% and 23.2% of the total population. Finally, the 37 integrated groups, representing 26% of all groups, comprise, by our calculations, a minimum of 25,400 and a maximum of 37,650 people, or from 37.2% to 37.7% of the total indigenous population.

It is to be emphasized that this last 37% represents a proportion of the indigenous population who, having achieved the condition of integration into the national society, present a certain demographic stability and in some cases even are experiencing appreciable population increases. The remaining 63% are still experiencing, to greater or lesser extent, the decline in population [13] that accompanies the various stages of the process of integration. In the light of these data we can infer, thus, that unless protective intervention becomes much more powerful and better oriented, the indigenous Brazilian population will continue to decline in the near future. Given the most optimistic hypothesis the Indian today comprises less than 0.2% of the Brazilian population. But it is predictable that not even this extremely low proportion will be maintained in the future.

However, correlating population totals with degree of integration, we observe that the average population per group tends to fall as the group passes from the condition of isolation to that of intermittent and permanent contacts, in the proportion of 1,000 to about 300 persons per group, and to rise thereafter, in integrated groups, to 600. These data confirm our observation that after the first contacts with civilization groups lose a substantial proportion of their population. But if they survive the first stages, they tend to make up at least part of their population, and are able even to exceed it once the principal causes of depopulation presently active among integrated groups have disappeared or become attenuated.

Thus it is seen that the indigenous Brazilian population is not condemned to disappear. Its survival and its increase depend directly on the assistance of which it may be assured.

Table V

Brazilian Indigenous Population, 1957, by Region: Minimum and Maximum Estimates

Regions	Groups	Population	
		Minimum	Maximum
AMAZONIA			
1—Amazonas	33	13,250	19,300
2—Pará	22	10,500	15,650
3—Maranhão	4	1,850	3,250
4—Acre	13	5,350	7,250
5—Rondônia	10	1,450	2,250
6—Rio Branco	7	9,750	12,500
7—Amapá	5	900	1,850
TOTAL	94	43,050	62,050
CENTRAL BRAZIL			
8—Mato Grosso	29	12,750	17,650
9—Goiás	5	2,100	3,750
TOTAL	34	14,850	21,400
EASTERN BRAZIL			
10—Northeast	8	4,700	7,500
11—Bahia	2	1,100	1,750
12—Minas	1	100	250
TOTAL	11	5,900	9,500
SOUTHERN REGION			
13—Total Southern	4	4,300	6,750
BRAZIL: TOTAL	143	68,100	99,700

Table V presents the same data arrayed by region to show the distribution of the indigenous population throughout the country.

The great majority is found in Amazonia—that is, 94 of the 143 groups (65.7%) with an estimated minimum population of 43,050 (63.2%), or an estimated maximum of 62,050 (62.2%). The States of Mato Grosso and Goiás, in Central Brazil, follow with 34 groups (23.7%)—a total population of 14,850 at minimum, 21,400 at maximum. Thereafter come the States of the Northeast, Bahia, and Minas Gerais, with 11 groups (7.0%) encompassing an indigenous population that we estimate at between 5,900 (8.5%) and 9,500 (9.5%). In the states of southern Brazil we find only 4 groups (2.8%), with an indigenous population varying between 4,300 (6.3%) and 6,750 (6.8%).

Correlating the regional distribution of indigenous population with degree of integration, we verify that all the *isolated* groups are found in the Amazon (26) and in Central Brazil (7) as are almost all the groups in *intermittent* and *permanent contact;* only 2 of the 72 groups in the latter stage appear in other regions. We may conclude therefore that the predicted reduction in indigenous population will be felt in the Amazon-Central Brazil area primarily, not only because the greater part of the indigenous population is concentrated here, but principally because the groups included are those that are most vulnerable to the lethal effects of epidemics and to other factors in decimation.

Table VI

Brazilian Indigenous Population, 1957, by Linguistic Family: Minimum and Maximum Estimates

Linguistic Family	Groups						Population	
	under 250	250 500	500 1,000	over 1,000	un-known	Total	Min.	Max.
Tupi	14	4	2	4	2	26	10,450	14,350
Aruak	6	6	3	2	6	23	11,500	16,150
Karib	8	3	1	3	7	22	10,250	14,150
Jê	5	4	4	4	1	18	9,950	15,600
Pano	1	2	3	—	6	12	4,600	8,750
Xiriuná	1	—	1	1	2	5	5,600	7,750
Others	17	2	4	5	9	37	15,750	22,950
Totals	52	21	18	19	33	143	68,100	99,700

Table VI, indigenous Brazilian population by linguistic stock, shows us that six of these stocks—the Tupi, the Aruak, the Karib, the Jê, the Xirianá and the Pano—comprise 106 of the 143 groups or about 70% of the total number of groups and an equivalent proportion of the entire Indian population. Representatives of all six are found in a state of isolation, for all the Xirianá are in this situation and none of the Pano groups appears to have achieved integration into the national society. These facts probably are explicable in the light of the Xirianá residence in an area which has remained unexplored until the present day, and of the Pano encounter with one of the most violent frontiers of expansion of the national society, that of the latex collectors of the Juruá and Purus river valleys.

Summary

1—The four categories of contact with civilization that we are using—*isolation, intermittent contact, permanent contact,* and *integration*—represent successive and necessary stages in the process of integration of indigenous populations into the national society. Some groups disappear before completing these stages. The duration of each group's permanence in a given stage depends on the historical incidents of its relations with the agents of civilization, certain of its cultural characteristics, and the particular economic variants of the national society with which it is confronted.

2—At each stage of integration, indigenous groups experience more or less uniform pressures. These stem from ecological and biotic factors in the first two stages, and progress cumulatively through economic and acculturative pressures in the successive phases of contact.

3—The final stage of integration does not correspond to the fusion of indigenous groups with the national society as an indistinguishable part of the latter, for this would be group assimilation. Group assimilation has not occurred in any of the cases examined. We are faced with, and have designated as a state or level of integration, a form of accommodation conciliating a certain degree of conservation of tribal cultural attributes with an increasing participation in the economic life and in the institutionalized spheres of national behavior. In extreme cases we are dealing with groups that speak only Portuguese and are highly Mestizo. Such groups are distinguished from the rural Brazilian populations with whom they coexist principally by virtue of the popular acceptance of their self-identification as Indian.

4—Analysis of the passage of indigenous Brazilian groups through the various stages of integration and of those groups that became extinct between 1900 and the present shows that they experienced substantial reduction in numbers and changes in composition. These modifications are expressed in the quasi-inversion of Lists I and II. The two columns that stand out are the first in List I and the last in List II, reporting respectively on isolated groups as constituting 45.6% of the known indigenous groups in 1900, and on the 37.8% that were extinct by 1957.

5—The proportion of tribes that have disappeared in their first collision with civilization during the past half-century indicates that the chances of survival were 7 in 10 for the isolated tribes and a bit higher, 3 in 4, for groups in intermittent contact. The principal factors of extinction that operate in the first stages of integration are conflicts with the agents of civilization and, above all, the high rate of depopulation resulting from the impact of epidemics of grippe, measles, whooping cough, etc., upon susceptible indigenous groups.

6—When indigenous groups reach the stage of permanent contact, in which forces of an ecological and biotic order accumulate with the compulsions of the process of acculturation, 3 in 10 groups decline; thereafter, in the stage of integration, 6 out of 10 groups become extinct. In all, 4 of each 10 tribes that were in existence in 1900 have disappeared, permitting the prediction that, if the same conditions persist, 57 of the current 143 groups will have become extinct before the end of the century.

7—Examination of the data by linguistic stock indicates that the Tupi groups were the most vulnerable to the constraints to which all were subject, for the Tupi lost a much greater proportion of their representatives reported in 1900. This fact perhaps can be explained by the relatively smaller cultural distance between these groups and representatives of the national society—a factor that facilitated communication, thereby intensifying contacts, resulting in an accumulation of the disorganizing pressures generated at each stage in integration. A substantially smaller decline characterizes the remaining linguistic stocks in contrast to the total disappearance of languages spoken by now extinct smaller populations.

8—Although their vocabularies have been modified to express the new experiences of the group, and their structure has been modified in coexistence with another language—given bilingualism—indigenous languages continue to be spoken, except where the group has become extinct or when extralinguistic pressures have prevailed.

The greater number of the integrated groups—even some of the most acculturated—continue to speak their original languages.

9—The national society presents such diverse characteristics, depending on whether it shows the face of its extractive, agricultural, or pastoral economy, that we cannot treat it as a constant. The difference in the pressures that each of these aspects of the economy can impose on indigenous groups is expressed in the proportion of indigenous groups that has disappeared in encounters with the several facets of the economy. Of the indigenous groups that came into contact with the frontiers of the agricultural economy, 60% have disappeared as compared with 45.7% of those who confronted extractive economies and 30.2% of those who were in the path of pastoral frontiers.

10—The proportion of indigenous groups in the areas of extractive economy (48.9%), pastoral (20.9%), and agricultural (2.8%) expresses, essentially, the degree of penetration and domination of the national society in each instance. These proportions demonstrate that the fundamental determinant of the destiny of indigenous groups is the dynamics of the national society's inexorable advance on the few unexplored geographic belts on which isolated groups (27.1%) still survive. In the measure that demographic concentrations increase, the number of indigenous groups and their population will decrease.

11—A bellicose defensive posture toward invaders in their territories and an aggressive stance against the pioneering fronts has enabled some indigenous groups to maintain their autonomy, but only at the cost of a rising mortality rate and profound changes in their ways of life. However, given the disparity between the two parties in confrontation, the Indians can deter the pioneering fronts only for a time, at a tremendous cost in terms of their own population. The deterrent is successful only until indigenous resistance has stimulated a concentration of forces capable of advancing on the Indians like an irresistible avalanche.

12—A docile and receptive attitude on the part of the Indians, facilitating contacts and creating the conditions for a rapid succession of stages of integration, stimulates an accumulation of disintegrating effects at each stage that condemns them to rapid extinction.

13—Intervention by the Serviço de Proteção aos Índios on behalf of indigenous groups at any stage of integration creates artificial conditions of integration. In many cases protection delays the natural order of events, assuring more time and greater liberty for Indian accommodation to the various forces impinging upon their society. Thus many tribes that would otherwise disappear are able to survive, establishing free and spontaneous relations with agents of the national society. Lamentably, the Serviço cannot operate throughout the entire country; its absence in areas like Juruá-Purus, Guaporé, and others is manifest in the higher proportions of groups that have disappeared during the twentieth century.

14—In the light of these facts we ought to conclude that indigenous cultures and languages can survive autonomously only in unexplored areas or areas of recent and tentative penetration, or under the artificial conditions of protective intervention. Indigenous cultures and languages are obsolescent and destined to lose their character as the national society grows and develops homogeneity.

15—There are between 68,100 and 99,700 Indians in contemporary Brazil; even if we accept the most optimistic hypothesis, indigenous Brazilians constitute less than 0.2% of the national population. About 30% of this indigenous population is isolated (21,750 to 26,100); about 11% lives in intermittent contact (7,800 to 12,750); about 21% maintains permanent contact (13,150 to 23,200); and about 38% is integrated (25,400 to 37,650).

16—A progressive reduction in the indigenous population is predictable to the extent that various groups move from a state of isolation to integration. This decline, however, will not condemn the indigenous portion of the Brazilian population to disappearance as a human group. Indigenous groups tend to experience a certain degree of demographic increase upon achieving integration. This increment, which presently permits some groups to regain part of their original numbers, can lead them to achieve and even surpass earlier population size in the future if they have assurances of better living conditions.

II. THE TASKS OF ETHNOLOGY AND OF LINGUISTICS

Examination of the behavior of Brazilian indigenous groups, in the face of the advance of civilization during the last fifty years and of the prospects for their survival, leads inevitably to the conclusion that tribal languages and cultures represent obsolescences in modern Brazil. It is only because the several geographic regions have developed at different rates of speed, and because our occupation of national territory has been discontinuous and irregular, that so many tribes (!) have survived and maintained their linguistic and cultural autonomy into the contemporary era.

We find the same contrasts of coexistence and contemporaneity of life styles that are not coetaneous in various other sectors of Brazilian life, for example, the African cultural survivals and the primary technology of certain areas; their respective ideological expressions appear in archaic beliefs and practices. How long will these archaisms continue to survive? What factors are responsible for their retention?

Given the rapid development of industrialization and urbanization, the expansion of means of communication and transportation, and the increase in the national population, their disappearance in the near future is to be predicted. Among the various anachronisms that might vanish, inevitably, are the autonomous indigenous languages and cultures whose coexistence with an ever more homogeneous industrial civilization is not feasible.

Brazilian indigenous tribes are numerically insignificant—in fact, none numbers over 5,000, and the great majority has a population of under 200. Their cultural diversity is reflected in the existence of about 35 independent languages, divided into more than 100 mutually unintelligible dialects. In view of this combination of factors, there would be no possibility of their autonomous cultural development in the direction of that domination of modern technology which would permit them to exist as independent peoples.

Protective intervention works through the imposition of artificial conditions of integration into the national society. Its occasional successes are the only factor in the maintenance of the original tribal cultural configurations in contact situations. The activities of the Serviço arise not from a conservationist zeal for tribal styles of life, but simply from interest in the salvation of the Indian as a human being. There is also the practical consideration that the Indians' survival frequently appears to be a function of a slower rate of culture change than is likely without intervention. Continuation of the protective orientation in relation to groups now entering into contact with the national society and its extension to presently isolated groups in the future may prolong the existence of indigenous languages and cultures.

Even so, we are merely postponing the inevitable. This postponement is fully justifiable and highly to be recommended for humanitarian reasons. But it must be recognized that the protective policy can do no more than delay the disintegration of the tribal world.

From these facts we must conclude that, if in our judgment Brazilian tribal languages and cultures ought to be documented, we must act promptly. It is fully certain that there will never again be an opportunity to do whatever is not done now in this respect. We face a task that is unquestionably of major scientific relevance, that of preserving dozens of autonomous indigenous languages and cultures by documentation—the sole form of preservation practicable here. These dozens of surviving languages and cultures are the last remnants of thousands that have disappeared in the wake of European expansion.

In other words, our task consists in salvaging leftovers in the wake of a hecatomb of worldwide proportions which eliminated a major part of the systems of verbal communication and of the cultural ways developed by man to satisfy human needs. If we consider the scientific description of natural zoological and botanical species important, if we value geological and other classifications, what weight must we give to the task of documenting the most singular human creations, languages and cultures, particularly these languages and cultures, the last to have kept themselves intact against the influences of our own standardized cultures?

This is the task facing our generation of ethnologists and linguists.

We shall point out some themes which appear to us to merit priority, some resources that can and should be mobilized, and some criteria that seem to us convenient for the accomplishment of this task.

Exploratory Inquiry

The difficulties encountered in the elaboration of the present balance of the situation of Brazilian tribes suggest that priority be given to studying all the regions of the country where tribal groups survive, or at least those regions of which our ignorance is greatest. The resultant overall and current view of tribes that subsist effectively would serve as a base for the formulation of a program of intensive studies. This study ought to cover a certain number of basic questions concerning demographic structure, conditions of integration into the national society, degree of acculturation, and culture and language of all the Brazilian tribes. A duly experimental model vocabulary like that of Morris Swadesh should be used in the last-mentioned effort.

Besides lending itself to the ends of genetic classification, the experimental model device has other advantages. Culture would be documented through the organization of collections of artifacts and the use of films and sound tracks recording the language and all the aspects of group life that are accessible to extensive research and are susceptible to this type of documentation.

This work will provide materials that permit not only the revision of current linguistic classifications, all of which are unreliable because the vocabularies upon which they are based are deficient, but also the sketching of a new, more complete, and current picture of Brazilian ethnology. The possibilities of successfully completing all the most intensive studies with the requisite speed are slight indeed. It is, however, all too probable that the accumulation of these data will come to constitute the greatest future patrimony of information on the ethnology and linguistics of the tribes of Brazil.

Given the character of this task and the data to be anticipated from it, it seems likely to capture the interest of a good many museums and universities throughout the world. It should also be of interest to various international institutions that encourage scientific research, especially on this continent. Moreover, the task is meaningful to the specialized agencies of the United Nations, for example UNESCO and the International Labor Office, both of which have manifested interest in problems of this order. Its practical execution could be left to an interinstitutional committee authorized to represent the various sponsors and to recruit the necessary field work staff. Such a committee should preferably be constituted of specialists who have already worked in certain areas. They should be assured the opportunity of a preliminary meeting to establish a uniform working methodology. In Brazil alone there are many ethnologists and Indianists to whom participation in a program of this type will be of interest.

Ethnological Research

However, the basic task of ethnology, for which there is no substitute, is intensive monographic study of cultures, particularly of cultures that have maintained their autonomy. In the light of earlier analyses, one can synthesize the conditions for the completion of this work and the priorities that should be assigned each type of study as follows:

a   *Isolated tribes*—These are the most conservative groups;

the conditions in which they live in general discourage immediate study, for the normal exigencies of safety in the intimate and continuing cohabitation imposed by intensive ethnological research need to be considered. However, it has already become practicable to carry out direct research on some secluded groups living in accessible regions. This is true for example of the *Xiriana* of the Aruak language group, of the *Waiká*[14] and the *Pakidái*[15] of the upper course of the Demeni, Marauiá, and Cauboris rivers and the sources of the Catrimani and the Uraricoera. The *Salumá* and *Tirió* Indians at the sources of the Cuminá and Trombetas rivers on the frontiers of Brazil with Dutch Guiana [now Surinam] are additional examples.[16] In this category two Tupi groups of the left bank of the Rio Tocantins, the *Asurini* and the *Parakanãn*[17] for whom we do not even have vocabularies, also can be included. For it was only in 1955 that the Serviço de Proteção aos Índios contacted some subgroups of these tribes. An ever increasing number of other groups reported as isolated on our list should be entering into peaceful relations with agents of civilization during the coming years, opening up new opportunities for research.

   b Tribes in intermittent contact—Conditions for research among these groups are ideal, as much because these Indians have not yet lost their basic culture traits as because at this stage it is possible to grasp their traditional mode of life in full swing. Although the disorganizing effects of epidemics and of other factors have already begun to affect them, rendering certain sectors of their culture inoperative, it is still possible to reconstruct these sectors through information taken from people who have participated in them. As a general rule, command of the tribal language is indispensable for studies of this type. This requirement and the difficulties of access to groups who live in remote areas are serious hindrances to research. Perhaps for these reasons there have been few studies of groups in intermittent contact.

   In this category, research on the two Kayapó groups, the *Xikrín* and the *Kubén-Kran-kegn* of southern Pará, pacified by the SPI[18] in 1952 and 1954 respectively, is particularly recommended. Also suitable are the *Xavante (Akuên)* pacified in 1949, who represent one of the most conservative Jê groups, and who, with the still hostile *Gaviões,* are the tribes of this linguistic family that are of major ethnological interest. Among the Tupi in intermittent contact are the *Aré* (Xetá), a small group recently discovered in the woodlands of Serra dos Dourados in the State of Paraná, a region which is rapidly being occupied by coffee planters. It is to be noted that these Indians still use stone axes; they appear to be the most conservative tribe of Brazil. Thanks to a combination of circumstances that is difficult to prearrange, they have been able to maintain their segregation in a very accessible area and to conserve much of their traditional culture.[19] Other Tupi groups at an equivalent stage of integration are the *Kaapor (Urubus),* located on the right bank of the Gurupí in an economically marginal zone, who conserve what is fundamental in their traditional culture,[20] and the *Kayabí* who are moving from the valley of the Rio Teles Pires to the tributaries of the Xingú, fleeing from the pioneers of the extractive economy to seek the type of assistance that the SPI gives to Xingu groups. The *Kayabí* have not yet been studied by ethnologists; research on this Tupi group can contribute much to the clarification of some basic problems of Brazilian ethnology.

The *Kamayurá* and *Awetí* are also found on the Rio Xingú. With the *Trumái* and the Aruak and Karib groups they will be given special consideration in the light of their experiences with a process of intertribal acculturation that has contributed considerable uniformity to their cultural heritage.

The *Nambikuára* Indians[21] of northwestern Mato Grosso, the *Xiriná*—an isolated language on the Rio Uraricoera—and the *Javaé* of the island of Bananal should also be assigned to this category of priority. These last constitute a *Karajá* subtribe that has enjoyed greater isolation and appears, therefore, to offer especially favorable conditions for intensive ethnological study.

To these groups can be added the *Kaxuiâna* of the middle Rio Trombetas, the *Katawiân* and *Sikiâna* of the Rio Cafuini, the *Waiwai*[22] and *Parikotó* of the upper Rio Mapuera, and the *Apalaí* on the Rio Jari further to the east.

   c *Tribes in permanent contact*—The groups in permanent contact with the national society already present profound modifications resulting from the cumulative effect of pressures of ecological, biotic, economic, and cultural order. They therefore offer special compensations and attractions for ethnological studies. The fact that many of their members are bilingual is the first of these.

Bilingualism in itself signals that cultural disintegration has proceeded to the point at which the group or isolated individuals are able to treat objectively aspects of their culture that they were unable to discuss earlier under pain of sanctions or out of simple shame. Moreover, by virtue of assimilation the group becomes more aware of the relativity of customs and is able to view itself less subjectively.

There are at least eight Tupi groups in these conditions of interaction: the *Tapirapé*[23] of Mato Grosso, four small groups who live on the tributaries of the left bank of the Guaporé,[24] the *Mundurukú*,[25] and the *Jurúna*. These latter are represented by a small nucleus living near the mouth of the Manitsauá-Mitsú River on the Xingú.[26] They are remnants of the great *Jurúna* tribe that faced the first impact of civilization in the seventeenth century at the mouth of the Xingú and that has been in constant flight with a continually declining population, since then.

Among the Aruak in permanent contact with the national society, there are five little-known tribes in the area of Juruá-Purus, two on the Rio Negro and the *Irantxe,* and a *Paresí* subgroup in northwest Mato Grosso, none of whom has yet been studied intensively.

Three Jê tribes are found in the same contact situation: the *Kayapó-Gorotíre* of southern Pará, the *Ramkókamekra* or *Canelas* who are the best studied indigenous group in Brazil,[27] and the *Krahó* who still await intensive ethnological study.[28]

The same comment holds for some subgroups of the *Taulipang* and *Wayâna,* both of the Karib linguistic group, and also for five Pano tribes and a Katukína group of Juruá-Purus, the *Tukána* and *Baníwa* tribes of the Rio Negro, the *Witóto* and *Tukúna* of Solimões.[29]

Table II classifies the *Karajá, Borôro,* and *Kadiwéu* Indians at the same level of interaction. A series of studies of these tribes has been published, but lively interest in them persists. Studies in depth are needed to permit clarification of a series of problems cited in available ethnographic essays on the *Borôro,* who are of special interest.

The *Maxakalí* Indians of Minas Gerais, the only group in Eastern Brazil that has conserved enough of its traditional culture to permit a study of the type we are discussing, are in the same category.[30]

d *Integrated* groups participate intensely in the economy and the principal forms of institutionalized behavior of Brazilian society. Their languages and cultures have been so profoundly affected by integration that they cannot profitably be the subject of the same order of studies we have been considering. Nonetheless, they present other facets increasingly within the purview of ethnology. These will be considered below.

It is now necessary to examine the possibilities of carrying out the most urgent of the studies enumerated above. The plain fact is that if we continue at our current pace it will not be possible to complete even a substantial portion of them. Under these circumstances, it becomes essential to ask what interventions would most effectively promote new research.

During recent years the study of ethnology has been integrated into the university system; despite some imperfections, it is now possible to train researchers. Effectively, throughout the world many young men capable of becoming professionals in this field are earning degrees. The basic problem is that there are only a limited number of institutions capable of offering employment opportunities or financing research. In Brazil until recently only museums and universities had a few openings for ethnologists on their staffs. Now the Serviço de Proteção aos Índios also recruits for some appointments. All in all, however, positions for ethnologists are very few for the vast task ahead. It is improbable that there will be considerable increases in their number during the next few years. It becomes necessary, therefore, to augment the sources of financing for the research of independent specialists and to stimulate greater collaboration with the ethnologists of other countries.

The means which, to our view, is most convenient would be to persuade institutions that sponsor research to make more ample funds available for ethnological studies and to establish priorities favoring the study of indigenous groups who are maintaining their cultural and linguistic autonomy.

Studies of Socio-Cultural Processes

Examination of the perspectives for survival of the indigenous languages and cultures of Brazil suggests, with the same character of priority, another order of research: research on certain socio-cultural processes which must be studied promptly, if ever, for the human contexts in which they operate are on the verge of extinction.

1—*Areas of intertribal acculturation*—On the borders of the Brazilian Amazon, in areas drained by the headwaters of some of the principal tributaries of the Amazon River, there are six confederations of indigenous tribes, each of which participates in an area of intense intertribal acculturation. The ethnological study of each tribal component of these constellations which we have treated up to now will contribute only material for the traditional studies of culture areas based upon bibliographic and museum sources. The opportunity that is offered, however, is that of focusing directly on the last of these still-evolving areas with the aim of achieving a more precise comprehension of how relations of dependence, complementarity, or symbiosis function when established among tribal units, welding them into supertribal combines. The direct study of these contexts would cast new light on the behavior of their components and perhaps also on factors in resistance or motivation which are capable of affecting the process of evolution on the tribal level.

We suggest below the areas which seem to be most indicated for this order of research:

a   In the region of the headwaters of the Xingú several tribes coexist and interact intensely, forming a true linguistic mosaic in which the Tupi are represented by two groups; the Aruak, by three; the Karib, by four; the Jê, by one; and there is yet another unrelated language, that of the Trumái.[31] The diversity of tribal languages contrasts with a cultural uniformity[32] which ranges from the participation of all in the same adaptive equipment to common forms of social organization and a world view that is essentially identical. Such uniformity can have resulted only from a secular process of interinfluence that culminated with the establishment of a true system of intertribal relations, today fundamental for the survival of each group. The direct study of this web of relations of interdependence of the tribes of the Upper Xingú is at least as important as ethnological studies of each component of the area.

b   Two similar supertribal confederations exist in the region which extends from the sources of the tributaries of the right bank of the Guaporé to the Rio Pimenta Bueno.

Here, too, tribes that are linguistically distinct were brought by reciprocal interinfluence to a profound uniformity of culture that is easily seen when artifacts and ethnological data are examined. We refer to the *Kepkiriwát, Mondé, Sanamaiká, Guarategaja, Kabixiâna, Huarí, Masaká, Amniapé, Arikapú, Wayoró, Makúrap, Tuparí,* and *Aruá* on the one hand, and the *Txapakúra, Urupá, Pakaánovas, Arikên,* and *Puruborá* groups on the other hand. Here, moreover, protective intervention has not exerted the same force as on the Upper Xingú. All these groups have been profoundly affected by civilization. The majority of tribes has disappeared, as can be seen from Table II. The survivors have conserved little of their cultural autonomy and failed to maintain the minimum population indispensable to the functioning of their ancient institutions. All in all, given the relevance of the problem, it is necessary to make an effort to reconstitute the ancient system of tribal interrelations.

c   The upper Juruá-Purus appears to have been another area of intense intertribal acculturation. Ethnographic data concerning the Pano, Aruak, and Katukína groups of that region reveal considerable uniformity and also the probable existence of a system of interdependence between distinct groups of tribes. However, it already may be too late to study this region directly, for the violence that accompanied colonization annihilated many tribes and left the greater part of the survivors in profound cultural disorganization.[33]

d   In the region of the tributaries of the Rio Negro—the Uaupés, the Tiquié, the Içana and their affluents—a long process of intertribal acculturation has intermixed the cultural heritages and at times even the languages of another block of tribes which were originally distinct. Here, it appears that various waves of distinct tribes followed upon each other. For example, the Makú, with a more rudimentary culture, launched themselves towards the periphery while the several Aruak groups which had a more advanced culture installed themselves along the banks of the great rivers. The most simply equipped Tukána tribes entered into competition with the Aruak and must have adopted much of the latter's culture. It is still possible today to distinguish representatives of these different waves of migration and to follow the process of acculturation.

In our times Tukána has been adopted by the Tariâna Indians who originally spoke a language related to Baníwa, of the Aruak language family.[34] This area affords a rich ethnographic documentation in addition to the possibility of direct research. The two sources in combination make feasible a reconstruction of the former pattern of intertribal relations.

e   On the high ground between the watersheds of the Orinoco and Uaupés rivers in the far north of Brazil, there is another combination of tribes that has experienced intensive interculturation. The tribes are the Xirianá, Waiká, Pakidái, Yabaâna, Mandawáka, and perhaps many others yet to be known. Because it has been one of the least explored belts of our national territory, this probably is the area of major demographic concentration of the Indians of Brazil. It has been penetrated only recently, and only by extractors of woodland drugs. Thus the indigenous occupants are not yet subject to the pressures that have liquidated so many languages and cultures in other areas.

f Finally, we highly recommend that this type of research be undertaken along the upper course of the Cuminá, Trombetas, and Cafuini rivers, on the frontiers of Brazil with the Dutch and British Guianas [now Surinam and Guyana]. There are several *Tirió* groups here (the *Marahtxo* or *Pianokotó, Aramayana, Proyana* or *Rangu-Pikí, Aramiatxo, Okomoyana* and *Aramihotó*,[35] *Salumá*, and *Sikiâna*), who also appear to depend on a system of intertribal relations that can be the subject of a field study.

2—*Process of Integration and Acculturation*—The study of certain aspects of the process of integration of indigenous populations into the national society is another order of phenomena that merits special consideration as an urgent task of ethnology in Brazil. Such studies frequently have been referred to as all that remains to ethnologists as tribal cultures decline. However, given the rate with which the national society is proceeding to integrate tribal groups, time for the scientific observation of the processes of acculturation and integration is running out.

We particularly need investigations of the kinds of pressure that affect tribal life before direct and permanent contacts have been established. The data analyzed in this article offers some hints of what is involved. Thus, we know that there are preacculturative factors, e.g., those proceeding from biotic and ecological interaction, to which a relevant role in the decimation of tribal groups and in cultural disintegration is to be attributed. An example is the disintegrating consequences of depopulation caused by epidemics. Another disorganizing factor is the abrupt and compulsory transformation of tribal economies originally devoted to subsistence production into economies productive of articles for commerce. This transformation appears to coincide with the entry of the group into permanent contact with civilization. These two "moments" in the process of integration can be fully understood only through field studies focusing on indigenous groups in various stages of integration. As isolated groups or groups in intermittent contact become more and more rare, studies from the viewpoint proposed here become increasingly urgent.

Considering the volume of the tasks we face and the limitations of resources available, studies dedicated exclusively to this proposition may not be practicable. If so, ethnographic research should be projected in such fashion that a specific concern with the problems of survival of tribal populations is built into the design. In other words, the meticulous investigation of demographic structure, of birth rates and fertility indices, of the disorganizing effects of epidemics, and of other factors that aid in the delineation of the first stages of integration should be incorporated into ethnological research design. These problems and facets of tribal life are as relevant to ethnological knowledge as the study of mythology or of the kinship system.

The perspective we propose requires ethnology to evidence greater interest in the destiny of the people it studies. It will benefit ethnological research, heightening the precision of our grasp of tribal situations, for the fact that must be kept in mind is that no group—not even the most isolated—is entirely immune to the influences of civilization. Here the task of ethnography is not the simple and more or less naive documentation of the tribal culture at a hypothetical point in time, but rather the delineation of that culture as it presents itself at the moment of observation. In other words, the ethnologist's aim is to understand how and why a tribal culture has assumed the configuration it presents to the observer.

Linguistic Studies

The most important contribution to be made to indigenous Brazilian linguistics is the elaboration of a new classification based on materials more adequate than those presently available. Only through an extensive inquiry, such as was suggested in the first topic covered above, will it be practicable to collect such materials with the necessary speed and required uniformity.

To perform the basic descriptive tasks for the study of the indigenous languages, a system of priorities inverse to that proposed for our ethnographic studies will be needed. It is preferable that ethnologists direct their attention to the most isolated groups in an effort to document the last manifestations of a culture not as yet affected by civilization. But linguists should seek out the most integrated groups, for their languages are the most immediately threatened with extinction.

This inversion is possible only because language constitutes the most persistent sphere of culture. Languages, although modified, continue to live in the greater proportion of groups; they disappear only with the death of the last components of the group. Moreover, the ethnologist must have functioning cultures to observe, while the linguist can, if necessary, satisfactorily reconstruct a language with the aid of only a single individual who speaks it.

Casual examination of the last column of List II, referring

to groups which became extinct between 1900 and 1957, gives us an idea of the considerable number of languages that have died. Lamentably, we do not even have linguistic material adequate for the genetic classification of the majority of the lost languages. However, that column reports the groups that have disappeared as ethnic entities and does not necessarily imply that none of their members survived; it is probable that individuals with whose aid it may be possible to reconstruct the original language can still be found.

Reconstruction of languages threatened with extinction will be the most urgent task of the linguist. From it follows the study of the language of groups that are presently integrated. Research on groups with fewer current survivors, who are in greatest danger of extinction, is of particular urgency.

There is, therefore, a relevant practical problem here. The majority of the most competent linguists in the field today are people who were especially trained to translate the Gospels[36] into indigenous languages. These specialists very naturally are interested in groups who have the greatest likelihood of surviving—groups capable of becoming literate and able some day to read the Bible in translation. Under these circumstances, the languages that are most clearly threatened with extinction are the least likely to be recorded. For the sum total of these reasons, it is desirable for institutions sponsoring research to make the study of languages on the verge of extinction attractive.

In our view the most desirable way to initiate an intensive program of descriptive linguistic studies would be to interest linguists—for example, those of the Summer Institute of Linguistics of Oklahoma—in specializing individually in a linguistic stock. Exhaustive study of one of the variations within this language stock should be followed by less detailed research on other representatives of the same stock. Were this done, we would promptly have model studies of languages of the Tupi, Karib, Aruak, Jê, Pano, Katukína, Tukána, Txapakúra, Xirianá, Mura, Makú, and Puináve linguistic stocks, and of the Borôro, Karajá, Mbayá-Guaikurú, Nambikuára, Tukuna, Maxakali, and Fulniô (Yatê), and perhaps also of the Mirânia, Guató, and Ofaié languages.

For this minimal program of descriptive studies of the principal variants of Brazil's indigenous languages we need at least 22 appropriately trained linguists. Research of this magnitude can be accomplished only through the collaboration of scientific institutions all over the world. We stand before a cultural inheritance that is only incidentally Brazilian, for the indigenous languages and cultures surviving here are the patrimony of science and of humanity. This fact alone justifies the proposal.

III. REPORT ON BRAZILIAN INDIGENOUS GROUPS

We present below a report on indigenous groups which has served as the base for our research. Coverage includes almost all the Brazilian tribes that have survived into the twentieth century.

Tribal designations, capitalized and in alphabetical order, are followed by data as indicated: (1) synonyms, when their inclusion seems necessary to avoid confusion; (2) a generic estimate of the current population by sizable classes (under 50, 50 to 100, etc.) which allows us to use information from various sources that frequently contradict each other; (3) a report on the linguistic affiliation of the group; (4) a summary of the most recent available data on location and assistance by the Serviço de Proteção aos Índios for each group with which contact has been direct and continuous; (5) finally, an indication of the type of relations the group presently maintains with the national society. The expression "extinct" is used here to refer to any group that has ceased to be an ethnic entity during the last fifty years. Its use does not imply that no detribalized individuals have survived the group's disappearance.

Our principal source for the location of indigenous groups, for population estimates, and for determination of the type of contact maintained with the national society, has been the archives of the Serviço de Proteção aos Índios. In the classification of tribe by linguistic family, we have followed Curt Nimuendajú. But for this and other purposes we at times have used the work of Paul Rivet, Chestmir Loukotka, Alden Mason, and Norman A. McQuown, as well as to the reports of K. G. Grubb and G. P. Murdock.

Tribal designations conform to our interpretation of the convention for the spelling of tribal names proposed by the Primeira Reunião Brasileira de Antropologia.

To facilitate consultation, the alphabetical report includes some allusions to linguistic families and indigenous groups not considered in this study. Such remarks are parenthetical and in lower case: they are provided only when the information available is unreliable.

We proposed this study in full knowledge that it could be brought to conclusion only at the risk of errors and imprecisions. Our research has been motivated by the inescapable need for a working instrument of this type and by the conviction that exploratory studies similar to the present effort offer the sole opportunity to contribute to precise reporting on contemporary tribes in the future.

This, then, is our appeal for the collaboration of every scholar who has direct knowledge of, or more precise data on, the several indigenous groups of Brazil.

AGAVOTOKUENG   *Aruak* (?)
> Referred to by the Xinguanos as "similar to the *Iawalapití*." Living between the Curisevo and Culuene rivers, sources of the Xingú. State of Mato Grosso. (Isolated)

AIPATSÊ   *Karib*
> Had their own settlement on the banks of the middle Culuene, but have been so decimated that the survivors were incapable of living independently and have united with the Kuikúro. State of Mato Grosso. (Extinct)

AIWATERÍ   *Xirianá*
> Mapulau and Totobí rivers, sources of the Demeni, tributaries of the left bank of the Rio Negro. State of Amazon, Venezuelan frontier. (Isolated)

AMAHUÁKA (100 to 250)   *Pano*
> Some small groups on the upper Juruá and the upper Purus rivers; the major part of the tribe lives in Peru. Territory of Acre. (Permanent contact)

AMANAYÉ (less than 50)   *Tupi*
> Along the Garrafão and Ararandeuára, tributaries of the Capim and Caiararé rivers, on the Rio Mojú. State of Pará. (Integrated)

AMNIAPÉ   *Tupi*
> Lived on the Rio Mequens. Territory of Guaporé. (Extinct)

APALAÍ (100 to 250)   *Karib*
> On the Jari and Paru rivers. Territory of Amapá. (Intermittent contact)

APÂNIEKRA Jê
Branch of the eastern *Timbira*. Lived in Porquinhos, on a small tributary of the Rio Corda. State of Maranhão. (Extinct)

APIAKÁ Tupi
On the banks of the upper Rio Tapajós, near the confluence of São Manoel. Northern Mato Grosso. (Extinct)

APINAYÉ (100 to 250) Jê
Branch of the eastern *Timbira*. In the region included in the angle formed by the lower Rio Araguaia with the Rio Tocantins. Indian Post Apinajés, near the Farinha, tributary of the Tocantins, in the municipality of Tocantinópolis. Extreme north, State of Goiás. (Integrated)

ARARAS Karib
Arara groups (Parirí? Timirem?) have been referred to at various locations in the woodlands between the Xingú and Tocantins (the Anapú, Pacajá and Panelas rivers). State of Pará. (Extinct)

(Araras) Unknown
Four other groups designated as "Arara," of unknown linguistic affiliation, are located on the Jamaxim, a tributary of the Rio Tapajós, on the Manicoré and on the Rio Prêto, tributaries of the middle and lower Madeira, and on the Rio Guaraibas, tributary of the Aripuanã, in the States of Pará and Amazonas.

ARAWÍNE Tupi
On the Rio 7 de Setembro, tributary of the Culuene, source of the Xingú, in the State of Mato Grosso. (Extinct)

ARÉ (XETÁ) (100 to 250) Tupi
In the Serra de Dourados, valley of the Rio Ivaí, beyond the Campo do Mourão, State of Paraná. First contacts with SPI in 1952. (Intermittent contact)

ARIKAPÚ or MAXUBÍ (50 to 100) Unknown
Headwaters of the Rio Branco, tributary of the right bank of the Guaporé. Territory of Rondônia. (Permanent contact)

ARIKÊN Tupi
Found by the Rondon Commission in 1913 between the Candeia and Jamarí rivers, tributaries of the right bank of the Madeira, from whence they were transferred to the Pôsto Rodolfo Miranda of SPI. Territory of Rondônia. (Extinct)

ARUÀ   *Tupi*
>Along the Rio Branco, tributary of the left bank of the Guaporé.
>Territory of Rondônia. (Extinct)

ASURINÍ (250 to 500)   *Tupi*
>Headwaters of the Rio Bacajá, tributary of the Middle Xingú.
>A subgroup was attracted to Pôsto Trocará on the embank-
>ment of the E. F. de Alcobaça, [Alcobaça Railroad] by SPI in
>1953. State of Pará. (Isolated)

ATRUAHÍ   *Karib*
>*Waimirí* subgroup on the Alalau and Jauaperí rivers, tributaries
>of the Rio Negro, in northern Amazonas. Have had sporadic
>contacts with Pôsto de Pacificação Barbosa Rodrigues, munici-
>pality of Itacoatiara. (Isolated)

AWETÍ (under 50)   *Tupi*
>On the left bank of the Rio Curisevo, one of the sources of
>the Xingú. Pôsto Capitão Vasconcelos. State of Mato Grosso.
>(Intermittent contact)

BAENÂN   *Baenân*
>On the left bank of the Rio Pardo; survivors were brought to
>the Pôsto Indígena Paraguassu and Caramuru in the municipality
>of Itabuna where fewer than twenty detribalized Baenân sur-
>vive. State of Bahia. (Extinct)

BAKAIRÍ (100 to 250)   *Karib*
>At the beginning of the twentieth century there were two
>distinct nuclei of *Bakairí* who maintained no communication
>with each other; one on the Novo and Paranatinga rivers,
>tributaries of the Teles Pires, was in contact with white men;
>the other on the Batovi and Curisevo rivers, sources of the
>Xingú, was entirely isolated. Today all the Bakairí are found on
>SPI's Pôsto Simões Lopes, on the right bank of the Rio Parana-
>tinga near the mouth of the Azul, in the municipality of
>Cuiabá, State of Mato Grosso. (Integrated)

(Baniwa) (Baniua do Içana)   *Aruak*
>Linguistic family of the Içana River: three principal variants:
>Karutâna, Kadaupuritana (Hohodene) and Korispaso.

BARAWÂNA   *Aruak*
>Upper Padauiri, tributary of the left bank of the Rio Negro.
>State of Amazonas. (Isolated)

BOCA NEGRA   *Tupi*
Kawahib tribe of the upper Machadinho, tributary of the Roosevelt. Previously occupied various locations between the Jiparaná (Machado) and Roosevelt (Dúvida) rivers, in the Territory of Rondônia. (Isolated?)

BORÔRO (500 to 1,000)   *Borôro*
One of the major tribes of Central Brazil whose territory crossed the center of Mato Grosso from the frontiers of Bolivia to the "Mineiro" triangle. Greatly decimated and now living on the Pôstos General Gomes Carneiro (Ex-Córrego Grande), Couto de Magalhães (ex-Perigara), General Galdino Pimentel and Pôsto Piebaga, all in the municipality of Leverger. Also a group at the Salesian Mission. Rio São Lourenço. Center of the State of Mato Grosso. (Permanent contact)

BOTOCUDOS (Aimoré, Borun, Gueren)   *Botocudos*
Includes several linguistically differentiated groups divided into bands some of which survived into the twentieth century, in the woodlands *(matas)* between the Rio Jequitinhonha and the valley of the Rio Doce, in the States of Bahia, Minas, and Espírito Santo. Survivors of the Jequitinhonha and Mucuri groups, now extinct, were brought together at the Itambacurí mission in Minas, site of the contemporary city of Itambacuri, and became extinct here. The Rio Doce groups were pacified by SPI in 1911 and resettled at the Pôstos Pancas in Espirito Santo and Cibrão and Guido Marlière (Crenaque or Eme) in Minas Gerais. Fewer than ten descendants of the Botocudos survive at the latter site, in the municipality of Resplendor. (Extinct)

CANOEIROS (Avá)   *Tupi*
Above the floodplains between the Formoso River and the eastern arm of the Araguáia. Island of Bananal, Goiás. (Isolated)

DESÂNA (100 to 250)   *Tukána*
Division of the *Wanâna* on the Papuri and Tiquié rivers, tributaries of the Uaupés. Receiving assistance from SPI Pôsto Melo Franco and the office of the SPI adjutant on the Rio Uaupés. Northwestern Amazonas. (Permanent contact)

DIÓRE (500 to 1,000)   *Jê*
Division of the northern *Kayapó*. The principal nucleus is on the Rio Paraopeba, tributary of the Itacaiunas which in turn

is a tributary of the Tocantins. Hostile, in conflict with the nut collectors of Marabá and the cattle raisers of Conceição do Araguáia in southern Pará. (Isolated)

EMERILON   *Tupi*

Between the sources of the Aproague, Marroni and Oiapoque rivers, in the far north of the Territory of Amapá. Survivors were found on Pôsto Luiz Horta, at the confluence of the Muripi and Oiapoque rivers. (Extinct)

ESPINHOS (Epinod)   *Pano*

Rio Corumahá, tributary of the Purus, in the Territory of Acre. (Extinct)

FULNIÔ (Carnijó) (1,000 to 1,500)   *Fulniô*

Largest and most conservative indigenous group of northeast Brazil. Pôsto Dantas Barreto, near the city of Aguas Belas in the State of Pernambuco. (Integrated)

GALIBÍ (250 to 500)   *Karib*

Rio Uaçá, tributary of the Oiapoque. Indian Post of the same name in the municipality of Clevelândia, in the far north of the Territory of Amapá. (Integrated)

GAVIÕES (1,500 to 2,000)   *Jê*

Today the principal division of the eastern *Timbíra*. Settled on the plains at the edge of the forests *(matas)* of the right bank of the middle Tocantins, between Mãe Maria and Jacundá, in southeastern Pará. (Isolated)

GOROTÍRE (100 to 250)   *Jê*

Division of the northern Kayapó, pacified in 1936. Rio Fresco, tributary of the Middle Xingú. Aided by SPI Pôsto Gorotire. Municipality of Altamira in the State of Pará. (Permanent contact)

GUAHARÍBO   *Xirianá*

Upper Cauaboris and Marauiá rivers, tributaries of the left bank of the Rio Negro, in the State of Amazonas. (Isolated)

GUAJÁ (100 to 250)   *Tupi*

Small bands living in the "babassu" palm tree zone on the eastern edge of the woodlands of the Gurupí and the upper Pindaré rivers. State of Maranhão. (Isolated)

GUAJAJÁRA (1,000 to 1,500)   *Tupi*
    Division of the *Tenetehara* on the Grajaú, Mearim, and Pindaré
    rivers. Aided by SPI Pôstos Gonçalves Dias, Manoel Rabelo,
    and Ararigboia. State of Maranhão. (Integrated)

GUARANÍ (3,000 to 4,000)   *Tupi*
    Principal concentrations in southern Mato Grosso, western
    Paraná and Northwestern Rio Grande do Sul on SPI Posts and
    in independent nuclei. Among the contemporary *Guaraní* of
    Brazil three subdivisions can be distinguished by variations in
    dialect: the NANDÉVA (Apopokuva, Tañyguá, Txiripá); the
    MBIÁ (Kaiwá, Tambéopé, Aputeré, Baticolas); and the KAIOVA
    (Teüi, Tembekuá, Kaiwá). The principal nuclei are in Mato
    Grosso on Pôsto Francisco Horta and in the village of Passa-
    rinho in the municipality of Dourados; on Pôsto Benjamin
    Constant and the Iguatemí, Cerro Peron, Sossoró, and Pirajuí
    reservations in the municipality of União; on Pôsto José Boni-
    fácio, in the municipality of Ponta Porã. In the State of São
    Paulo on Pôsto Curt Nimuendajú, in the municipality of Avaí;
    and on Pôsto José de Anchieta. There are several small nuclei
    in Itarirí and Itanhaem along the Paulista coast. In the State
    of Paraná, on Pôsto Barão de Antonina in the municipality of
    Araiponga; on Pôsto Rio das Cobras in the municipality of
    Iguassú; on Pôsto Mangueirinha in the municipality of Man-
    gueirinha. In the State of Santa Catarina: a nucleus on Pôsto
    Duque de Caxias in the municipality of Ibirama. In the State
    of Rio Grande do Sul: on Pôsto Guarita and several half-
    civilized settlements in the municipality of Palmeiras and in
    Erechim, Lagoa Vermelha, and Passo Fundo. On Pôsto Guido
    Marlière in the municipality of Resplendor in the State of
    Minas Gerais, a small nucleus relocated here by SPI. (Inte-
    grated)

GUARATEGAJA   *Tupi*
    On the Rio Mequens, tributary of the right bank of the Gua-
    poré, in the Territory of Rondônia. (Extinct)

GUATÓ   *Guató*
    On the banks of the Rio Paraguai, sometimes going up the
    Rio São Lourenço, in the State of Mato Grosso. (Extinct)

HOHODENE (500 to 1,000) *Aruak*
On the middle Içana and Ayarí several groups who speak Baníwa—the *Hohódene, Kadaupuritana, Sucuriyu-Tapuya, Siusy-Tapuya, Irá-Tapuya, Acutí-Tapuya* and *Kawá-Tapuya.* Aided by SPI Pôsto Içana. State of Amazonas. (Permanent contact)

HUARÍ *Huari*
On the Rio Corumbiára, tributary of the right bank of the Guaporé, in the Territory of Rondônia. (Extinct)

IAWANO (Iawavo) *Pano*
On the Rio Amcniá, tributary of the Juruá, in the Territory of Acre, on the frontier with Peru. (Permanent contact)

INGARIKÓ (250 to 500) *Karib*
On the Rio Maú and the abutments of the Serra do Sol, on the frontier between the Territory of Rio Branco and British Guiana [now Guyana]. (Permanent contact)

IPEWÍ *Unknown*
"Ipewí" is the *Kayabi* designation for unknown Indians of the Rio Peixoto Azevedo, tributary of the Teles Pires in the State of Mato Grosso. C. Villas Bôas has flown over their settlements. (Isolated)

IPURINÂN (Kangite) (500 to 1,000) *Aruak*
Right banks of the Acre and the Seruini, and left bank of the Ituxí, in the State of Amazonas. A division of the tribe was pacified in 1913 by SPI and settled on Pôsto Seruini. (Permanent contact)

IRÁNTXE (100 to 250) *Aruak*
Paresí subgroup on the headwaters of the Rio Cravari, tributary of the Rio Sangue which in turn is a tributary of the Rio Juruena. State of Mato Grosso. (Permanent contact)

ITOGAPÚK (Ntogapig) *Tupi*
Tupi-Kawahib subgroup on the Rio Madeirinha, tributary of the Castanha which flows into the Aripuanã. State of Amazonas. (Extinct)

IPOTEWÁT *Tupi*
Tupi-Kawahib subgroup of the upper Cacoal between the Riosinho and the Tamuripú, tributary of the Rio Jiparaná. Territory of Rondônia. (Extinct)

JABUTIFÉD   *Tupi*
    Tupi-Kawahib subgroup that lived between the Cacoal and Riosinho, tributaries of the Jiparaná. Territory of Rondônia. (Extinct)

JABUTÍ   *Unknown*
    On the headwaters of the Rio Branco, tributary of the right bank of the Guaporé, in the Territory of Rondônia. (Extinct)

JAVAÉ (250 to 500)   *Karajá*
    Karajá subgroup on the east side of the Island of Bananal. SPI Pôsto Damiana da Cunha. State of Goiás. (Intermittent contact)

JURÚNA (50 to 100)   *Tupi*
    Originally settled along the Middle Xingú. Today near the mouth of the Manitsaua-mitsu River, on the Upper Xingú, in northern Mato Grosso. (Permanent contact)

KABIXÍ   *Unknown*
    Seen on the slopes of the Planalto dos Parecís, on the right bank of the upper Guaporé, in the neighborhood of Vila Bela. Conflicts of the Kabixí with the inhabitants of Vila Bela and with woodland drug collectors resulted in the creation of the Pôsto Barbosa de Faria to pacify the former. To date they have remained unpacified. (Isolated)

KABIXIÂNA   *Tupi*
    At the source of the Rio Corumbiara, tributary ·of the right bank of the Guaporé. Territory of Rondônia. (Extinct)

KADIWÉU (Édiu-Adig) (100 to 250)   *Mbayá-Guaikurú*
    In the territory included between the Serra of Bodoquena and the Rio Nabileque, on the left bank of the Paraguai, and on SPI Pôsto Presidente Alves de Barros. Another Mbayá-Guaikurú (Édiu-ewud) group living with the Terêna Indians on the Lalima Post has lost command of their language. Both in southern Mato Grosso. (Permanent contact)

KAINGÁNG (Coroado, Guaianá) (3,000 to 4,000)   *Jê*
    One of the major indigenous groups of southern Brazil, the *Kaingáng* has three principal divisions. The *Kaingáng* of the State of São Paulo, pacified by SPI in 1910, now number under 100 persons and are settled on Pôsto Icatú in the municipality

of Penápolis and on Pôsto Vanuire in the municipality of Tupã, both in São Paulo. The southern *Kaingáng* who have been living in contact with civilization for more than a century, are on several indigenous posts and in semicivilized settlements in the southern States, as follows: in the State of Paraná, on Pôsto Barão de Antonina in the municipality of Araiponga; Pôsto Queimadas, in the municipality of Reserva; Pôsto Ivaí, municipality of Pitanga; Pôsto Fioravante Esperanca, municipality of Palmas; Pôsto Rio das Cobras and Pôsto Boa Vista, municipality of Iguassú; Pôsto Apucarana, municipality of Londrina; Pôsto Mangueirinha, municipality of Mangueirinha; Pôsto José Maria de Paula, municipality of Guarapuava. On Pôsto Xapecó in the municipality of Xapecó, in the State of Santa Catarina; SPI Pôstos Cacique Doble, Ligeiro, Nonoai and Guarita and on reservations or in semicivilized settlements under state administration in all the municipalities of the far northwest of the State of Rio Grande do Sul. Another division of the *Kaingáng* is composed of the *Xokleng* of Santa Catarina. (Integrated)

KALAPÁLO (100 to 250)   *Karib*
On the left bank of the Rio Culuene, source of the Xingú. Aided by SPI Pôsto Capitão Vasconcelos. State of Mato Grosso. (Intermittent contact)

KAMAKÂN (Catathoy, Cutasho, Masacará, Menian)   *Kamakân*
Some survivors of small hostile groups attracted by SPI on the Gongori, Cachoeira and Pardo rivers are now living on SPI Pôsto Caramuru in the municipality of Itabuna of the State of Bahia. (Extinct)

KAMAYURÁ (100 to 250)   *Tupi*
Near Lake Ipavu close to the Rio Curisevo, source of the Xingú, in the State of Mato Grosso. Aided by SPI Pôsto Capitão Vasconcelos. (Intermittent contact)

KANAMARÍ   *Katukína*
On the upper Inauini, tributary of the Purus, and on the left bank of the Juruá, as well as on the Rio Massipira, tributary of the right bank of the Tarauacá (Wiri-Diapá) and between the Jurupari and the Pauiní rivers; also a branch between the Tapauá and the upper Tefé. (Extinct)

KANAMARÍ (250 to 500)   *Aruak*
    Between the headwaters of the Acre and Iaco rivers in the
    Territory of Acre. (Integrated)

KAPANÁWA   ·   *Pano*
    On the upper Juruá in the Territory of Acre, along the frontier
    with Peru. (Integrated)

KARAJÁ (Javaé, Xambioá) (500 to 1,000)   *Karajá*
    Along the length of the Rio Araguáia, from Leopoldina to
    Conceição do Araguáia. Divided into several local groups
    (see Javaé). States of Goiás and Pará, on the frontiers of Mato
    Grosso. (Permanent contact)

KARIPÚNA   *Pano*
    Lived on the Rio Capivari, tributary of the Jaci-Paraná and
    the Mutum Paraná; were settled on SPI Pôstos Coronel Ti-
    búrcio and Rodolfo Miranda. Territory of Rondônia. (Extinct)

KARIPÚNA (250 to 500)   *Tupi*
    Survivors on the Rio Curipi, tributary of the Uaçá, aided by
    SPI Pôsto Luiz Horta in the municipality of Clevelândia in the
    far north of the Territory of Amapá, on the frontier of French
    Guiana. (Integrated)

(Kariri)   *Kariri*
    Extinct linguistic family that included the *Kamarú, Dzubukuá,
    Kipea* and *Sapuya*. Kariri survivors, a highly Mestizo group who
    had forgotten their language and preserved nothing of their
    culture, were dislocated from the settlement at Pedra Branca,
    near Amargosa in Bahia. They joined Tupinaki (?) survivors in
    São Bento at the headwaters of the Catolé, from whence some
    went to SPI Pôsto Paraguassú in the municipality of Itabuna in
    southern Bahia.

KARITIÂNA   *Tupi*
    At the sources of the Candeia and Jací Paraná, tributaries of
    the Madeira. State of Amazonas. (Extinct)

KARUTÂNA (100 to 250)   *Aruak*
    Baníwa subgroup represented by various clans on the lower
    Içana (*Yawareté-Tapuya, Yuraparí-Tapuya, Urubu-Tapuya,
    Arara-Tapuya*) in northeastern Amazonas. (Permanent contact)

KATAWIÂN   *Karib*

On the Anumu, tributary of the Trombetas, in northwest Pará along the Dutch Guiana [now Surinam] frontier. (Intermittent contact)

KATIÂNA   *Aruak*

Upper Rio Purus, in the Territory of Acre. (Extinct)

KATUKÍNA (500 to 1,000)   *Katukína*

This designation is specific for the *Kutia-Diapá, Pidá-Diapá* and other groups of the middle Jutaí and its tributaries, the Mutum and Biá rivers. The *Tukum-Diapá* groups of the Rio Pedras, tributary of the Javarí; the *Ben-Diapá* of the São Vicente River, affluent of the left bank of the Juruá; the *Puku-Diapá* or *Tawaí* and the *Wadiuparanin* and *Urubú-Daipá* of the Restauração, tributary of the Juruá, also speak Katukína. The *Amena-Diapá* and the *Kadiu-Diapá* are found near São Felipe. The *Katawixi,* also Katukína, are located on the Mucuim, tributary of the Ituxi. See *Kanamarí* (Katukína), *Katukína* (Pano) and *Parawa.* Territory of Acre. (Permanent contact)

KATUKÍNA (500 to 1,000)   *Pano*

Between the middle Gregório and the Juruá rivers. State of Amazonas. (Permanent contact)

(Kawahib)   *Tupi*

Curt Nimuendajú found historical and linguistic evidence of the existence of a *Kawahib* or *Cabahiba* tribe occupying an extensive area at the tip of land formed by the Teles Pires and Juruena rivers. When they were dislodged by the *Mundurukú* in the eighteenth century they divided into several groups. The principal subdivisions are known as *Parintintin-Kawahib* and *Tupi-Kawahib.* See *Parintintin, Paranawát, Boca-Negra, Tapayúna, Wiraféd, Takuatép, Itogapúk, Ipotewát, Tukumanféd, Mialát, Jabutiféd, Rama-rama.*

KAXARARÍ   *Aruak*

Ipurinân subgroup. At the headwaters of the Curuquetê, tributary of the right bank of the upper Ituxí, and on the Rio Abunã. State of Amazonas and Territory of Acre. (Extinct)

KAXINÁWA (250 to 500)   *Pano*

Several groups dispersed within an extensive strip along the upper Rio Envira and its tributaries; on the Paraná do Ouro, and the upper Muru and its tributaries: the Iboaçu and Humaitá. Also on the upper courses of the Tarauacá, Rio Gregório and Rio Liberdade. Territory of Acre. (Integrated)

KAXUIÂNA (under 50) *Karib*

Along the Cachorro River, tributary of the Trombetas; northwestern Pará. (Intermittent contact)

KAYABÍ (250 to 500) *Tupi*

Pacified by the SPI in 1924 in the region between the Verde and São Manoel rivers. A group has been living at SPI Pôsto Pedro Dantas or José Bezerra on the bank of the Verde, tributary of the Teles Pires. They are now being transferred to the Manitsáua-assu, tributary of the left bank of the Xingú. State of Mato Grosso. (Intermittent contact)

(Kayapó) (Cayamo, Coroá) *Jê*

Two principal divisions: the Southern Kayapó represented by several groups that are now extinct, in southern Goiás, southern Mato Grosso, northwestern São Paulo and the Mineiro Triangle; and the Northern Kayapó. The latter include several groups; some Kayapó in southern Pará and northern Mato Grosso are still hostile. See *Kayapó do Sul, Kayapó-Kradaú, Gorotíre, Kubén-kran-kegn, Kubén-kragnotíre, Mentuktíre, Xikrín* and *Dióre.*

KAYAPÓ-KRADAÚ *Jê*

Division of the Northern Kayapó of Ribeirão Pau d'Arco, tributary of the Araguáia. Aided by the Dominican Mission which gave way to the founding of the city of Conceição do Araguáia in southern Pará. (Extinct)

KAYAPÓ DO SUL *Jê*

This subgroup survived until the early years of the twentieth century near the mouth of the Rio Grande above Paraná, on the boundaries of the States of Minas Gerais and São Paulo. (Extinct)

KAYUIXÂNA *Aruak*

On several sites between the Japurá and Solimões rivers. State of Amazonas. (Extinct)

KÊNKATEYE *Jê*

Branch of eastern *Timbíra*. Along the Rio Alpercatas before 1908; after the massacre of the Chinelo settlement in 1913 the survivors joined a *Ramkókamekra* settlement. (Extinct)

KEPKIRIWÁT   Tupi
Pacified by the Rondon Commission in 1912, on the Pimenta
Bueno, tributary of the Jiparaná. Territory of Rondônia. (Ex-
tinct)

KINIKINÃO   Aruak
The last group to survive lived in the Paraíso settlement in
Agaxí, in the municipality of Aquidauana. The survivors joined
forces with the Terêna and the Layâna on Pôsto Lalima in the
municipality of Miranda. Southern Mato Grosso. (Extinct)

KOBÉWA (500 to 1,000)   Tukána
Includes several clans living on the Rio Querari and along the
upper Ayari. Aided by SPI Pôstos Querari and Içana. Northwest Amazonas. (Permanent contact)

KOKÁMA   Tupi
Survivors on the banks and islands of the Solimões, near the
mouths of the Japurá and the Içá. State of Amazonas. (Extinct)

KORIPAKO (100 to 250)   Aruak
Baníwa subgroup consisting of the Paku-Tapuya of the Acuti-
igarapé, tributary of the Rio Içana, the Coaty-Tapuya, Tapiíra-
Tapuya, Ipeca-Tapuya, and Tatu-Tapuya of the upper Rio
Ayari and the Yawareté-tapuya on the upper Rio Guainia.
Northwest Amazonas and Colombia. (Permanent contact)

KRAHÓ (500 to 1,000)   Jê
One of the principal branches of the eastern Timbíra. On the
Craolândia reservation or SPI Pôsto Manoel da Nóbrega on
the Rio Manoel Alves Pequeno in the municipality of Pedro
Afonso. Northern Goiás. (Permanent contact)

KREM-YÊ   Jê
Branch of the eastern Timbíra living to the west of Bacabal as
far as the Mearim and Grajaú rivers; one group reached Rio
Cajuapara and went down it as far as Gurupi and Pôsto Felipe-
Camarão (Jararaca) where some detribalized survivors are still
to be found. States of Maranhão and Pará. (Extinct)

KREEN-AKARORE   Unkown
According to the Mentuktire this is an isolated group living
between the headwaters of the Peixoto de Azevedo and the
Jarina in northern Mato Grosso. (Isolated)

KRIKATÍ   Jê
   Timbíra group of the Barra do Corda in the municipality of
   Grajaú. State of Maranhão. (Extinct)

KUBÉN-KRAN-KEGN (Cabeça pelada) (250 to 500)   Jê
   Division of the Northern Kayapó living above the Cachoeira da
   Fumaça on the Riosinho, tributary of the Rio Fresco that runs
   into the Xingú. Pacified in 1952, they were brought to Pôsto
   Nilo Peçanha in the municipality of Altamira. Southern Pará.
   (Intermittent contact)

KUBÉN-KRAGNOTÍRE (100 to 250)   Jê
   Division of the Northern Kayapó living along the tributaries
   of the left bank of the Xingú, near the sources of the Rio Irirí
   in southern Pará. (Isolated)

KUJIJENERÍ   Aruak
   Between the upper Envira and the Curumahá, tributaries of the
   headwaters of the Purus. Territory of Acre. (Extinct)

KUIKÚRO (100 to 250)   Karib
   On the left bank of the Culuene, source of the Xingú, in the
   State of Mato Grosso. Aided by Pôsto Indigena Capitão Vas-
   concelos. (Intermittent contact)

KULÍNA (Culino) (250 to 500)   Aruak
   Several groups between the lower Tarauacá and the Gregório,
   along the course of the Mararí and Eiru, and at the confluence
   of the Tarauacá and the Envira, all on the right bank of the
   upper Juruá. Aided by SPI Pôsto Rio Gregório. State of Amazonas. (Permanent contact)

KUNÍBA   Aruak
   Between the Juruasinho and the Jutaí rivers. State of Amazonas.
   (Extinct)

KURÍNA (or Culino)   Pano
   Along the Rio Jutaí and the lower Jundiatuba. State of Amazonas. (Extinct)

KURUÁYA   Tupi
   Several groups lived along the Jamaxim, tributary of the
   Tapajós and along the Curuá, tributary of the Middle Xingú.
   Southern Pará. (Extinct)

KUSTENÃO *Aruak*
On the Batovi and Ronuro rivers, sources of the Xingú. State of Mato Grosso. (Extinct)

KUYANÁWA *Pano*
Between the Môa and Paraná dos Mouras rivers, in Juruá. In the Northwest of the Territory of Acre. (Extinct)

LAYÂNA *Aruak*
Guaná subgroup on the banks of the Miranda River; some survivors live on Pôsto Lalima, others have joined forces with the Terêna at several SPI posts in southern Mato Grosso. (Extinct)

MÁKU *Máku*
Several linguistically unaffiliated groups about whom little is known have been located along the Rio Auarí, tributary of the left bank of the upper Uraricoera in northwestern Amazonas. (Isolated)

MAKUNABÖDÖ (Makú Mansos and Makú bravos) *Puináve*
At the headwaters of the Iurubaxí, Mariá, and Curicuriarí rivers, tributaries of the right bank of the Rio Negro. Those who live in the interior on the left bank of the Japurá between Puré and Cumapi are called Makú-Bravos (hostile or angry Makú). (Isolated)

MAKURÁP *Tupi*
There may still be a few dozen along the Rio Branco, tributary of the right bank of the Guaporé. Territory of Rondônia. (Extinct)

MAKUXÍ (1,500 to 2,000) *Karib*
Several nuclei along the Tacutú, Cotingo, and Surumú and their tributaries. Aided by SPI Pôstos at Fazenda São Marcos and on the Rio Seruini. Territory of Rio Branco, along the British Guiana [now Guyana] frontier. (Integrated)

MANDAWÁKA *Aruak*
On the upper Cauaboris, tributary of the Rio Negro. State of Amazonas. (Isolated)

MANITENERÍ   *Aruak*
Lived on both banks of the Rio Purus, between the mouths of the Yaco and the Curinahá. Were also found along the Rio Caspahá and the Rio da Maloca, tributaries of the upper Acre. Territory of Acre. (Extinct)

MANITSAWÁ   *Tupi*
Inhabited the area of the Manitsaua-missu, tributary of the Upper Xingú. State of Mato Grosso. (Extinct)

MAOPITYAN (Mapidian)   *Aruak*
Between the sources of the Cafuini and the Mapuera in the far northwest of Pará, along the frontier of Dutch Guiana [now Surinam]. (Isolated)

MARAKANÁ   *Unknown*
In the mountainous zone to the south of the Rio Uraricoera. Territory of Rio Branco. (Extinct)

MARAWÁ   *Aruak*
Along the lower Jutaí and the small rivers between the former and the Rio Juruá. State of Amazonas. (Extinct)

MARINÁWA   *Pano*
Along the upper Envira, tributary of the Tarauacá, in the Territory of Acre. (Integrated)

MARÚBO (250 to 500)   *Pano*
Along the headwaters of the tributaries of the Curuçá, Ipixuna and Javari, near the Peruvian frontier. State of Amazonas. (Permanent contact)

MATANAWÍ   *Matanawí*
Along the lower Marmelos, tributary of the Madeira. State of Amazonas. (Extinct)

MATIPUHY (under 50)   *Karib*
Along the right bank of the Rio Curisevo, source of the Xingú. State of Mato Grosso. Aided by SPI Pôsto Capitão Vasconcelos. (Intermittent contact)

MAWÉ (Maué, Andirá, Arapium) (1,000 to 1,500)   *Tupi*
Several groups on the Andirá, Urupadi and Mamuru rivers in the region of the lower Madeira. Aided by Pôsto Abacaxis of the municipality of Maues. State of Amazonas. (Integrated)

MAXAKALÍ (Caposho, Cumanasho, Macuni, Monaxó) (100 to 250)

Maxakalí

In the region of the headwaters of the Itanhaem River. Aided by Pôsto Eng. Mariano de Oliveira of the municipality of Machacalis in the State of Minas Gerais, near the frontier shared with Bahia. (Permanent contact)

MAYONGONG (Iekuana) (500 to 1,000) *Karib*

Several settlements between the upper Uraricoera and the Uraricapará rivers. Northwestern Rio Branco on the Venezuelan frontier. (Isolated)

MAYORÚNA *Pano*

Occupied several sites between the Solimões and Javari rivers and along the Javari. State of Amazonas, along the Peruvian frontier. (Extinct)

MEIINÁKU (50 to 100) *Aruak*

To the left bank of the Rio Curisevo, source of the Xingú. Aided by SPI Pôsto Capitão Vasconcelos. State of Mato Grosso. (Intermittent contact)

MENTUKTIRE (Gente preta) (500 to 1,000) *Jê*

Division of the *Northern Kayapó* located on the left bank of the Xingú at Cachoeira von Martius. From this location the Mentuktire launched their attacks upon the cattle raisers of the plains of Araguáia and on the Indians of the region of the sources of the Xingú River whom they call the *Txukarramãe*. Pacified in 1954 by SPI. Southern Pará. (Isolated)

MIALÁT *Tupi*

Tupi-Kawahib subgroup of the upper Leitão, tributary of the Jiparaná. Territory of Rondônia. (Extinct)

MIRÂNIA *Witóto*

Near the Solimões, between the Tefé and Caiçara rivers. They have also been referred to as living along the Brazilian course of the Rio Içá. State of Amazonas. (Extinct)

MONDÉ (Sanamaiká) *Tupi*

In the woodlands *(matas)* of the right bank of the Pimenta Bueno in the Territory of Rondônia. (Extinct)

MUDJETÍRE (50 to 100)   *Tupi* (?)
Kayapó name *(estojo peniano grande)* for a group, possibly Tupi, found along the Sororosinho, tributary of the Rio Sororó emptying into the Vermelho, tributary of the right bank of the lower Itacaiuna. State of Pará. (Isolated)

MUNDURUKÚ (1,000 to 1,500)   *Tupi*
Along the middle and upper Tapajós River and on the system of canals of the lower Madeira, on the Maué-Assu, the Abacaxis and the Canumã rivers. Contemporary concentrations on the Cururú and Tropas, tributaries of the right bank of the upper Tapajós where the Pôsto Indígena Mundurukú and the Franciscan Mission of Cururú are located. State of Pará. (Permanent contact)

MURA (1,000 to 1,500)   *Mura*
Several small *Mura* groups have been reported along the Autaz, Marmelos, Mataurá, Carapanã, Urubu, and Coary rivers of lower Amazonas, aided by SPI Pôsto Lodo d'Álmeida. The *Mura-Pirahá* are living along the Maicí and Marmelos, tributaries of the Madeira. Aided by SPI Pôstos Antônio Paulo and Major Amarante. State of Amazonas. (Integrated)

NAHUKUÁ (50 to 100)   *Karib*
Right bank of the Rio Curisevo, source of the Xingú. Aided by SPI Pôsto Capitão Vasconcelos. State of Mato Grosso. Fleeing from the attack of a hostile group (*Txikão*), they took refuge in a *Matipuhy* settlement. (Intermittent contact)

NAMBIKUÁRA (500 to 1,000)   *Nambikuára*
In northwestern Mato Grosso near the so-called Serra do Norte, between the Rio Juruena and the upper courses of the sources of the Aripuanã, in the region crossed by the telegraph line constructed by the Rondon Commission, which pacified them in 1910. Divided into many subgroups, some of which are aided by Pôsto Pirineus de Souza of the municipality of Alto Madeira and by a Jesuit Mission of Utiarití. (Intermittent contact)

NARAVÚTE   *Karib*
Along the middle Culuene, source of the Xingú. State of Mato Grosso. (Extinct)

NATÚ *Unknown*
Some detribalized survivors are living with Indians who identify themselves as *Xokó,* in Pacatuba. State of Sergipe. (Extinct)

NUKUINÍ *Pano*
From the upper Mõa to the Rio Sungarú in Juruá. Northwestern Acre. (Permanent contact)

OFAIÉ (Opaie-Xavante) *Ofaié*
Several nuclei along the Verde, Vacaria, and Ivinhema rivers have been cited. The latter received aid from SPI Pôsto Laranjinho near the mouth of the S. Bento. In 1948 about a dozen were living on a reservation conceded to them along the Rio Samambaia in southern Mato Grosso. (Extinct)

OTÍ (Otí-Xavante) *Otí*
In the Campos Novos of Paranapanema in the State of São Paulo. (Extinct)

OYANPÍK (Wayapí) *Tupi*
Originally from the valley of the Xingú, they relocated along the Oiapoque and have been almost completely assimilated by the *Karib* of French Guiana. (See Emerion.) Northern Amapá. (Extinct)

PAKAÁNOVAS (Jaru, Uómo) (500 to 1,000) *Txapakúra*
Between the Pacaás Novas and Ouro Preto, tributaries of the Mamoré in the Territory of Rondônia. The SPI is maintaining two posts for the purpose of pacifying the Pakaánovas. (Isolated)

PAKANÁWA *Pano*
At the headwaters of the Envira, tributary of the Juruá, in the Territory of Acre. (Permanent contact)

PAKARARÁ (100 to 250) *Unknown*
In the sierras of Cacaria and of Arapuá, near Vila Riacho do Navio there is an indigenous group called the Pakarará that has forgotten its language and traditional culture. Municipality of Floresta, State of Pernambuco. (Integrated)

PAKIDÁI (Surára) *Xiriana*
This is the name used to refer to several little-known indigenous groups living along the Demeni, Aracá, and Padauirí

rivers, tributaries of the left bank of the middle Rio Negro. For some time they were aided by SPI Pôsto Ajuricaba in the municipality of Barcelos. State of Amazonas. (Isolated)

PALIKÚR (250 to 500)   *Aruak*
Along the Uaçá River, tributary of the Oiapoque. Aided by Pôsto Uaçá in northern Amapá, on the frontier with French Guiana. (Integrated)

PALMELAS   *Karib*
Right bank of the Rio Guaporé between the mouths of the Branco and the Mequens. Territory of Rondônia. (Extinct)

PANKARARÚ (1,500 to 2,000)   *Pankararú*
On SPI Pôsto Pancararus in Brejo dos Padres, municipality of Tacaratú. State of Pernambuco. Another similarly mestizo group calling itself Panakaré, likewise characterized by the complete loss of language and the absence of any trace of their original culture, lives in Brejo-do-Bugre, municipality of Santo Antônio da Glória (formerly Curral-dos-Bois) in the State of Bahia. (Integrated)

PARAKANÃN (250 to 500)   *Tupi*
Between the upper Jacundá and the left bank of the Tocantins. A subgroup was attracted to SPI Pôsto Pacificação Pucurui near the E. F. Alcobaça [Alcobaça Railroad] in 1953. State of Pará. (Isolated)

PARANAWÁT (Pawaté, Majubim) (50 to 100)   *Tupi*
Kawahib group on the Muqui and Leitão and Riosinho rivers, tributaries of the Jiparaná (Machado). Another group was settled on the Rio do Sono. Territory of Rondônia. (Permanent contact)

PARAWÁ   *Katukína*
Includes the *Hon* and *Maro-Diapá* clans of the seringal (rubber reservation) Adélia, on the left bank of the upper Juruá. State of Amazonas. (Extinct)

PARESÍ (250 to 500)   *Aruak*
Originally included three divisions: the *Kaxiniti* of the Rio Sumidouro; the *Waimaré* of the upper courses of the Rio Verde and the Rio Sacre; and the *Kozarini* who lived at the headwaters of the Rio Cabaçal and of other sources of the Juruena. It is impossible to differentiate among the survivors

now living at the ancient Telegraph Line stations and on Pôsto
Major Coloizoroce in the municipality of Diamantina and Pôsto
Fraternidade Indígena in the municipality of Barra dos Bugres,
in the State of Mato Grosso. (Integrated)

PARIKOTÓ   *Karib*

Rio Tauiní, affluent of the Mapuera, tributary of the Trombetas,
in the State of Pará on the frontier between Brazil and British
Guiana [now Guyana]. (Isolated)

PARINTINTÍN (100 to 250)   *Tupi*

This *Kawahib* group lived in the region bounded by the Madeira, Jiparaná, and Marmelos rivers until they were pacified
in 1922 by Curt Nimucndajú on SPI Pôsto Rio Maicí. There
were three divisions: the *Kawahib* on the Ipixuna and Maicí;
the *Odiahub* of the upper Maicí and the tributaries of the Marmelos, and the *Apairandé* between the Rio Jiparaná and Rio
Maicí. Survivors are living along the Ipixuna, tributary of the
Madeira. State of Amazonas. (Permanent contact)

PASÉ   *Aruak*

On the lower Rio Içá. State of Amazonas. (Extinct)

PATAXÓ-HAHAHÃI   *Pataxó*

Originally inhabited the *matas* (woodland region) of Jequitinhonha from the Mucuri to the Arassuaí rivers. Some small
autonomous bands survived until the twentieth century in the
zone between the right bank of the Rio das Contas from
Pontal to the Rio do Peixe on the one hand, and the upper
Almada, on the other. After they had been pacified by SPI
some survivors were brought to Pôsto Paraguassu in the municipality of Itabuna. State of Bahia. (Extinct)

PAUMARÍ (Purupurú) (250 to 500)   *Aruak*

On the islands and sand banks of the middle Rio Purus, from
the mouth of the Jacaré to the Hiutanaham. State of Amazonas.
(Permanent contact)

PAUXÍ   *Karib*

Above the flood lands on the right bank of the middle Cuminá
in the State of Pará. (Extinct)

PAUXIÂNA (Pawixana)   *Karib*

Between the Mocajaí and Catrimani rivers in the Territory of
Rio Branco. (Extinct)

PIANOKOTÓ (250 to 500) *Karib*
Tirió subgroup self-designated as the *Marahtxó*. On the Panamá, Marapi, and Cucharé rivers, tributaries of the Trombetas. State of Pará, on the Brazilian frontier with Dutch Guiana [now Surinam]. (Intermittent contact)

POKANGA (Pokangá-Tapuya or Bará) (50 to 100) *Tukána*
Two groups on the upper Tiquié, tributary of the Uaupés, speaking Tukána dialects. Aided by SPI Pôsto Tiquié and by Catholic and Protestant missionaries. (Permanent contact)

POTIGUÁRA (500 to 1,000) *Tupi*(?)
Pôsto Nísia Brasileira on the Baía da Traição, in the municipality of Mamanguape. Profoundly mestizo. Have lost their tribal culture and their command of their language. State of Paraíba. (Integrated)

POYANÁWA *Pano*
Upper Rio Môa, tributary of the Jumá. Pacified in 1913 on SPI Pôsto Tauacuera. Territory of Acre. (Extinct)

PURUBORÁ (50 to 100) *Tupi*
On the headwaters of the Rio São Miguel, tributary of the right bank of the Guaporé. Territory of Rondônia. (Intermittent contact)

PURUKOTÓ *Karib*
Near the island of Maracá on the Rio Uraricoera. Survivors of *Wayumará* and *Sapará* groups live in the same area. Territory of Rio Branco. (Extinct)

RAMA-RAMA *Tupi*
Kawahib group on the Anari and Machadinho rivers, tributaries of the Jiparaná. Territory of Rondônia. (Extinct)

RAMKÓKAMEKRA (250 to 500) *Jê*
Timbíra tribe known as the *Canelas,* who originally inhabited the area between the Rio Itapecuru and the Rio do Corda, in the region of Pastos Bons. State of Maranhão. Now living on SPI Pôsto Capitão Uirá of the municipality of Barra do Corda and on Pôsto "Arariboia," of the municipality of Grajaú. (Permanent contact)

SAKUYA *Pano*

Also known as the *Remo*, the *Sakuya* lived between the sources of the Javari and the upper Juruá-mirim, in the extreme northwest of the Territory of Acre. (Extinct)

SALUMÁ *Karib*

On the upper Anamu, source of the Trombetas, in northwest Pará along the frontier with Dutch Guiana [now Surinam]. (Intermittent contact)

SANAMAIKÁ *Tupi*

On the tributaries of the left bank of the Pimenta Bueno, tributary of the Jiparaná. Probably a subdivision of the *Mondé*. Territory of Rondônia. (Extinct)

SIKIÂNA *Karib*

Between the Rio Cafuini and the sources of the Turuna and the Itapi, in the far northwest of Pará, along the frontier with Dutch Guiana [now Surinam]. (Intermittent contact)

SUYÁ *Jê*

To the east of the headwaters of the Rio Culuene, source of the Xingú, in the State of Mato Grosso. (Isolated)

TAKUATÉP *Tupi*

Tupi-Kawahib subgroup on the Rio Tamuripa, tributary of the right bank of the Jiparaná. Territory of Rondônia. (Extinct)

TAPAYÚNA *Unknown*

Probably a *Tupi-Kawahib* group. Living at the confluence of the Tapajós and Teles Pires. Sometimes called the *Raipe-Xixí*. Another group known as *Tapayúna* has settled on the left bank of the Rio do Sangue, tributary of the Juruena. State of Mato Grosso. (Isolated)

TAPIRAPÉ (under 50) *Tupi*

On the Rio Tapirapé, western tributary of the Araguáia, aided by SPI Pôsto "Heloisa Alberto Torres," on the left bank of the Araguáia. State of Mato Grosso. (Permanent contact)

TARIÂNA (500 to 1,000) *Aruak*

Group on the middle Uaupés. With their *Yuruparí-Tapuya* vassals they spoke a language related to Baniwa; today both speak Tukána. (Integrated)

TAULIPANG (Jaricunas) (1,000 to 1,500)   Karib
    Several nuclei on the Surumu and Cotingo rivers and along the
    sources of the Maú, near the slopes of the mountain Roroima,
    on the Parimé-Maruá and Majari rivers, in the mountainous
    region of Paracaima. Aided by SPI Pôstos Surumu and Cotingo.
    Territory of Rio Branco, along the frontier with British Guiana
    [now Guyana]. (Permanent contact)

TEMBÉ (100 to 250)   Tupi
    Division of the Tenetehara tribe whose settlements were lo-
    cated in the area between the sources of the Gurupi and the
    middle Gurupi. Today the few remaining groups are gathered
    at Pôstos Felipe Camarão and Pedro Dantas on the Rio Gurupi
    and at Pôsto Tembé on the Rio Guamá. A few families are
    scattered throughout the region. (Integrated)

(Tenetehara)   Tupi
    Tupi tribe on the eastern edge of the Amazon forest, in the
    States of Pará and Maranhão. Two divisions: the Tembe on
    the Gurupi, Capim, and Guamá rivers and the Guajajára on the
    Pindaré, Grajaú, and Mearim rivers.

TERÊNA (3,000 to 4,000)   Aruak
    Survivors of the Terêna division of the Guaná group; also sur-
    vivors of other tribes of the same language family whose
    population has been decimated to the point where they can
    no longer maintain themselves independently (Layâna, Kini-
    kináo) and who have therefore joined the Terêna settlements.
    The Terêna are the largest indigenous group in southern Mato
    Grosso. They live on Pôstos Cachoeirinha and Lalima and in
    the Passarinho, Moreira, and União settlements of the munici-
    pality of Miranda; on Pôstos Taunay and Ipegue and in the
    Lima Verde settlement in the municipality of Aquidauana; on
    Pôsto Capitão Vitorino in Nioac, Pôsto Buriti in Sidrolândia,
    and Pôsto Francisco Horta in Dourados; with two nuclei of
    Kadiwéu Indians on Pôsto Presidente Alves de Barros; also on
    Pôsto Curt Nimuendajú in the municipality of Avaí, State of
    São Paulo, where the SPI relocated one group. (Integrated)

(Timbíra)   Jê
    Division of the northern Jê. Includes a western division, the
    Apinayé and an eastern, the Timbíra. The latter are themselves
    divided into several tribes. See Apinayé, Gaviões, Krahó,

Ramkókamekra (Canelas), *Krem-yé* of Cajuapára, *Krem-yé* of Bacabal, *Timbíra* of Arapiritiua, *Apâniekra*, *Kênkateye*, *Krikatí* and *Txakamekra*.

TIMBÍRA of Araparitiua   Jê
   Timbíra subgroup that has uprooted itself from the plains of Maranhão and relocated in the forest area of the Rio Gurupí, principally along the Araparitiua, tributary of the right bank of the Gurupí. State of Pará. (Extinct)

TIRIÓ (2,000 to 3,000)   Karib
   Several groups at the sources of the Trombetas, Cuminá, and Parú de Este rivers on the frontier of the State of Pará with Dutch Guiana [now Surinam]. Includes the *Marahtxó* or *Pianokotó* groups on the Panamá, Marapi, and Cucharé rivers, tributaries of the Trombetas; the *Aramayâna* on the bank of the Parú de Oeste; the *Proyâna* or *Rangu-Pikí* groups of the serra of Avararí near the Igarapé Cumaruvini, tributary of the Parú de Oeste and the Aramiatxó of the Igarapé Apuguina, tributary of the Parú de Este; and the *Okomoyâna* and the *Aramihotó* groups, both of which are practically extinct. (Isolated)

TORÁ   *Txapakúra*
   On the lower Marmelos, tributary of the Rio Madeira. State of Amazonas. (Extinct)

TRUMÁI (under 50)   *Trumái*
   One solitary settlement on the right bank of the lower Culuene, source of the Rio Xingú, in Mato Grosso. Aided by Pôsto Capitão Vasconcelos of SPI. (Intermittent contact)

TSUVA   Karib
   Lived on the middle Culuene, near the *Kuikúro*, in the region of the sources of the Xingú. Mato Grosso. (Extinct)

(Tukána)
   Tukána-speaking tribes who inhabited all of the Brazilian basin of the Uaupés, and adjacent areas in Colombia and Peru. Some representatives of these tribes reached the Rio Içá and the upper Aiari. See also *Kobéwa*, *Wanâna*, *Desâna*, *Tuyuka*, *Pokanga*, *Waikíno*, *Tukára*, and *Tukána*.

TUKÁNA   *Tukána*
   The Indians properly called *Tukána* (Datxea) are found at various sites along the Uaupés, Tiquié, and Paporis rivers. They

speak the same language as the *Tukána-Datxea,* the *Arapáso,* the *Kurawa-Tapuya,* the *Uçá-Tapuya,* and the *Yi-Tapuya.* The languages of the *Mirití-Tapuya,* the *Yurupary-Tapuya,* and the *Tariâna* were influenced by Tukána. The *Kobéwa (Dyurémana* or *Yiboya-Tapuya)* of the upper Aiari were also linguistically or culturally assimilated by the *Tukána.* Aided by Pôsto Melo Franco in the municipality of São Gabriel, State of Amazonas. (Permanent contact)

TUKUMANFÉD (under 50)   *Tupi*
Tupi-Kawahib subgroup at the mouth of the Cacoal, tributary of the Jiparaná. Territory of Rondônia. (Permanent contact)

TUKÚNA (Tikuna) (1,000 to 1,500)   *Tukúna*
At various sites along the bank of the streams that run into the Içá and Solimões, at the junction of the two rivers, in both Peru and Brazil. Aided by SPI Pôsto Ticunas, in the municipality of São Paulo de Olivença. Basin of the Solimões River, State of Amazonas. (Permanent contact)

TUPARÍ (under 50)   *Tupi*
In the forests on the right bank of the Rio Branco, tributary of the left bank of the Guaporé, in the Territory of Rondônia. (Permanent contact)

(Tupinaki?)   *Tupi*
Detribalized survivors of a group thought to be *Tupinaki.* On the Santa Rosa settlement near Jequié, on the Rio das Contas, Bahia. A highly mestizo group that retains no trace of its language and its traditional culture. The Tupinaki (?) had joined the *Karirí* in São Bento at the headwaters of the Catolé. Some Indians of this group have moved to Pôsto Paraguassú in the municipality of Itabuna of the State of Bahia.

TURIWÁRA   *Tupi*
In the mid-nineteenth century the *Turiwára* migrated from Maranhão to Pará, settling on the bank of the Capim; they next moved to the junction of the Acará Grande and the Acará Pequeno rivers. The so-called *Turiwára* of the Turi River are a subgroup of the Urubus or Kaapor. (Extinct)

TUXÁ (100 to 250)   *Unknown*
At SPI Pôsto Indígena Rodelas, near the city of Rodelas, on the bank of the São Francisco. The Indians who call themselves

Tuxá are highly mestizo. They have forgotten their language and their traditional culture. State of Bahia. (Integrated)

TUXINÁWA *Pano*
On the tributaries of the upper Envira, tributary of the Juruá. In the Territory of Acre. (Integrated)

TUYUCA (50 to 100) *Tukána*
On the upper Tiquié, tributary of the Uaupés, along the Colombian frontier. State of Amazonas. (Permanent contact)

TXAKAMEKRA (Mateiros) *Jê*
Timbíra subgroup which inhabited the savannahs along the Rio das Flores, small tributary of the Mearim. Survivors joined with the Ramkókamekra. State of Maranhão. (Extinct)

(Txapakúra) *Txapakúra*
Groups of the Txapakúra language family are scattered from the right bank of the Guaporé to the tributaries of the right bank of the middle Madeira: the *Huayan, Torá, Urupá* and *Pakaánovas*.

TXIKÃO *Unknown*
An unknown tribe living along the tributaries of the Jatobá. This is the base from which they set out to attack the Xinguanos of the Rio Curisevo. State of Mato Grosso. (Isolated)

UAMUÉ (Aticum) (1,000 to 1,500) *Unknown*
These highly acculturated Indians who have lost both their language and their tribal culture live on SPI Pôsto Indígena Aticum on the Serra de Umã, in the municipality of Floresta, in the State of Pernambuco. Another highly acculturated group, the *Baixóta* of the Serra do Catolé, near the city of Maniçobal, appears at the Pôsto from time to time. (Integrated)

UMOTÍNA (Barbados) (100 to 250) *Borôro*
The *Umotína* were pacified by SPI in 1918 in the woodlands between the upper Paraguái and the Sepotuba rivers. For some years they maintained their cultural autonomy. Thereafter they gathered at Pôsto Fraternidade Indígena in the municipality of Barra dos Bugres; survivors have remained at this Pôsto. State of Mato Grosso. (Integrated)

URUBUS-KAAPOR (500 to 1,000) *Tupi*
At the end of the last century the *Urubus-Kaapor* migrated from Pará to Maranhão, and settled on the banks of the rills

that run into the Gurupi, the Pindaré, and the Turiaçu. They were pacified by the SPI in 1928. Contemporary Urubus-Kaapor are aided by Pôsto Pedro Dantas on the left bank of the Gurupí in the Paraense municipality of Vizeu and by Pôsto Felipe Camarão on the right bank of the Gurupí, in the Maranhense municipality of Carutapera. State of Maranhão. (Intermittent contact)

URUMÍ   *Tupi*
On the right bank of the Jiparaná, between the Tarumã and Madeirinha rivers. Territory of Rondônia. (Extinct)

URUPÁ (100 to 250)   *Txapakúra*
On the Urupá, tributary of the left bank of the Jiparaná. Some survivors were taken to Pôsto Rodolfo Miranda on the upper Jamari. Territory of Rondônia. (Permanent contact)

WAIKÁ (over 4,000)   *Xirianá*
Several groups composing one of the densest indigenous populations of Amazonia, between the sources of the Uraricoera, Mucajaí, and Demeni in Brazil and the Mavaca, Ocamo, Matacuní, and Padamo rivers in Venezuela. Far northwest, Territory of Rio Branco. (Isolated)

WAIKÍNO (Pirá-Tapuya) (100 to 250)   *Tukána*
Tukána tribe speaking a dialect close to that of the *Wanâna;* on the Rio Uaupés, tributary of the Rio Negro. State of Amazonas. (Permanent contact)

WAIMIRÍ (Yawaperí, Atruahí, Krixaná)   *Karib*
In the woodlands along the Alalaú and Jauaperí, tributaries of the Rio Negro. Some subgroups have been in contact with SPI posts, but the majority remain hostile. State of Amazonas. (Isolated)

WAINUMÁ (Uainumá)   *Aruak*
On the middle Japurá, along the frontier between the State of Amazonas and Colombia. (Extinct)

WAIWAI (Tapióca) (100 to 250)   *Karib*
On the banks of the upper Mapuera, tributary of the Trombetas, in the State of Pará and on the R. Essequibo in British Guiana [now Guyana]. (Intermittent contact)

WAKONÁ (500 to 1,000) *Unknown*
On Pôsto Palmeira dos Índios and the Serra da Cafurna, in the municipality of Palmeira dos Índios. They have lost both their language and their tribal culture. State of Alagoas. (Integrated)

WANÂNA (Kótedia) (100 to 250) *Tukána*
Includes the *Pirá-Tapuya* and other groups of the lower Uaupés who speak a Tukána dialect. Northwest Amazonas, along the frontier with Colombia. (Permanent contact)

WAPITXÂNA (Vapidiana) (1,000 to 1,500) *Aruak*
Several nuclei along the Tacatú, Uraricoera, Amajarí, Parimé, and Cauamé rivers, settled in the plains near the mountains. Aided by SPI posts on the Majari River and Lake Caracaranã. Territory of Rio Branco, along the frontier with British Guiana [now Guyana]. (Integrated)

WAREKÉNA *Aruak*
On the Içana and Xié, tributaries of the Rio Negro. Survivors are found on the Guainía River in Venezuelan territory. (Extinct)

WAURÁ (100 to 250) *Aruak*
One settlement on the east bank of the Batoví, one of the sources of the Xingú. Aided by SPI Pôsto Capitão Vasconcelos. State of Mato Grosso. (Intermittent contact)

WAYÂNA (50 to 100) *Karib*
Includes the *Urukuiâna* and *Wayâna* groups on the Parú de Este in the Territory of Amapá, and others living in French Guiana. (Permanent contact)

WAYORÓ *Unknown*
In the woodlands beginning at the sources of the Branco and Colorado rivers, tributaries of the right bank of the Guaporé, in the Territory of Rondônia. (Extinct)

WIRAFÉD (under 50) *Tupi*
Tupi-Kawahib subgroup on the Riosinho and Muqui, tributaries of the Jiparaná. Territory of Rondônia. (Permanent contact)

WITÓTO (50 to 100) *Witóto*
On the highlands along the left bank of the lower Tefé, tributary of the right bank of the Solimões. State of Amazonas. (Permanent contact)

XAVANTE (Akuên) (2,000 to 3,000)   Jê
With the *Xeréntes* from whom they detached themselves over
half a century ago, the *Xavante* formed the Akuên, the principal
group of the *Jê central*. Occupied an extensive region bounded
by the Mortes and Culuene rivers. Some subgroups are aided
by SPI Pôsto Pimental Barbosa which entered into peaceful
relations with them in 1946. State of Mato Grosso. (Intermittent contact)

XERÉNTE (250 to 500)   Jê
Division of the Akuên group which also includes the *Xavante*
and the now extinct *Xakriabá*. Now living between the Rio do
Sono and the Rio Tocantins, they are aided by SPI Pôsto
Tocantínia in the municipality of Tocantínia, in the State of
Goiás. (Integrated)

XIKRIN (250 to 500)   Jê
Division of the *Northern Kayapó*. Several nuclei along the
tributaries of the right bank of the Itacaiunas which flows into
the Tocantins near the city of Marabá. Some subgroups were
persuaded to enter into contact with Pôsto Las Casas, on the
plains of Conceição do Araguáia, in 1954. From Pôsto Las
Casas they migrated to SPI Pôsto Gorotire in the municipality
of Altamira in southern Pará. (Intermittent contact)

XIPÁYA   *Tupi*
Included several groups located along the Irirí and Curuá
rivers, tributaries of the Middle Xingú, in the State of Pará.
(Extinct)

XIPINÁWA   *Pano*
Between the upper Liberdade and the upper Valparaiso, and
along the Amoaca and Grajaú, all tributaries of the Juruá in
southern Amazonas and the Territory of Acre. (Integrated)

XIRIÂNA   *Aruak*
Several little-known groups along the Mapulau and other tribu-
taries of the Demeni, tributaries of the left bank of the Rio
Negro in the State of Amazonas on the frontier with Venezuela.
(Isolated)

XIRIANÁ (500 to 1,000) *Xirianá*
Several groups in the valleys of the Majarí and the Uraricoera in northwestern Rio Branco on the frontier with Venezuela. See also *Guaharíbo, Pakidái, Waiká, Aiwaterí.* (Intermittent contact)

XOKLENG (*Aweikoma, Bugre, Botocudos* or *Kaingáng*) (100 to 250) *Jê*
Tribe of the *Kaingáng* group which lived in the forests along the Rio Itajaí until they were pacified by SPI in 1914 and joined the Indians at Pôsto Duque de Caxias in the municipality of Ibirama, State of Santa Catarina. Survivors of a subgroup of these Indians who lived in the valley of the Rio Cinzas were pacified by SPI and taken to Pôsto Laranjinhas in the municipality of Bandeirantes in the State of Paraná. (Integrated)

XOKÓ (100 to 250) *Unknown*
Highly acculturated survivors who have lost both their language and culture live on SPI Pôsto Padre Alfredo Damaso in the city of Pôrto Real do Colégio, State of Alagoas. Two other small groups, likewise acculturated, live in Ôlho d'Água do Meio, also in Alagoas. Another lives in São Pedro in the State of Sergipe. (Integrated)

XUKURÚ (1,000 to 1,500) *Unknown*
Mestizo survivors who have lost their tribal language and culture inhabit the region of the Serra de Urubá (Arobá) in the neighborhood of the city of Cimbres, in the State of Pernambuco. (Integrated)

YABAÂNA *Aruak*
At the headwaters of the Marauiá and Cauaboris, tributaries of the left bank of the Rio Negro. State of Amazonas on the frontier with Venezuela. (Isolated)

YAMAMADÍ (250 to 500) *Aruak*
Between the Juruá and Purus rivers, at several sites along the Mamoriá, Pauiní, Tuini, upper Tapauá, and Xiruá rivers, in the State of Amazonas. (Permanent contact)

YAMINÁWA (500 to 1,000) *Pano*
Includes several nuclei scattered along the tributaries of the Envira, Tarauacá, Humaitá, Valparaiso, all tributaries of the upper Juruá, in the Territory of Acre. (Permanent contact)

YAWALAPITÍ (under 50)   *Aruak*

On Rio Curisevo, near the Lagoa dos Kamaiurá, on the Upper Xingú. Aided by SPI Pôsto Capitão Vasconcelos. State of Mato Grosso. (Intermittent contact)

YUBERÍ   *Aruak*

Also called *Purupuru*. Lived along the beaches of the lower Tapauá and on the middle Purus, below the confluence of the Mamoriá, in the State of Amazonas. (Extinct)

YUMÁ   *Unknown*

Small groups, also called *Arara,* in the woodlands of the upper Ipixuna and the Tabocal, tributaries of the Purus in the State of Amazonas. (Extinct)

YURÍ   *Yurí*

On the watershed between the Içá, Japurá, and Solimões. (Extinct)

BIBLIOGRAPHY

Classificações Lingüísticas e Culturais e Obras de Sintese Bibliográfica da Etnologia Brasileira

BALDUS, Herbert
1954   *Bibliografia Crítica da Etnologia Brasileira*
        Publ. da Comissão do IV Centenário da Cidade de São Paulo, S. Paulo, 859 págs., Introdução; 1785 indicações bibliográficas; índices de matérias, geográfico, de tribos e de autores, comentadores e tradutores; 11 estampas.

COOPER, John M.
1944   "Areal and Temporal Aspects of Aboriginal South American Culture"
        The Smithsonian Report for 1943, Washington, págs. 429/462, 2 mapas no texto, 10 figuras em pranchas fora do texto. Bibliografia.

PRIMEIRA REUNIÃO BRASILEIRA DE ANTROPOLOGIA
1953   Proposta de Convenção para a Grafia dos Nomes Tribais, *in Revista de Antropologia*, vol. 2, no. 2, dezembro de 1954, págs. 150/152 e vol. 3, no. 2, dezembro de 1955, págs . 125/132, S. Paulo.

GRUBB, K. G.
1927   *The Lowland Indians of Amazonia.*
        A survey of the location and religious condition of the Indians of Colombia, Venezuela, The Guianas, Ecuador, Peru, Brazil and Bolivia. London, 159 págs., 14 mapas, 5 apêndices, índice alfabético.

LOUKOTKA, Chestmír
1939   "Línguas Indígenas do Brasil"—*Revista do Arquivo Municipal,* LIV, S. Paulo, págs. 147/174, 1 mapa. Bibliografia.
1950   "Les langues de la Famille Tupi-Guarani". Boletim no. 16 de Etnografia e

língua tupi-guarani da Faculdade de Filosofia, Ciências e Letras da Universidade de São Paulo, São Paulo, 42 págs., índice alfabético de línguas e tribos. Bibliografia.

MASON, J. Alden
1950   "The Languages of South American Indians"—*in Handbook of South American Indians*, Vol. 6, Smithsonian Institution, Bureau of American Ethnology, Bulletin 143, Washington, págs. 157/317, Bibliografia e um mapa em côres.

MCQUOWN, Norman A.
1955   "The Indigenous Languages of Latin America"—*American Anthropologist*, vol. 57 no. 3 parte 1, junho de 1955, págs. 501/570. Bibliografia. Mapas.

MURDOCK, George P.
1951   *Outline of South American Cultures.*
        Behavior Science Outlines II. New Haven, 148 págs. 29 mapas no texto, índice alfabético de tribos.

NIMUENDAJÚ, Curt
1932   "Idiomas Indigenas del Brasil"—*Revista del Instituto de Etnologia*, II págs. 543/618. Universidad Nacional de Tucumán. Tucumán.
1950   "Reconhecimento dos Rios Icana, Ayari e Uaupés. Relatório apresentado ao Serviço de Proteção aos Índios do Amazonas e Acre", 1927—*Journal de la Société des Américanistes*, N.S., XXXIX, Paris, págs. 125/182.

Inédito *Mapa Etno-Histórico com índice Bibliográfico e de tribos*, pertencente ao Museu Nacional do Rio de Janeiro.

PERICOT Y GARCIA, Luis
1936   *América Indígena*, I, Barcelona, xxxii, 732 págs., 341 figuras, 8 pranchas coloridas, 56 mapas. Bibliografias.

RIVET, P. et TASTEVINI, C.
1921   "Les Tribus indiennes des bassins du Purús, du juruá et des régions limitrophes". *La Géographie* XXXV, Société de Géographie. Paris, págs. 449/482. Bibliografia. Um mapa lingüístico.

RIVET, P. et LOUKOTKA, C.
1952   "Langues de l'Amérique du Sud et des Antilles"—in *Les Langues du Monde*, par un groupe de linguistes sous la Direction de A. Meillet et Marcel Cohen. Paris, págs. 1.099/1.160. Bibliografia. Mapas.

VÁRIOS AUTORES
1946/48 Handbook of South American Indians. Julian H. Steward, Editor. Smithsonian Institution. Bureau of American Ethnology, Bulletin 143. Vol. I: *The Marginal Tribes*, Washington, 1946, xix, 624 págs., 69 figuras, 7 mapas, 112 pranchas, bibliografia, vol. III: *The Tropical Forest Tribes*, Washington, 1948, xxvi, 986 págs., 134 figuras, 8 mapas, 126 pranchas, bibliografia.

FOOTNOTES

1. This report is based upon data assembled in the course of the author's exhaustive study of reports and other documents of the Directory, Regional Inspectorates, and local action posts of the Serviço de Proteção aos Índios (SPI) relevant to his research on the process of assimilation of indigenous populations in modern Brazil. The research project was sponsored by the Department of Social Sciences of UNESCO.

2. Within the limits of an article it is impracticable to publish these sources. For bibliography on the tribes included in this study, see Herbert Baldus, 1954.

3. This figure naturally reflects known tribes; the existence in the unexplored areas of Brazil of tribes as yet unknown must be assumed. For example, C. Villas Boas called the *Ipewí* to my attention when this article was already on the presses— beyond the deadline for additions to the tables. It is probable that still other groups will come to our attention in the future.

4. See my study "Convívio e Contaminação—Efeitos Dissociativos da Depopulação provocada por Epidemias em Grupos Indígenas." *Sociologia*, vol. XVIII No. 1, São Paulo, 1956, pp. 3-50.

5. We refer to the pacification of the *Nambikuára* Indians (1912); the *Urubus-Kaapor* (1928); the *Xavante* (1946); the *Kubén-kran-kégn* (1952); the *Xikrín* (1954) and the *Kayabí* (1956).

6. These Xingu groups are the *Waurá, Mehináku, Trumái, Yawalapití, Kalapálo, Kuikúro, Matipuhy, Kamayurá,* and *Awetí.*

7. Between the date of their pacification and the contemporary period the São Paulo *Kaingáng* population declined from 1,200 to 87; the *Xokléng* from 800 to 189; and the *Umotína* from over 1,000 to under 200.

8. The decline of the Tupari population from 2,000 prior to contact to 180 in 1948 to 15 presently (1957), as estimated by Franz Caspar, suggests the tragedy of the decimation of these groups.

9. Our category *extinct* essentially refers to the disappearance of the group as an ethnic entity. Individuals who speak the language of the *Ofaié* or of other *extinct* groups perhaps may still be found dispersed throughout the region in which these groups lived.

10. Steward, Julian H. "South American Cultures: An Interpretative Summary" *Handbook of South American Indians*—Bul. 143 Smithsonian Institution, Washington, D. C., 1949, Vol. V, p. 666.

11. Darcy Ribeiro, "Assistência aos Índios no Brasil" *Américas,* Vol. 6, No. 4 (1954), p. 16.

12. Nota mimeografada no. 249 de 5 de janeiro de 1954 do Conselho Nacional de Estatística.

13. On the depopulation of indigenous groups, see my study "Convívio e Contaminação," *loc. cit.*

14. Otto Zerries had done a field study of the *Waiká, Guaharíbo* and *Xiriána* reported in a preliminary communication to the XXXI International Congress of Americanists, São Paulo, 1954.

15. Hans Becher has studied the Pakidái.

16. Data obtained from Frei Protásio Frikel who has visited the region and studied these Indians.

17. Carlos de Araujo Moreira Neto was studying the characteristic forms of the expansion of the national society in this area and completing a concomitant ethnological survey. See also Expedido Arnaud.

18. Alfred Métraux studied the *Kubén-kran-kegn.* Specialized studies have been made by Horace Banner (mythology) and Simone Dreyfus (musicology).

19. José Loureiro Fernandes visited the Aré immediately after their first contacts with agents of civilization. He has continued a meticulous documentation of their culture with special attention to its material aspects.

20. The author has made an intensive ethnological study of this group; he was in their settlements in 1949 and in 1951, and has promoted the documentation on moving picture film and sound tracts of those aspects of their culture that lend themselves to such documentation.

21. The *Nambikuára* have been studied by Rocquette-Pinto (1912), Claude Lévi-Strauss (1938) and, more recently, Kalervo Oberg.

22. Thanks to W. Neill Hawkins we have a linguistic study of the *Waiwai* which satisfies modern scientific requirements.

23. These groups have been studied by Herbert Baldus, Charles Wagley, and Eduardo Galvão.

24. Among these groups, only the *Tuparí* have been studied intensively. See Franz Caspar's monograph.

25. Robert and Yolanda Murphy have published a monograph on the *Mundurukú*.

26. Eduardo Galvão undertook an exploratory study of the Jurúna.

27. We refer to Curt Nimuendajú's study, *The Eastern Timbira*, Berkeley, University of California Press, 1946. William Crocker also is studying the Timbira.

28. Harald Schultz studied the *Krahó* and provided some photo-ethnographic documentation.

29. For these tribes we have only Curt Nimuendajú's exhaustive monograph on the *Tukúna*, and a study of Tukúna acculturation by Roberto Cardoso de Oliveira. Two other studies by Paul Fejos (1941) and Irving Goldman (1939-40) focus, respectively, on the *Witóto* and the *Kobéwa*.

30. Marcelo Moretzsohn de Andrade and Marcos Rubinger have contributed ethnographic studies of this group.

31. According to Claudio Vilas-Boas of the Serviço de Proteção aos Índios, there are two additional typical Xinguana tribes that have not yet established contact with civilization. These are the *Agavotokueng*, whose name means *"other Yawalapití,"* living between the Curisevo and Culuene rivers, and the Jatobá River group called *Txikão* or *Tonorê* by the *Kamayurá*. The former may be Aruak; no information is available concerning the latter.

32. Eduardo Galvão analyzed the traits common to Xinguana cultures and proposed the designation *área do uluri*. See "Apontamentos sôbre os Índios Kamayurá"— Publ. Avulsas do Museu Nacional no. 5, Rio de Janeiro, 1949, pp. 31-48.

33. In Vol. IX of the *Revista do Museu Paulista*, Harald Schultz published a report of his trip on the upper Purus in which he notes some groups not previously listed in ethnological bibliographies, and records the progressive extinction of other groups.

34. Curt Nimuendajú, "Reconhecimento dos rios Içana, Ayari, and Uaupés," *Journal de la Société des Américanistes de Paris*, N.S. XXXIX, Paris, 1950, pp. 125-182.

35. Information obtained from Frei Protásio Frikel.

36. We refer to the *Summer Institute of Linguistics* of Oklahoma, whose entry into Brazil was an auspicious event for linguistic studies among indigenous Brazilians, and to the *New Tribes Mission* which in recent years has been interested in similar studies in Brazil.

INDIGENOUS CULTURE AREAS OF BRAZIL, 1900-1959

by Eduardo Galvão

Museu Paraense Emílio Goeldi

Translated by Janice H. Hopper from the Portuguese text: "Áreas culturais indígenas do Brasil; 1900-1959," in the *Boletim do Museu Paraense Emílio Goeldi,* Nova Série, Antropologia, N.º 8, Janeiro, 1960. Belém, Pará, Brasil: Instituto Nacional de Pesquisas da Amazônia, Conselho Nacional de Pesquisas.

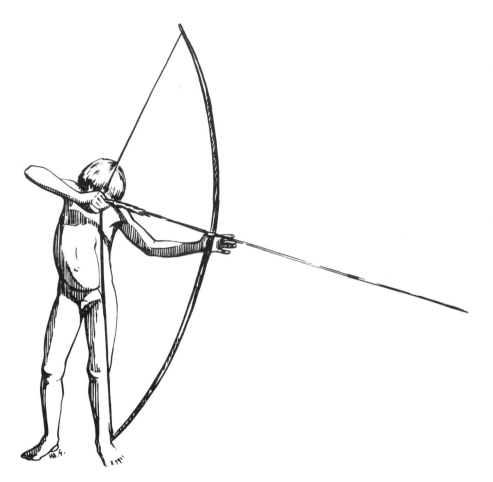

INDIGENOUS CULTURE AREAS OF BRAZIL, 1900-1959

by Eduardo Galvão

To the extent that the emphasis of Brazilian ethnology shifts from descriptive monographs on indigenous tribal groups to problems of a comparative order, particularly those of acculturation processes and culture change, the need for cultural classifications of broader perspective and greater accuracy than those currently in use is underscored.

For some time it has been apparently satisfactory to classify indigenous tribes into linguistic groups in which other cultural aspects were also implicit, at least in relation to the principal phyla. Brazilian ethnography continues to use the classical linguistic scheme—Tupis, Caribes, Aruaques, Jês, and Isolates—as synonymous with different culture types. We speak of a "Tupi culture" in contrast to an "Aruaque culture" or a "Caribe culture."

There was and is a certain rationale for this procedure.* Awareness of the distortion inherent in the use of linguistic criteria to define cultural configurations notwithstanding, the fact that some of these linguistic groups are distributed in geographic belts of exclusive occupancy contributes to this identification between language and culture. Such is the case of the Tupi Indians, who in the period of exploration and discovery occupied the shoreline from

---

* In a paper for the IV Meeting of the Associação Brasileira de Antropologia (A. B. A.), Matoso Câmara, Jr. (MS 1959), basing his thesis on Greenberg (1957), stressed interest in the areal type of classification used in modern linguistics, given "the evident correlation between linguistic areas, so obtained, and cultural areas, as one or the other comes under the influences of contact, the linguistic criteria which serve to establish an areal group of languages can be used for anthropology, along with nonlinguistic criteria, to determine a culture area."

south to north, in contrast to the Jê of the interior, who continue today to dominate an extensive area of the states of Maranhão, Goiás, and Pará which has been practically exempt from the intrusion of other groups. Given the irregular geographic distribution of the Aruaque and Caribe, the identification of these respective cultures was or is less correct. Nonetheless, the Aruaque commonly are stereotyped as "civilizing," able potters, weavers, and horticulturists, and the Caribe, as warlike and pioneering.

This classification, which bears the vice of its origin and has been little improved by the dearth of studies in depth similar to those of Alfred Métraux (Tupi) and Max Schmidt (Aruak), has no instrumental function in ethnological taxonomy. Its use persists, however, because Brazilian ethnologists, preoccupied with the study of individual Indian tribes and considerably averse to generalization, have not sought a systematic comparative base. In any such effort, the focus of Brazilian interest is the diffusion of specified culture traits.

There are certain difficulties in the application to Brazilian Indian cultures of the concept of culture area as it has been developed, principally by North American anthropologists. These difficulties are inherent in the lack of factual information regarding a considerable number of tribes, and in the added circumstance that the force of Luzo-Brazilian expansion concentrated indigenous survivors of the most dissimilar origins in the same area.

While Wissler's pioneering attempt (1922) to apply the concept of culture area derived particularly from his interest in its application to North American tribes, he did extend it to South America, identifying a single culture area, the *Amazonian,* in Brazil. His delineation was based on the concept of food area; the region was defined as the manioc area. Kroeber (1923) revised Wissler's general scheme; he retained the Amazon area, but designated it the Tropical Forest area. The limited utility of this scheme in application to problems of Brazilian ethnography was glaringly apparent; it aroused no interest.

Other classifications on a cultural base followed, always on the initiative of foreign (i.e., non-Brazilian) anthropologists. These scholars took an overall view of South America; they were known for their emphasis on problems of the historical development of Amerindian societies. In general their taxonomies were not specific in relation to Brazil. Stout (1938) established 11 areas; Cooper (1942), 3 areas; Kroeber (1948), 4 areas; Bennett and Bird (1949), 3 areas; Murdock (1951), 24 areas.

Map 1—Areas of Native Culture in South America according to Kroeber (1948:791)

Differences in method and conceptualization in these schemes need to be made explicit. These are brought into bold relief when the culture areas of Cooper and Steward are contrasted with those of Murdock. Although both of the former explicitly mention areas (cultural areas, culture-type area), they superimpose on this concept a diachronic notion of cultural development, with a concomitant emphasis on ecological relations and the level of socio-cultural integration. Murdock is more insistent on assigning value to the distribution of specified material traits (pottery, basketry, loom-weaving, subsistence techniques, etc.) and such nonmaterial traits as linguistic affiliation, social classes, kinship, and so on; in this respect he follows the model developed by Wissler.

Cooper's object, in actuality, was a model of cultural sequences. *Sierral* (Andean Altiplano), *Silval* (Amazonas-Orinoco), and *Marginal* (prairie-plains) simultaneously designate areas and indicate levels of development. Peoples of the *Marginal* culture included, beside the Jê tribes (provisionally), the Botocudo, Masakali, Pataxó, Puri, and other groups of the Brazilian east, the Bororo, Guató, Guaiaki, peoples of the Chaco, the Pampa, and Patagônia, considered "externally marginal" to the *Sierral* and *Silval* areas. Other groups, like the Yaruro, Maku, Xiriana, Waika, and Mura, were classified as "internally marginal" to the *Forest (Silval)* area. Cooper suggested the possibility of considering the Jê groups as retrogressed *Forest* types.

Cooper recognized as basic uniformities in marginal groups traits which can be summarized as follows: hunting, fishing, and gathering. *Horticulture* lacking or rudimentary. Absence of domestic animals, with the exception of the dog. Generally, the absence of stimulants (alcohol, tobacco, coca). Pottery frequently absent or very simple. Loom weaving absent. Simple shelters, sleeping on the ground (coarse grass mats or skins). Exceptionally long arrows. Absence of cannibalism. Monogamy or simple polygamy. Basic social unit, the band.

People of the *Forest* culture, including most of the Amazon Forest tribes, are characterized by *horticulture* (manioc, maize, and potatoes) and the presence of a great many of the traits shown as negative for the *Marginal* type. Cooper brought together comparative data adequate, in his view, to demonstrate that the *Marginal* culture is older than the *Forest* type. He cited the so-called Pan-American culture elements, found in South America but absent in the *Forest* area, which reappear in North America.

Steward amplified Cooper's scheme, superimposing on the concept of area another more general concept of types representing levels of socio-cultural integration. On this basis he redefined the Forest, Mountain, and Marginal areas in terms of Tropical Forest Type, Andean Type, and Marginal Type, and included a new type, the Circum-Caribbean. Discussing the culture-environment relationship in depth, he called attention to, among other facts, the differences in subsistence resources of the seacoast and interior areas which act as determinants of population density and have a bearing on socio-political patterns.

Steward's classification is based on the occurrence, distribution, and integration of socio-economic and religious patterns. He relegated to secondary importance culture elements taken in isolation because ". . . too many of them are independent variables. Their distributions were dissonant with those of the socio-political and religious patterns, and they occurred in quite different patterns. They were the building materials of culture and did not greatly affect the architecture" (Steward 1949, V: 674).

Like Cooper's, this scheme has developmental implications in the sense that ". . . some institutions and practices were necessarily antecedent to others, but it is not a unilinear scheme . . . a strong historical tradition carried certain socio-political institutions and probably several technologies throughout a considerable portion of South America, but the acceptance and patterning of such institutions was always contingent upon local potentialities" (Steward 1949, V: 674).

Steward recognized the necessity of area subdivisions within these "types" of culture, as follows:

TROPICAL FOREST TYPE

Guianas—considered the center of dispersal because a major number of culture traits are included.
Three possible subdivisions:

a) coast

b) mountain-savannah area

c) Amazon area

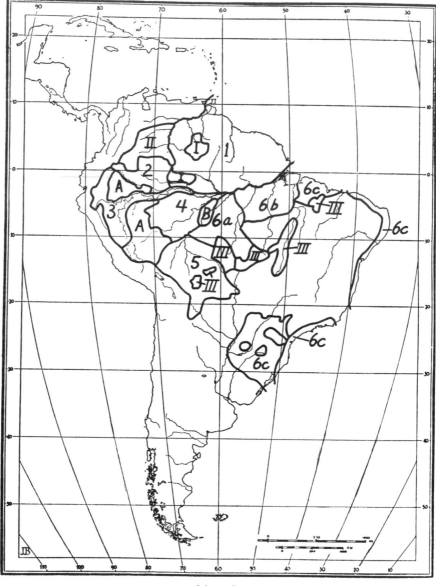

Map 2

Northwest Amazon—the Eastern Tukanos and their neighbors of the Uaupés-Caquetá region. Witotos, Tukuna and probably Yurimagua (more or less marginal insofar as their technology is concerned).

Mura—Impoverished material culture (described as nomads without horticulture). Some distinctive traits in their social and religious organization.

Juruá-Purus—a block of Pano, Aruak, and Katukina tribes.

Tupi Tribes—three subgroups:
      a) Tupinambá and Guarani
      b) smill tribes of the lower Tocantins
      c) tribes of Tapajós and Madeira. The Tupi of the Solimões are classified within the Montaña area.

Mojos-Chiquitos and Montaña, two areas of incidental interest to Brazilian ethnology.

MARGINAL TYPE

Marginal tribes of the southern Amazon periphery. Groups on the tributaries and headwaters of the Tocantins, Xingú, Tapajós,

---

Map 2—Cultural Divisions according to Steward (1948:884)

1—6:   Basic Tropical Forest cultures:
1—   Guianas
2—   Northwest Amazon
3—   Montaña
4—   Juruá-Purús
5—   Mojos-Chiquitos
6—   Tupían: a) Madeira-Tapajóz
                  b) lower Xingú-Tocantins
                  c) Tupinamba and Guaraní

A, B—   Submarginal tribes:
        A—Western Marginals
        B—Mura

I - III—   Marginal tribes:
        I—Guiana Internal Marginals
        II—Northwestern Marginals
        III—Southern Amazon Marginals

Madeira, and Guaporé rivers—Carajá, Tapirapé, Alto Xinguanos, Nambikwara, Bororo, Jê tribes, Guajá, and Tenetehara.

Guiana Internal Marginals. Southern headwaters of the Orinoco and northern headwaters of the Rio Negro—Xiriana, Waika, Guaharibo, Auake, etc.

Northwestern Amazon Marginals. In Brazil *perhaps* the Catapolitani, Huhuteni (Hohodene), and other groups possibly of Maku origin, assimilated by the Aruaks, are included.

Western Marginals. Two groups—(a) on the north bank of the Marañon as far as the Putumaio; (b) Panos and Aruaks on the Ucaiale, Madre de Dios, and Juruá-Purus.

Even when account is taken of the divergence between a classification based on levels of socio-cultural integration and one that stresses the contiguous diffusion of culture traits and complexes, there is a certain incongruity in a scheme such as the one just presented above. Thus in the inclusion of Tupi tribes in a single group or area, the linguistic criterion is definitive, although a more or less continuous distribution of part of these tribes is implied. The Mura culture area, actually that of a highly mobile tribe of whose culture little is known (cf. Nimuendajú, 1948:257), cannot be regarded as similar. The Marginals, especially those of the first subdivision or area, are tribes of quite diverse culture elements bracketed as a single type. The marked contrast between the Tenetehara of the Maranhense rain forest, the Timbira of the southern plateau of Maranhão, the Kaiapó of the plains between the Tocantins and Xingú rivers, the Xinguanos of the headwaters of the Xingú, and the Nambikuara of northern Mato Grosso has been observed. Steward himself refers to the heterogeneity of these groups; nevertheless, he lumps them together on the grounds of their differentiation from other South American tribes, given the absence of culture traits such as horticulture, loom-weaving, more complex types of basketry, canoes, etc., present in these latter cultures (cf. Steward 1949: 671-2). With rare exceptions (among them the Bororo and Guajá) the groups mentioned have, in greater or lesser degree, a form of cultivation directly related to the potentialities of the geographic area they inhabit, in which the rain forest, the gallery forest, or the scrub-woodland of the plains predominates. In terms of socio-cultural patterns, the point is illustrated by a comparison of the extensive bilateral family of the Tenetehara and the Xinguanos with the dual organization of the Timbira and Kaiapó and the Nambikuara bands. Similarly, the differences in religious systems and in the development of shamanism are considerable.

This classification can be revised to improve upon the ethnological description of the various tribes. If possible, it should be amplified to include a third "type" intermediary between the Tropical Forest and Marginal area groups. One of the two main factors suggesting the utility of this third "type" is acculturative; the other, adaptive. Marginal groups have assimilated some of the culture elements of the Tropical Forest groups, thus becoming acculturated. The development of a technology specialized to a specific geographic panorama * is adaptive. A typology such as is suggested here provides a more adequate approach to problems of a general comparative order and of culture development throughout the continent. However, even this revised typology is too generalized to be an effective instrument for a cultural taxonomy of Brazilian Indians.

A more recent scheme, more closely approximating the traditional conception of culture area, is that of Murdock (1951). Murdock criticizes the earlier attempts on two basic points: variation in the quality of ethnographic data, and classification resting upon negative traits (absences). He proposes other criteria which are summarized in the following enumeration:

      linguistic affiliation
      subsistence techniques
      domestic animals and cultivated plants
      participation of the sexes in agriculture
      ceramics, loom-weaving, and basketry
      type of dwelling
      social classes, political institutions
      marriage, kinship

-----

* An example of this intermediate type is suggested to us by the eastern Timbira and the Kaiapó. These are Indians of the plains (campo) and of the scrub woodlands (cerrado), whose subsistence, however, depends in large measure on the slash-burn cultivation of small plots (roça) in the gallery forests. They have villages of a certain permanence and a technology specialized for the environment of the savannahs. During part of the year a population superior to that common among the modern societies of the Tropical Rain Forest type gathers in the villages. The Canela until a few years ago numbered 400 individuals to a village; the Xavante (Xerente), about 600; the Kubenkrankegn, a little over 400; and according to data from the Second Regional Inspectorate of the Indian Protective Service (SPI), a Kaiapó group of Iriri had more than 700 people in its village base.

On the basis of these diagnostic elements, Murdock distinguishes 24 culture areas in South America; of these, 11 include Brazilian areas and tribes (Murdock, 1951 b: 133, 55).

Map 3—Culture Areas of South America according to Murdock
(1951 b:134)

Eastern Lowland—Guarani, Tupi (São Francisco), Tupinambá.

Atlantic—Kaingang, Maxakali, Aweikoma, Botocudo, Kamaka, Guataka, Gueren, Pataxo, Puri.

Goyaz—Akroa, Apinayé, Bororo, Karajá, Kariri, Kayamo, Kaiapó, Coroa, Fulnio, Jeiko, Opaye, Xakriaba, Xerente, Suya, Tapirapé, Tarairu, Teremembe, Timbira.

Pará—Amanaie, Apiaka, Arara, Kawahyb, Guaja, Maué, Munduruku, Tenetehara.

Xingú—Arawine, Aueto, Bakairi, Nambikwara, Trumai, Waura, Yaruma.

Bolivian—Arikem, Xapakura, Xane, Paressi.

Juruá-Purus—Amahuaka, Kaxinaua, Katukina, Ipurina, Maioruna, Mura, Paumari, Iamamadi, Iuma.

Amazon—Kokama, Manao, Omagua, Wairaku, Yurimagua.

Caquetá—Achagua, Baniwa, Betoi, Tukano, Tukuna.

Savannah—Auaké, Puinave, Guahibo, Maku, Xiriana.

Guiana—Apalaí, Aruak, Arua, Barauna, Kamarakoto, Karib, Emerillon, Makuxi, Palikur, Rukuyen, Taulipang, Waiwai, Wapixana, Yekuana.

In this scheme some areas need to be better defined. As Rowe (1953: 52) points out, the inadequacies derive from lack of information on some tribes, differences in the data and quality of information sources, and inconsistency in the application of definition criteria. The tendency, common to many classifications, to use historic descriptions of the first stages of occupation indiscriminately with current data results in the location of different stages of acculturation and of culture change along the same plane. In consequence both geographical distribution and ethnological characterization are distorted.

In Murdock's classification, for example, this is seen in the excessive extension of areas like Goyaz, Pará, and Guiana, and in the inclusion of historic and contemporary tribes in the same frame, thereby creating difficulties in the geographic or cultural definition of the area. But these difficulties are hard to overcome in any model spanning a long historical period.

Archaeological findings enabled Bennett (1949) to define Andean cultural provinces in a space and time which goes far beyond the available historical information—the "co-traditions"—but there is very little archaeological knowledge of the greater part of Brazil. The nature of the culture of the forests and the plains, both highly mobile, must also be considered. Withal, we already are able to point to some results which can serve to orient future classifications. See for example Meggers and Evans (1955); their findings demonstrate the difficulties inherent in Steward's view of the Guianas as a center of dispersion of the Tropical Rain Forest Type.

In our view, a classification of indigenous culture areas of Brazil will have to proceed by stages. In the first place, a census of the surviving tribes on a specified time base is necessary. The interval between 1500 and 1950 is too large. Changes of all kinds occurred during four centuries of our history; if these changes are not taken into account, the comparative picture is distorted. Let us keep in mind the example of the Plains Area in North America, initially defined by Wissler as constituted essentially of nomadic tribes which took over the horse introduced by the Europeans and developed a unique type of culture. On the basis of archaeological investigation, Strong (1933) showed that an agricultural complex had existed earlier and had been destroyed in historic times by nomads on horseback, who, having increased their mobility, had left the periphery of the area to occupy it totally, absorbing and dominating the primitive cultivators. The delimitation of historic epochs also will contribute to uniformity and to selectivity of sources. Cultures thus reconstituted will have a more solid base.

Secondly, and depending on the period chosen, the definition, however tentative, of the contact situation of tribes selected as representative of the area becomes necessary. *Internal contact,* that is, intertribal relations and their acculturative results, and *external contact,* between tribal societies and the national society, equally induce changes.

On the basis of historical and current data, some tribes have been described without any consideration of the phenomenon of intertribal acculturation, which can be observed only when the researcher proceeds from the study of individual tribes to comparative area research. Intertribal acculturation processes characterized the past and continue to operate in the present. Maku, Tukano, and Aruak groups in the region of the Rio Negro have integrated their cultural elements in a new configuration. Distinguishing between a

Tropical Rain Forest type (Tukano and Baniwa) and a Marginal Internal type (Maku) permits us a somewhat historical inference of occupation and settlement, but affords very little insight into the phenomena of cultural dynamics. Frikel (1959) refers to his observation of the same intertribal acculturation phenomenon among Carib groups of Guiana. Tribes or large sibs of the same linguistic family (Carib influenced) living in contiguous territory are found in different culture phases, from the most simple level in the process of acculturation to the most developed. The general processes of diffusion, acculturation, and integration that operate here are more significant than the count and delineation of "absences" in these more simple groups. We also can cite the case of the Upper Xingú, where tribes of diverse origin, history, and language became the nucleus of a culture area, facilitating the process of intertribal acculturation. This phenomenon, which we call "cultural compression" (Galvão, 1953:10), is an indirect effect of the expansion of national pioneer intrusions upon these groups.

From the point of view of external contacts, it is necessary not only to define the contact situation, but also to clarify its nature. We shall use Darcy Ribeiro's categories (1957: 7-14) for this purpose: isolated groups, groups in intermittent or permanent contact, and integrated groups. Characterization of the regional manifestation of each of the types of pioneering frontiers—the extractive, the pastoral, and the agricultural—and of its differential effects upon the acculturative process becomes equally urgent.

Beginning in the seventeenth century when contacts between the colonists and the indigenous population were firmly established, the spatial distribution, cultural configuration, and demographic density of the latter were substantially modified. A look at the vast areas along the coastline, on the banks of the Amazon, and along the middle and lower tributaries, all of which have no Indian population, is sufficient to make the point. Lack of documentation renders the task of reconstructing the traditional culture of groups which are already integrated or are now extinct a hazardous enterprise. The reduction of a population of almost two million Indians in the era of discovery to less than one hundred thousand in contemporary Brazil has brought about equally profound modifications in the context of the surviving tribal societies.

Taking into account the preceding exposition, we have attempted to divide Brazil into culture areas on a limited temporal base—1900 to 1959—the same period utilized by Ribeiro in the study cited above. It is not our intent to relegate the historical sources and processes of long-term culture change to a secondary place, nor to affirm the impossibility of developing a model appropriate to the analysis of a longer time frame. We wish to stress the necessity of establishing a first stage in the classification and description of a culture area. Once the contemporary picture has been clarified, linkages and historical inferences may be used to expand the dimensions of our perspective in time and space.

This preliminary study does not develop a new classification; it does, rather, adapt the schemes elaborated by Steward and Murdock. Some groups have been relocated, and the boundaries of some areas have been revised. We have emphasized the contiguous spatial distribution of culture traits, both material and socio-cultural, as the decisive criterion. Although specific details of the geographic environment of each area are not covered in this summary description, they were taken into account. Definition of the contact situation * and of the cultural context of the pioneering national frontiers is equally important. We consider the occurrence of intertribal acculturation phenomena to be of major significance. With the exception of Ribeiro (1957:58) the various authors mentioned here have neglected to discuss this point explicitly. Ribeiro's study is essential to an understanding of the dynamics and the processes of the integration of culture elements in an area or regional configuration. For a static typology is of little use when, as in the Amazon areas especially, the process observed is the meeting of cultures and the absorption of groups which are considered marginal into other groups belonging to more complex configurations in the same area.

The 11 divisions presented constitute large areas; their subdivision is suggested with greater or lesser specificity by available ethnographic data. The inclusion of some groups in these areas may appear arbitrary. For example, the Karajá are classified in the Tocantins-Xingú area, in which Timbira-Kaiapó elements predominate. Rather than considering the former "atypical" or isolating them in a provincial autonomy, we think that in addition to possessing some traits in common, they represent specialization to a sector of the geographical environment, the Araguaia River.

----

* We are using Ribeiro's categories to define the types of external contact (1957: 7 ff.) *isolated* (accidental contacts); *intermittent* (occasional relations); *permanent* (direct and permanent contacts); *integrated* (Indians incorporated in the labor force or as specialized producers).

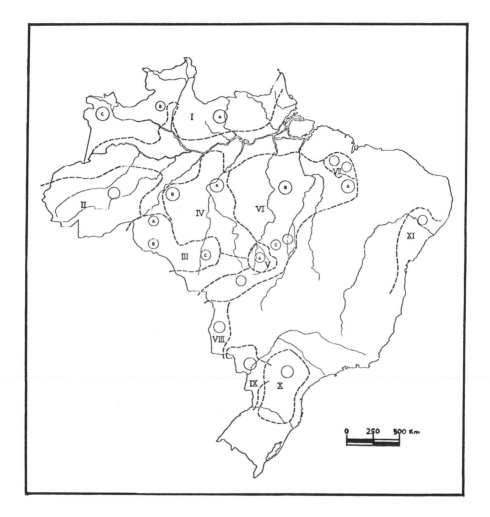

Map 4—Indigenous Culture Areas of Brazil, 1900-1959

I—North Amazonian   II—Juruá-Purus
III—Guaporé   IV—Tapajós-Madeira
V—Upper Xingú   VI—Tocantins-Xingú
VII—Pindaré-Gurupi   VIII—Paraguai
IX—Paraná   X—Tietê-Uruguai
XI—Northeast

Culture area	Nucleus	Tribes

I—North Amazon	A	Parukoto-Xaruma, Warikyána, Pianokotó-Tiriye, Urukuyana, Aparai (Karib)
		Oeste—Makuxi, Taulipang (Karib)
		Leste—Oiampi, Emerion (Tupi)
		    Palikur (Aruak)
		    Galibi (Karib)
		Norte—Kalina
		    Waiwai (Karib)

	B	Xirianá, Waiká, Waharibo, Pakidai (Xirianá)
	C	Baniwa (Aruak), Tariana (Aruak), Tukano, Desana, Kobewa, Piratapuio (Tukano-Betoya) Maku Tukuna
II—Juruá-Purus		Ipurinã, Paumari, Iamamadi (Aruak), Marinawa, Kaxinawa, Iaminawa, Katukina (Pano); Katukina (Katukina)
III—Guaporé	A	Grupos Txapakura
	B	Tupari (Tupi)
	C	Nambikwara (Nambikwara)
IV—Tapajós-Madeira	A	Munduruku, Maué (Tupi)
	B	Grupos Kawahyb (Tupi)
V—Upper Xingú		Kamaiurá, Aueti (Tupi) Waurá, Mehinaku, Iawalapití (Aruak) Kalapalo, Bakairí, Kuikuro (Karib) Suiá (Jê) [ancient encroachment] Juruna (Tupi, mixed blood) [recent encroachment]
VI—Tocantins-Xingú	A	Timbira, Canela, Apinayé, Kraho (Jê)
	B	Xerente, Akwê-Xavante (Jê)
	C	Grupos Kaiapó, Gavião (Jê); Parakanã, Asuriní (Tupi) Tapirapé (Tupi) Karajá (isol.)——specialization Bororo (Otuke)—?

Culture area	Nucleus	Tribes
VII—Pindaré-Gurupi		Tenetehara: Tembé and Guajajara; Urubú-Kaapor; Guajá (Tupi)
VIII—Paraguai		Kaduveo (Mbaya); Terena (Aruak)
IX—Paraná		Nandeva, Kaoivá, Mbua (Guarani)
X—Tietê-Uruguai		Grupos Kaingang (Jê)
XI—Northeast		Fulniô (Carnijó); Potiguara (Tupi); Pankararu (Pankararu); Atikum (?); Xokó (?); Pataxo (Pataxo); Tuxá (?); Kariri (Kariri); Xukuru (?); Maxakali (Maxakali)

I. North Amazon

Belt north of the Amazon River between the sources of the Rio Negro to the west and the Atlantic Coast to the east. Tropical forest region with interspersed plains.

National pioneering frontier with an extractive base. The gathering of natural products has determined the pattern of occupation and exploration in the area since the beginning of the seventeenth century. Rubber and nuts are the principal contemporary products. Brazilian penetration between the Jari and Trombetas rivers is limited to their lower course. Indian groups here have remained relatively isolated, save for occasional incursions of the balata tappers from the south or the Saramacás Negroes from the northeast. In the region of the Rio Branco, a cattle-raising nucleus has been established but has not penetrated far into the interior; it principally affects the Makuxi Indians. Savannahs occupied exclusively by isolated Indian groups who have been contacted only in recent years by SPI agents and by missionaries, extend from the right bank of the Rio Branco to the Cauaboris. The western part of the area, centered between the Içana and Uaupés rivers, has undergone the greatest penetration, and its Indian population has maintained permanent contact over a long period. These differences in situation of external contact are reflected in more accentuated acculturation among the western groups (Baniwa and Tukano) and relative conservation of tribal patterns among the tribes of the east and center. Differences in origin and language notwithstanding, the several groups surrounded and pressured by the national society have developed an intense process of intertribal acculturation. Its outcome has been the cultural uniformity characteristic of the area.

Subareas and tribes—three cultural nuclei:
A—Brazilian Guiana—Karib
B—Savannah (Rio Branco-Cauaboris)—Xirianá
C—Rio Negro Aruak—Betoya

A. *Brazilian Guiana.* Predominantly Karib groups, the Pianokotó-Tiriyó can be considered the nucleus of the subarea. Parukotó-Xarúma, Warikyána, Urukuyána, Aparaí (Karib). Wapichiyana (Aruak). On the eastern periphery, the Oiampik, Emerion (Tupis), Palikur (Aruak), Galibi (Karib) are somewhat differentiated culturally. To the west, in an intermediary location between this subarea and the Savannah are the Makuxi and Taulipang (Karib).

Population estimated at 8,000 Indians. Intertribal acculturation in process. External contacts varying from isolated and intermittent (groups of the center) to integrated (Makuxi, Galibi, Palikur).

Manioc cultivation, pottery, basketry, hammock weaving (use of tucum and cotton fibers), navigation (bark canoes), benches. Use of curare, but absence of blowgun (*sarabatana*). Bows, arrows, and small war clubs. Various types of houses, from rounded to rectangular, used by the same group. Villages of 20 to 30 persons. Patrilineal sibs, except among the Warikyána, who are matrilineal. Religion fundamentally monotheistic. Shamanism considerably developed. Use of *paricá* (Piptadenia) for ritual purposes. Various forms of direct burial (Warikyána, Pianokotó-Tiriyó), cremation (Urukuyána), endocannibalism (Purukotó).

B. *Savannah*—Xirianá groups: Xirianá, Waiká, Pakidái, and Waharibos located between the Demeni and the Cauaboris, tributaries of the Rio Negro. Population estimated at over 4,000 Indians, an estimate we find highly dubious. Eastern Xirianá groups maintain contacts with the Makuxi and Taulipang. Small slash-burn plots of manioc and bananas. The cultivation of manioc, use of canoes and of blowguns appear to be recent borrowings. Generally isolated, except for intermittent contacts on the Uraricocra, Demeni, and Cauaboris rivers.

Seminomadic horticulturists with a gathering, hunting, and fishing base. Basketry twined ("*torcido*"). Large bows. Use of curare. Blowgun, attributed to borrowing. House of a rectangular or ring shape, the circular roof converging to an interior, uncovered patio. Information extremely unreliable, making it difficult to delineate this subarea culturally.*

---

* Judging from these data, the Xirianá can be incorporated into Steward's Marginal type and thus considered in a separate area. However, we prefer to include

C. *Rio Negro*—Baniwa tribes, Tariana (Aruak); Tukano, Desana, Kobewa, and smaller groups of the same linguistic family (Betoya); Maku groups. Population estimated at 3,500 Indians. Cultural and linguistic acculturation between Aruaks and Tukanos as a result of territorial contiguity, commerce, and manufacturing specialization. Aruak groups like the Tariana were Tukan-ized. The Maku, possibly the primitive inhabitants of the region, were in large part absorbed by one of the two great stocks. External contacts varying from intermittent to permanent, with assimilation of part of the population into rural nuclei.

Manioc horticulture. Technology similar to that of the Brazilian Guianas, varying only in accessory elements or details of form. Circular baskets in this subarea, four-sided baskets in Guiana. Greater development in pottery, with two types: one black and simple, the other white-red. Use of curare and of the blowgun. Large rectangular habitations (*malocas*), occurrence of a circular type generally superseded today by individual dwellings of a neo-Brazilian type. Settlements of 20 to 50 people. At the beginning of the century each dwelling housed an entire lineage of about 100 persons. Exogamous patrilineal sibs. Religion based on an ancestral cult (Kobewa) and mythological heroes, of whom the principal, Kowai, is identified as Jurupari (the devil of the Tupis). Influenced by Christian ideas. Messianic movements. Moderate shamanism. Use of masks personifying supernatural spirits and of sacred flutes, both forbidden to the women. Use of *paricá* (Piptadenia), ipadu (coca), and kaapi (ayahuasca), besides tobacco. Burial in urns in the past, within the dwelling or in cemeteries at present. Evidence of endocannibalism (bone ashes mixed with *chicha*) in the past.

Frikel, Protásio

1958—Classificação linguístico-etnológica das tribos indígenas do Pará setentrional e zonas adjacentes. Rv. Antropologia v. 6 n.º 2.

Galvão, Eduardo

1959—Aculturação indígena no Rio Negro. Bol. Museu P. E. Goeldi, N.S., Antropologia, n.º 7.

---

them in the larger North Amazon area because they have absorbed culture elements of the Brazilian Guiana and represent a special form of adaptation to the environment of the savannahs within these geographical limits. To a certain extent they correspond to the "nonaccessible" Tiryó, to whose primitive culture Frikel refers in his communication, or to the Maku of the Rio Negro, among whom some groups were "tukanizados" or "aruaquizados" (cf. Galvão). From our point of view, the individualization of static cultures is less interesting than evidence of a process of intertribal acculturation.

Gillin, John
1948—Tribes of the Guianas. H.S.A.I., v. 3, pp. 799-858.

Goldman, Irving
1948—Tribes of the Uaupés-Caquetá region. H.S.A.I., v. 3, pp. 763-798.

Koch-Grünberg, Theodor
1909-10—Zwei Jahre unter den Indianern. Reise in Nordwest Brasilien
          1903-5.—Berlin. 2 v.

Métraux, Alfred
1948—The hunting and gathering tribes of the Rio Negro basin.
          H.S.A.I., v. 3, pp. 861-867.

Zerries, Otto
1955—Some aspects of Waicá culture. Anais do XXXI Cong. Int.
          Americanistas. São Paulo, pp. 73-88.

II. Juruá-Purus

Region of southwestern Amazon, encompassing the basins of
the Juruá and Purus rivers. Forest zone with lowlands predominant.

National pioneering frontier of extractive activity; latex of the
Hevea and the inferior latex of the Avore Moráceas are the principal
products. Exploration and occupation of the area gained momentum
only in 1860, and became firmly established at the turn of the century
with the intense search for rubber. Northeasterners from Ceara and
Maranhão, and, on a lesser scale, Bolivians and Peruvians constitute
the nucleus of this frontier. In the precipitate occupation of this
geographic area a majority of the Indian groups were liquidated
or compulsorily enlisted as rubber tappers.

Ethnographic and linguistic data inadequate, impeding a more
precise delineation of the area.* A subdivision of the area into two

---

* For lack of sufficient information upon which to base a more adequate
delineation or subdivision, we are retaining the classification of this area proposed
by Steward and Murdock. As Métraux warned (1948:658), "The inclusion of the
Purus tribes within the same area as those of the Juruá may seem arbitrary. It is
very likely that the Arawakan Indians and the Panoans presented differences which
might have justified their separation in two different chapters. Actually, our information is too patchy to allow a sharp line to be drawn between them." The first
historic data date from the second half of the twentieth century, the era in which
these tribes were dislocated and subjugated during the influx of Brazilian pioneers.
A fact to which we wish to call attention is the repetition here of Frikel's observation

nuclei consisting of the Aruak and Pano tribes is admissible. However, in each nucleus there are tribes classified as Tropical Forest culture type and as Eastern Marginals situated at the headwaters of the Juruá, Acre, and Madre de Dios rivers. There is little ethnological evidence to indicate the occurrence of a process of intertribal acculturation among the several tribes. Extra-tribal contacts vary from isolated, in rare cases, to permanent or integrated. Among the former, the still hostile Yaminawa on the upper Curanja are cited; among the latter, the Ipurinã, Yamamadi, and Marinawa.

> Tribes: Paumari, Ipurinã, and Yamamadi (Aruak)
>
> Kaxinawa, Yaminawa, Marinawa (Pano)
>
> Dyapa Groups (Katukina)

Population: exceedingly fragmentary data make it difficult to estimate the total. The data available indicate, however, that their numbers have been greatly reduced.

Subsistence based on the *roça* (a small, slash-and-burn cleared plot on which subsistence crops are grown), however, the products cultivated vary in importance. Predominance of sweet manioc (*macacheira*) over bitter manioc. Pano groups generally horticultural. Small fields *(roçados)* among Aruaks, Ipurinã. The Paumari live exclusively off fishing and gathering. Pottery of various types; simple without decoration (Yamamadi, Paumari); oval forms with painting (Ipurinã); black with geometric designs (Kaxinawa). Basketry, twilled. Weaving of nets (cotton and fibers), absent among the Paumari. Use of venom (probably curare). Irregular distribution of the blowgun. Canoes of bark and of fire-hollowed wood, lanceolate oars.

Houses of various types, conic or "beehive" predominating. The Paumari are distinctive for their floating houses, constructed on rafts *(jangadas)*. A local group consists of an extended family. Groups of families joined together and identified by a name, generally the name of an animal. Belief in a Supreme God among the Pano groups, whose rituals are simpler than those of the Aruak. Use of flutes similar to those of the northern area, prohibited to the women. Flagellation among the Canamari and Curina. Shamanism. Use of tobacco, *paricá*, and chicha. Endocannibalism among the Pano groups (flesh and cremated bones), various forms of primary and secondary burial.

---

in the Guiana subarea—tribes of the same linguistic stock, in more or less contiguous territory, present different levels of culture development. A second fact is that of the slight emphasis on horticulture among the Aruak tribes, equated with the specialization to a type of river life as illustrated by the Paumari.

Capistrano de Abreu, J.
1938—Os Caxinauas. Ensaios e estudos. Ser. 3, pp. 275-357: Rio de Janeiro.

Métraux, Alfred
1948—Tribes of Juruá-Purus basins. H.S.A.I., v. 3, pp. 657-686.

Schultz, Harald and Chiara, W.
—Informações sôbre os índios do alto rio Purús. Rev. Museu Paulista N.S.V. IX, São Paulo, pp. 181-202.

III.   Guaporé

Area including the territories of the right bank of the Guaporé River and the southern part of the basin of the upper Madeira. Region of forest (*mata*) and *campo cerrado* (vegetation transitional between savannah and woodland), [See Waibel, Leo, "Vegetation and Land Use in the Planalto Central of Brazil," *Geographical Review* Vol. 38, 1948, pp. 529-554], which marks the transition belt between the plateau and the *hiléia* [Humboldt's name for the Tropical Rain Forest].

Pioneering frontier of extractive base (two qualities of latex, borracha and caucho); penetration dates from the beginning of the century. Seventy percent of the tribes extinct.

Lévi-Strauss (1949:371) distinguished between two subareas, the first on the lower Guaporé, between the Rio Branco and the Mamoré, occupied by Txapakura groups; the second including the basins of the Rio Branco, the Mequenes, and the Corumbiara, dominated by groups whose language probably is Tupi.

A.   Txapakura Groups—Pakaanovas and Urupá; the others generally mentioned in the literature, e.g. Kotemoka, Rokorona, Huanyam, Jaru, are practically extinct.

B.   Tupi Groups—Aruá, Makurap, Waioró, Amniapé, Guarátegajá, Kepkiriwat, Sanamaiká, Huari, Tupari. Only the last named have survived. The Jaboti and Puruborá have been culturally influenced by the Tupi, but are of uncertain linguistic affiliation.

C.   The Nambikuara, divided into various subgroups and constituting a linguistic unit which is as yet undefined, have a distinctively simple culture, but Lévi-Strauss considers them to be integrated into the Guaporé area.

Population estimates are unreliable but suggest a total of about 2,000 Indians. Acculturation is in process, but intertribal relations are characterized by hostilities. The Parecí-Kozarini on the south-western periphery of the area appear to be a Nambikuara subgroup that has been absorbed by the Aruak. External contacts vary from isolated (Pakaanovas), to intermittent (Nambikuara), and to permanent (Tupari).

Horticulture of maize and peanuts. Manioc secondary. Simple pottery, absent among the eastern Nambikuara. Cylindrical baskets of skins. Woven bags. Hammock weaving, except among the Nambi-kuara. General use of canoes among the river tribes. Use of curare for arrow-tips. Houses of the beehive type most common. Patrilineal exogamous sibs. Moieties. Nomadic bands for the Nambi-kuara. Belief in a supernatural force that can be manipulated by the shaman. Use of snuff (paricá and tobacco) for shamanistic purposes. Chicha. Primary burial among some groups of Nambikuara; secondary (bones).

Gaspar, Franz
n.d.—Tupari. Ed. Melhoramentos. São Paulo.

Métraux, Alfred
1948 The Chapacuran tribes. H.S.A.I., v. 3, pp. 397-406.

Lévi-Strauss, Claude
1948—Tribe of the right bank of the Guaporé River. H.S.A.I., v. 3, pp. 371-379.
1948—The Nambikwara. H.S.A.I., v. 3, pp. 361-9.

Roquette Pinto, E.
1938—Rondônia. Série Brasiliana, vol. 39. São Paulo.

IV. Tapajós-Madeira

Territory between the upper middle course of the Tapajós and the Madeira.

Forest zone with plains.

Pioneering national frontier on an extractive base with extensive penetration along both rivers.

Two subareas: one formed by the tribes called Kawahyb; the other, by the Munduruku. The Maué of the northwest of this area appear to be more closely linked to the latter. All speak Tupi.

A. Kawahyb. Of the ancient Kawahyb groups dislocated from the Tapajós by the Munduruku, which by the contemporary period had been driven back to the Madeira, only the Parintintin and the Tupi-

Kawahyb (Paranáwat, Bôca Negra, Wiraféd, Tukumanfed) remain. We also are including the Kajabi, located on the Xingú.

Population estimated at about 500 Indians. External contact varying from isolated (Bôca Negra) to permanent.

Cultivation of maize and sweet manioc (*macaxeira*). Maize flour. Pottery absent among some groups. Basketry little developed. Hammock weaving. Bow and arrows. Use of bark canoe. Houses open at the sides. Patrilineal exogamous moieties. Extended families. Resemblances between some motifs of Kawahyb mythology and the mythologies of the Jê groups. Tobacco unknown. Use of maize *chicha*. Primary burial.

The Tupi-Kawahyb cultivate both varieties of manioc. They are divided into patrilocal patrilineal sibs.

B.   Munduruku. The Munduruku of the Cururú River and the tribe in the interior called Campineiros are culturally differentiated only by the greater conservatism of the latter. Population estimated between 1,000 and 1,500. Originally concentrated on the Rio das Tropas, the Munduruku began to expand in 1750, pushing the Kawahyb toward the Madeira. Munduruku incursions extended to the south as far as the Nambikuara territory, and to the north and east as far as Santarém, Gurupá, and possibly the banks of the Tocantins.

Presently, the greater part of the population is integrated with rural nuclei of rubber tappers.

Cultivation of manioc. Pottery of poor quality. Basket weaving. Netting. Rectangular houses and double lean-tos, and another type with a conic top, all replaced by the contemporary neo-Brazilian model. Bows, arrows, lances, clubs. Use of venom? Feather art extraordinarily developed in the past. Tattooing of body and face. Exogamous half-sibs. Patrilineal sibs. Society of "warriors" with head-quarters in the men's house. Ancestor cult. Shamanism. Primary and secondary burial.

Lévi-Strauss
1948—The Tupi-Cawahib. H.S.A.I., v. 3, pp. 299-305.

Murphy, Robert
1954—As condições atuais dos Mundurucú. Publ. Inst. Antrop. Etnol. Pará n.º 8.

Nimuendajú, Curt
1948—The Cawahib Parintintin and their neighbors. H.S.A.I., v. 3, pp. 283-297.

Horton, Donald
1948—The Mundurucú. H.S.A.I., v. 3, pp. 271-282.

V. Upper Xingú

Region between the Suiá-Misu River to the north, the Parana-tinga to the south, the Ronuro to the west, and the Culisevu-Culuene to the east—sources of the Xingú River. Predominance of plains and scrublands. Gallery forests. Lakes.

Territory practically isolated until 1947 when the first settlements and bases of the Fundação Brasil Central were established here. Intermittent contact with agents of the FBC, SPI, and teams of topographic surveyors. Access of nonindigenous cultural elements was by way of the extreme south of the area, through contact with the Bakairí Indians (Paranatinga River).

Tribes: Kamaiurá, Aueti (Tupi), Waurá, Mehinaku, Iawalapití (Aruak); Bakairí, Kuikuro, Kalapalo, Nahukwá (Karib); Suiá (Jê); Trumai (isolated). A Juruna group recently settled a short distance below the Suiá-Misu, maintaining intermittent contacts. Culturally different from the Xinguanos (i.e., the nine tribes at the headwaters of the Xingú River). To the west are various groups whose classification is uncertain, labeled generically Kawahyb. To the south and east are the Xavantes, with whom, however, contacts are not reported.

Population of about 800 Indians. Despite their isolation, contagious diseases have decimated a good part of the earlier population, estimated at about 3,000 by von Steinen (1870). Some tribes are in the process of dying out—Iawalapiti, Trumai, and Aueti with fewer than 30 individuals. None of the others number much over 100. Intertribal ceremonials and joint game contacts are quite frequent.

The intertribal acculturation process has resulted in the emergence of a uniform pattern of culture.

Cultivation of manioc; consumption of tapioca cake (beiju) in preference to farinha. Pottery (Waurá specialization) of circular shape, flat bottom, everted lips, decorated; small zoomorphic vases. Very primitive basketry. Absence of tipiti press (a long, tubular squeezer used to extract the liquid starch from the manioc mash); substitution of a hand press. Hammock weaving (compact weave for the men, special texture for the women). Bow, arrows, cylindrical clubs (bordunas). Ceremonial use of spear thrower (atlatl). Bark canoes. Long oars. Houses with an oval ground plan, thatched walls and double arched ceiling, built in a circle, housing 30 to 40 persons under a single roof. Village populations varying from 20 to 140 individuals. Bilateral extended family. Mythology featuring twins identified with the sun and the moon. Shamanism developed. Feast of the dead. Use of tobacco and absence of fermented drinks (present among the Juruna). Use of dance masks. Ceremonial flutes prohibited to the women. Primary burial.

Galvão, Eduardo
1949—Apontamentos sôbre os índios Kamaiurá. Pub. Avulsas do Mus. Nac. n.⁰ 5, pp. 31-48.
1952—Breve notícia sôbre os índios Juruna. Rev. Mus. Paul. N.S., v. 6, pp. 469-479.
1953—Cultura e sistema de parentesco das tribos do alto Rio Xingú. Bols. Mus. Nac. N.S. Antropologia 14. Rio.

Lévi-Strauss, Claude
1948—Tribes of the upper Xingú river. H.S.A.I., v. 3, pp. 321-348.

Lima, Pedro E.
1955—Distribuição dos grupos indígenas do alto Xingú. Anais do XXXI Cong. Int. Amer. São Paulo.

VI.   Tocantins-Xingú

The area is bordered on the north by a line running roughly from the Mearim River as far as the Iriri (tributary of the Xingú), on the west by the watershed between the Tapajós and Xingú rivers, on the east by the Tocantins, and on the south by the large plateau that extends from Mato Grosso to Goiás. Plains predominate in this zone.

Pioneering frontier on a pastoral base, along the eastern edge of the area. Penetration as far as the plains (campos) of the Pau d'Arco by the end of the last century. Northeastern antecedence. Settlement proceeded slowly, and contacts with the Indians were peaceful. More recently gold, diamond, and crystal mining and the exploitation of rubber and nuts, radiating out from the Tocantins. Among the several important centers of fixed rural population along this river, Marabá, with 4,536 inhabitants, stands out. The colonizing enterprise here is symbolized by the Tocantins Railroad, linking Tucuruí with Jatobal. Penetration up the Xingú River was intensified at the beginning of the century under the stimulus of the rubber market (borracha and caucho). Settled population is restricted to a few unimportant villages; even so, occupation has been characterized by consistently hostile contacts with Kaiapó bands. These armed encounters have spread as far as the Tocantins River; the uneasy situation continues.

This area can be divided into three nuclei:
A. Oriental: Timbira (Canela and Apinayé)
B. Central: Akwẽ (Xerente, Xavante)
C. Occidental: Kaiapó (Gorotire, Xikrin—Diore, Menkranotire, Kubenkrankegn)

In addition to these Jê speaking tribes, the Asurini, Parakanã, Tapirapé (Tupi), Karajá (isolated), and Bororo (Otuke) are included in this culture area. With the exception of the first two groups, about which too little is known to permit description, these tribes differ in important aspects of their culture. The Tapirapé, encamped on the Xavante-Kaiapó dividing line, probably are recent arrivals. Nonetheless, some of their cultural traits—moieties, plaza groups (*grupos de praça*), age-grades, and various material elements—suggest the possible influence of neighboring groups. The Karajá, bound to the banks of the Araguaia, represent a special type of adaptation to a style of life based upon the resources and potentialities of the river. The Bororo, on the southern periphery, were included here provisionally on the basis of similarities in socio-economic structure. Possibly they had better defined links with the now extinct southern Kaiapó.

This division into three nuclei notwithstanding, the uniformities present permit a single schematic description for the entire area.

Population estimated at 12,000 Indians. External contacts varying from isolated (Kaiapó groups of the Xingú) to permanent (Timbira). Marked hostility, both intertribal and between villages of the same group. Resistance to neo-Brazilian acculturation. Between Jê tribes in the area, neither intertribal acculturation nor marked differences in level of development are observed. The diffusion of a basic pattern common to all the tribes is noted. Accessory elements identify and differentiate the various groups.

Manioc cultivation; greater emphasis on potato planting, *inhame* (Timbira), maize (Xavante). Pottery absent among the Jê; simple among the Bororo; polychrome among the Karajá. Basketry "twilled" and "coiled." Strip weaving only: belts, bands. Hammocks absent; sleeping on crude beds made from wooden rods (*jiraus*), cots, or mats. Feather art developed. Bows, arrows, and cylindrical or lanceolate clubs. Semilunar axes no longer in use as weapons of war. Absence of navigation, except among the Apinayé in historic times, and among the Karajá. Double lean-tos or houses of the "beehive type" (Xavante). Multifamily residence (Apinayé, Canela, Kaiapó); individual (Xerente). Habitations arranged in a circle or semicircle with a communal plaza. Man's house (Kaiapó, Xavante, Bororo, Tapirapé). Large villages—400 inhabitants (Canela, Kubenkrankegn), 600 (Xavante), 700 (Iriri). Dual organization: matrilineal (Canela, Apinayé, and Bororo). Age-grades or classes. Feast groups. Societies with ceremonial functions. Log races and sports competitions. Quite rich and complex ritual, but of a markedly profane nature. Belief in solar and lunar divinities. Shamanism inconsequentially elaborated among the Timbira, important among the Kaiapó, Xerente, Bororo, and Tapirapé. Use of tobacco but absence of tobacco cultivation among the majority of these tribes. Other narcotics or stimulants unknown. Use of various types of dance masks. Primary and secondary burial.

Baldus, Herbert
1944-49—Os Tapirapé, tribo tupi no Brasil Central. Rev. Arq. Mun. São Paulo, v. XCVI-CV, CVII-CXXVII.

Colbacchini, Antônio e Albisetti, César
1942—Os Bororos orientais. Brasiliana grande formato, v. 4. S. Paulo.

Lipkind, William
1948—The Carajá. H.S.A.I., v. 3, pp. 179-191.

Lowie, Robert
1946—The Bororo. H.S.A.I., v. 1, pp. 419-434.
1946—The Northwestern and Central Gê. H.S.A.I., v. 1, pp. 477-517.

Nimuendajú, Curt
1941—The Eastern Timbira. Univ. Calif. Public. in Amer. Archael. and Ethn., v. LI.
1956—Os Apinaié. Bol. Mus. Paraense E. Goeldi, v. 12.

Wagley, Charles
1955—The Tapirapé social and culture change, 1940-53. Anais XXXI Cong. Int. Am. São Paulo.

Wagley, Charles and Galvão, Eduardo
1948—The Tapirapé. H.S.A.I., v. 3, pp. 167-179.

VII. Pindaré-Gurupi

Area bounded by the Pindaré and Gurupi rivers, stretching west to the Guamá and Capim rivers, and east from the course of the Grajaú and Mearim rivers; bounded to the south by the Timbira territory. Forest zone. Terra firma.

Cabôclo population (Mestizos of Indian and white blood) engaged in agriculture and extraction (palm oil) whose settlement and stabilization dates from the second half of the nineteenth century. Gold mining in Maracassumé and Gurupi. Part of the territory has remained unexplored; however, it is a matter of record that the Urubú-Kaapor were not pacified until 1928, and that the contemporary Guajá have remained aloof until the present time.

Tribes: Tenetehara (Guajajara and Tembé). Urubú-Kaapor, Guajá, and possibly some surviving Amanaié and Turiwara. All tribes speak Tupi, although dialects differ.

Population estimated at 2,500 Indians. Guajajara and Tembé in permanent contact with the national society. Urubú-Kaapor pacified in 1928, still somewhat wild. Guajá, scattered in small bands; sporadic contacts in recent years. Intertribal relations between the Tenetehara and Urubú-Kaapor limited to occasional contacts on SPI posts. The Guajá, caught between these two groups, are plagued by persecution and hostility on both sides. The two principal groups present cultural differences, their sharing of basic common elements notwithstanding; the differences probably are attributable to their divergent historical origin and to adaptative factors. The Urubú-Kaapor are Indians of the forest, while the Tenetehara are by preference riverine. The Guajá are distinctive by reason of the difference in level of development: they are nomadic hunters and gatherers. Ethnographic documentation on the Guajá is almost nonexistent.

Cultivation of manioc, maize, pumpkin, sweet potato; use of the *tipiti* and of *farinha,* excepting only the Guajá, who are gatherers and hunters. Simple pottery, present among the Urubú-Kaapor, abandoned by the Tenetehara. Basketry inconsequential. Weaving of sleeping hammocks. Quite elaborate feather art among the Urubú-Kaapor, practically abandoned by the Tenetehara. Formerly used bark canoes and fire hollowed wooden canoes (Tenetehara). Double lean-tos, open at the sides (Urubú); neo-Brazilian houses (Tenetehara). Settlements of 15 to 60 inhabitants (Urubú); larger among the Tenetehara. Extended family. Matrilocal (Tenetehara). Maíra, principal figure in their mythology; twin sons of Maíra.

Honey and maize feast (Tenetehara). Fermented alcoholic beverages made with manioc and other fruit. Cauinagens (Urubú). Shamanism highly developed among the Tenetehara; of slight importance among the Urubú-Kaapor. Primary burial.

Lopes, Raimundo
1934—Os Tupís do Gurupí. Atas del XXV Cong. Int. Amer. La Plata, 1932, pp. 139-171.

Nimuendajú, Curt
1948—The Turiwara and Aruã. H.S.A.I., v. 3, pp. 193-198.

Nimuendajú, Curt and Métraux, Alfred
1948—The Amanayé. H.S.A.I., v. 3, pp. 199-202.

Ribeiro, Darcy
1955—Os índios Urubús. Anais do XXXI Cong. Int. Am. São Paulo. 1954, pp. 127-158.

Wagley, Charles and Galvão, Eduardo
1949—The Tenetehara Indians of Brazil. New York.

VIII.   Paraguai

Territory situated south of the Pantanal (swamps) of Mato Grosso, along the banks of the Paraguai River. Predominantly a plains area.

National pioneering frontier on a pastoral and agricultural base, characterized by large latifundi.

Tribes: Kadiueo (Mbayá-Guaikuru) and Terena-Guaná (Aruak).

Population estimated at 3,700 Indians. Contemporary survivors live on SPI reservations, the Kadiueo maintaining permanent contact and the majority of the Terena being integrated into regional society. Historically these two culturally different tribes had established a symbiotic relationship, the Terena being vassals of the Kadiueo. Today this type of relationship has been practically obliterated by the effects of extra-tribal acculturation.

Following the pattern of the Chaco, the Kadiueo are organized in nomadic bands dependent for subsistence on the products of gathering, hunting, and fishing. The introduction of the horse reinforced this style of life, simultaneously facilitating warlike activities ·for the domination and conquest of more sedentary tribes. The Kadiueo who conquered the Terena-Guaná obtained cultivated products from the latter. As early as the nineteenth century their sedentary life forced them to cultivate small plots of maize, beans, and manioc. Basketry. Weaving of cloth, polychromatic belts and bands. Pottery simple in form, but with quite elaborate decorative patterns. Bows, arrows, lances. Riverine groups have canoes.

Simple shelters, made of coarse grass mats mounted on poles. In their ancient encampments, houses placed in a horseshoe pattern. Migratory bands under the leadership of a chief whose status is hereditary.

Class stratified society: nobles (by inheritance or by granted title), warriors, servants (captives from vanquished tribes). The Guaná share some Chacoan elements, but their sedentary life with its agricultural base is distinctive. Dual division, endogamic moieties. Shamanism. Use of tobacco and fermented drinks. Primary burial.

The acculturative process was more accentuated among the Terena-Guaná, who, despite the maintenance of a rather high demographic level, on the order of about 3,000 Indians, lost their economic autonomy, modified their residence pattern, abandoned the dual division in moieties and the social class system, and adopted forms of the Christian religion. Shamanism stands out among the surviving traits.

Altenfelder Silva, Fernando
1949—Mudança cultural dos Terena. Rev. Museu Paulista. N.S., v. 3. São Paulo.

Belaieff, Juan
1946—The present-day Indians of the Gran-Chaco. H.S.A.I., v. I, pp. 371-9.

Métraux, Alfred
1946—Ethnography of the Chaco. H.S.A.I., v. I, pp. 197-370.

Oberg, Kalervo
1949—The Terena and Caduveo of Southern Mato Grosso, Brazil. Smithsonian Inst. Institute of Social Anthropology. Publ. 9.

Oliveira, Roberto Cardoso
1957—Preliminares de uma pesquisa sôbre assimilação dos Terena. In Rev. de Antropologia, n.º 2, vol. 5.

Ribeiro, Darcy
1950—Religião e mitologia Kadiéu. Conselho Nac. Prot. Índios. Pub. 106. Rio.

IX. Paraná

Area bounded by the frontiers of Paraguay and Argentina, extending from southern Mato Grosso to Rio Grande do Sul. The Paraná and its tributaries constitute the axis of this province. Zone of open plains ("*campanha*") and sparse forests.

The national population already has expanded and settled permanently in all but a few sectors in this area, and the rural nuclei are numerous. The three principal types of activity are represented here by the extractive industries of *ervamate* and wood cutting, by intensive agriculture, and by great latifundia devoted to the breeding of cattle.

Guarani-speaking tribes present common elements. Nonetheless, they can be divided into three large groups—*Nandeva:* banks of the upper Paraná and north of Iguaçu; groups are still found in the São Paulo littoral (Itariri and Bananal) and interior (Arariba). *Mbua:* serra de Maracaju, settlements in the states of Paraná, Santa Catarina, Rio Grande do Sul, and São Paulo (near Itariri). *Kaiová,* southern Mato Grosso. Differentiated on linguistic grounds and with respect to some cultural characteristics, they nonetheless may be treated as a unit.

Estimated population: between three and four thousand Indians. Messianically motivated migrations led to their dispersion in small groups and in differing situations of contact and acculturation. In permanent contact, or already integrated. The spatial contiguity of this linguistic group permitted the formation of a common cultural patrimony. Differences among local groups were accentuated during the colonial period and augmented by migratory movements (Schaden, 1954). The greater part of the population now lives on Indian reservations.

Maize is the cultivated product of greatest importance. Beans and sweet potatoes. Sweet manioc (*macaxeira*). Bitter manioc and *farinha* only in the littoral villages. Pottery practically abandoned today. Indifferent basketry. Weaving of hammocks, chiripas, belts or bands, and litters (cotton and croatá). Dugout canoes but, generally speaking, navigation is slightly developed or absent. Bows, arrows, and pellet-bows.

Large *malocas* on an oval base are still encountered; however, backwoodsman *(sertanejo)* type structures predominate. Settlements vary from 40 to 200 individuals. Extended family, bilateral descent. Chief-medicine men. Traditional emphasis on a system of collective labor. Acculturation to Christian religious ideas and practices. Mythical themes: fire, flood, and the existence of a "land without evil." Belief in a "land without evil" has motivated both migrations and messianic movements. Use of tobacco and of *chicha*. Burial in urns or within the *malocas*.

Métraux, Alfred
1948—The Guarani. H.S.A.I., v. 3, pp. 69 94.

Schaden, Egon
1954—Aspectos fundamentais da cultura Guarani. Bol. Fac. Filos. Ciências e Letras. Univ. São Paulo, n.º 188, Antrop. 4.

Watson, James B.
1952—Cayuá culture change: a study in acculturation and methodology. Am. Anthr., v. 54, n.º 2 p. 2.

X. Tietê-Uruguai

Area between the Tietê River (São Paulo), the interior of the states of Paraná and Santa Catarina, and the northern frontier of Rio Grande do Sul. Forests, predominance of Brazilian pine; plains formations to the west and south.

The region is characterized by extensive agricultural development based on the monoculture of coffee and on increasing industrialization. From the point of view of contacts with migratory currents, the distinctive experience of the area is that it has been extensively settled by European and Asiatic colonists of recent immigration and extraction.

Kaingang is the generic name that historically includes the tribes known as Guayana, Coroado, Bugre, Xokleng, Tupi, and Botocudo-Aweikoma. The Kaingang can be divided presently into the Kaingang of the State of São Paulo (Penapolis and Tupã), pacified in 1910; the southern Kaingang (states of the South); and the Xokleng (Santa Catarina).

Population estimated at between 3,000 and 4,000 Indians. The indigenous nuclei which suffered considerable losses during the first centuries of colonization are presently hemmed in by rural and urban centers of the national society, rather than by pioneering frontiers. The majority participates actively in the regional economy and lives on Indian posts under the direct jurisdiction of the SPI. The process has not operated uniformly in all groups; several levels of accommodation and integration are observable. There has been considerable modification and loss of traditional elements.

Cultivation of slash-burn plots; traditionally maize appears to have been the most important crop. With the exception of the Aweikoma, gatherers and hunters. Pine nut harvesting. Cane or bamboo-sprout basketry. Elongated or cone-shaped black pottery, now abandoned. Houses varying from the simple shelter of the single lean-to, to the double lean-to without walls, to the Guarani long-house (maloca) type: today houses built to the rural model have supplanted these types of shelter.

Bands divided in exogamic moieties, patrilinear affiliation sub-divided into two more groups (Tôldo das Lontras—Baldus). Division into moieties, and of the moieties into three classes (Tietê, Ijuí—Nimuendajú, I:462). Five groups suggestive of ancient patrilineal sibs (Aweikoma, Henry, 1941:59, 88, 175 ff.). Shamanism inconsequentially developed. Use of tobacco and fermented drinks. Burial mounds, conically shaped, with chambers for burial in the fetal position. Cremation among the Aweikoma. Feast of the dead, strongest expression of the spiritual culture of the Kaingang (Baldus).

Baldus, Herbert
1937—O culto dos mortos entre os Kaingang de Palmas. Ensaio de Etnologia brasileira. Brasil, v. 101, pp. 112-130.

Henry, Jules
1941—Jungle people. A Kaingang tribe of the highlands of Brazil. Virginia.

Métraux, Alfred
1946—The Caingang. H.S.A.I., v. 1, pp. 445-475.

XI. Northeast

Groups scattered through the states of Paraiba, Pernambuco, Alagoas, Bahia, and along a strip between the São Francisco River and the shore in Minas Gerais. Scrub-growth and forests.

Long established agricultural and pastoral frontier. The several surviving tribes are settled at SPI posts; in some instances, as for example at Águas Belas, where there are 1,264 Fulniô Indians, and Aticum where there are 1,026 Aticum Indians, the posts are heavily populated.

Tribes: Potiguara (Tupi), Baía da Traição, Paraiba; Pancararu (Pankararu), Petrolândia, Pernambuco; Fulniô (Karnijo), Águas Belas, Pernambuco; Atikum, Carnaubeira, Pernambuco; Xokó, Kariri (Kariri), Pôrto Real do Colégio, Alagoas; Pataxó (Pataxó), a Mestizo group,

Itabuna, Bahia; Tuxá, (?) Ilha da Viuva, Bahia; Maxakali (Maxakali), Minas Gerais. Kariri, Ribeira do Pombal, Bahia.

Population estimated at 5,500 Indians. The major part is integrated into the regional environment; there are reports of considerable miscegenation and of the loss of traditional cultural elements, including language. The Fulniô are the most conservative.

Given the effects of acculturation into the national society and the diversity of languages and origins of these groups, we have certain reservations about their inclusion in a single culture area.

Tentatively we shall take the Fulniô as representative, resting our case upon Pinto's affirmation (1956:67) that these Indians "are within a circle of cultural elements which if not identical are at least related, of which probably the Pancararu, Shucuru, Tusha, Shoco, etc., are part." Cultivation of maize, beans, sweet potatoes, manioc. Pottery, specialization of the Indians of Colégio Real. Baskets (Palmeira dos Índios). Pouches, coarse grass mats, hats, sandals of ouricuri straw *(palha de ouricuri)*. Basketry, checkered or twilled. Reed cots for sleeping. Two types of habitation: "settlement"—brick and tile; "ouricuri"—huts of straw, raised for the ceremonial season of September to November. Dual organization no longer in effect. Patrilineal sibs. Marriage in "classes" preferred. Ouricuri festival, prohibited to strangers and to children of marriages of the Fulniô with other "races," apparently linked to the ancestral cult. A temporary village *(rancharia)* is specially constructed for this purpose, next to a sacred *juazeiro* tree. Shamanism (cure by blowing smoke and magic touch). Use of smoke and of an intoxicating drink, made from the sap of the *"jurema"* tree. Use of dance masks.

Lowie, Robert
1946—The Cariri. The Pancararu, The Tarairio. H.S.A.I., v. 1, pp. 557-566.

Métraux, Alfred and Nimuendajú, Curt
1946—The Mashacali, Patashó and Malali linguistic families. H.S.A.I. v. 1, pp. 541-545.

Métraux, Alfred
1946—The Fulniô. H.S.A.I., v. 1, p. 571.

Pinto, Estevão
1935-38—Os indígenas do Nordeste. Bras., v. 44 e 112. São Paulo.
1956—Etnologia brasileira (Fulniô, os últimos Tapuia). Bras., v. 285.

BIBLIOGRAPHY

BENNETT, Wendell C.
1953   New World culture history. South America. Anthropology Today, p. 211-225. Chicago.

BENNETT, Wendell C. and BIRD, J.
1949   Andean culture history. American Museum of Natural History. Handbook series n.º 15. N.Y.

COOPER, J.
1942   Areal and temporal aspects of aboriginal South American culture. In Primitive Man, v. XV, n.º 1-2.

FRIKEL, Protásio
1959   Os Tiriyó (Notas preliminares). Bol. Museu Goeldi, N. S., Antropologia, 9, Belém.

GALVÃO, Eduardo
1953   Cultura e sistema de parentesco das tribos do alto Rio Xingú. Bol. Museu Nac. N. S. Antropologia 14. Rio.

GREENBERG, J.
1957   Essays in Linguistics, New York, pp. 66-85.

KROEBER
1923   Anthropology. New York.
1948   Anthropology. New York. 2nd ed. rev.

MATOSO CAMARA Jr. J.
1959   Classificação das Línguas Indígenas do Brasil. MS. Communicação à IV Reunião Bras. Ant., Curitiba.

MEGGERS, Betty J. and Clifford EVANS
1955   Preliminary results of archaeological investigations in British Guiana. Timehri n.º 34. British Guiana.

MURDOCK, G. P.
1951a   South American culture areas. Southwestern Journ. of Anthropology, v. VII, n.º 4.
1951b   Outline of South American Cultures. Behavior Science Outlines, vol. II, New Haven.

NIMUENDAJÚ, Curt
1948   Handbook of South American Indians, v. 3. B. A. E., Bul. 143, Washington.

RIBEIRO, Darcy
1957   Culturas e línguas indígenas do Brasil. Educação e Ciências Sociais, v. 2, n.º 6. Rio.

ROQUETTE PINTO, E.
1938   Rondônia. Série Brasiliana, vol. 39. São Paulo.

ROWE, L.
1953   Negative and positive criteria in setting up culture areas. An Appraisal of Anthropology Today. Ed. Sol Tax and others. Chicago.

STEWARD, Julian
1948   Handbook of South American Indians. B. A. E. Bul. 143, vol. 3. Washington.
1949   H. S. A. I., v. 5.
1955   Theory of cultural change. University of Illinois Press. Urbana.
STEWARD, J. and FARON, L. C.
1959   Native Peoples of South America. New York.
STOUT, D. B.
1938   Culture types and culture areas in South America. Acad. Sc. Arts and Letters. Pap., v. 23, pp. 73-86. Michigan.
STRONG, W. D.
1933   The Plains area in the light of archaology. AA, v. 3, n.º 2.
WISSLER, Clark
1938   The American Indian.

NOTE:

This study was in press when the author received the article by Betty Meggers and Clifford Evans—"Identification of culture types and culture areas based on ceramics from archaeological deposits," in Arquivos do Museu Nacional, vol. XLVI, 9-33, 4 est., Rio—analyzing the correlation of levels of ceramic development "with the Tropical Forest, Circumcaribbean and Andean culture areas and with the respective levels of culture development in Steward's classification." *(op. cit. :30)*

SYNOPSIS OF THE CRITICAL
BIBLIOGRAPHY OF BRAZILIAN ETHNOLOGY
1953-1960

by Herbert Baldus
Museu Paulista

Paper read on June 26, 1961, at the V Reunião
Brasileira de Antropologia in Belo Horizonte.
Translated by Janice H. Hopper from the Portuguese
text: "Sinopse da Bibliografia Crítica da Etnologia
Brasileira 1953-1960," Universidade do Rio Grande
do Norte, Separata dos Arq. Inst. Antrop. Natal,
v. 1, n. 2, p. 5-22, dez. 1964.

SYNOPSIS OF THE CRITICAL BIBLIOGRAPHY OF BRAZILIAN ETHNOLOGY, 1953-1960

by Herbert Baldus

In 1954, when I published an 859-page volume entitled *Bibliografia Crítica da Etnologia Brasileira (Critical Bibliography of Brazilian Ethnology)*, I declared in the introduction that I had begun a task that would never be completed—a task without end. In point of fact, new publications on the Indians of Brazil made their appearance with little delay. My paper today is based on 385 of these subsequent studies, but it is worth noting that I examined many dozens more which I have not taken into consideration because they include only passing references to the topic.[1]

I take special pleasure in informing you, as concrete evidence of the development of anthropology in our midst, that of the 385 works in discussion no fewer than 185 appeared in Portuguese. Of this number, there are, properly speaking, 120 publications in the subfield of ethnology, 36 in prehistory and archaeology, 19 in linguistics, and 10 in physical anthropology. The second largest number of publications is in German: there are 76, of which 68 are in ethnology, 5 in prehistory and archaeology, 2 in linguistics, and 1 in physical anthropology. The third largest number of publications is in English, 63 in all: 52 in ethnology, 8 in prehistory and archaeology, 2 in linguistics, and 1 in physical anthropology. In Spanish there are 30 publications: 21 in ethnology, 4 in prehistory and archaeology, 3 in linguistics, and 2 in physical anthropology. Of the 22 French-language publications, 14 are in ethnology, 5 in prehistory and archaeology, and 3 in linguistics. In addition, there are 3 ethnological publications in Italian, 3 in Russian, 2 in Dutch, and 1 in Danish.

---

[1] The bibliographic notes will be published within a few years in the second volume of the *Bibliografia Crítica da Etnologia Brasileira (Critical Bibliography of Brazilian Ethnology)*.

Before these hundreds of recent publications are classified with respect to the various aspects of culture discussed and the geographic areas covered, some works on the history of Brazilian ethnology will be mentioned.

At the 1954 meeting of the Congress of Americanists in São Paulo, Egon Schaden read a paper entitled "Problemas fundamentais e estado atual das pesquisas sôbre índios do Brasil" ("Research on the Indians of Brazil: Fundamental Problems and Current Status"), in which his principal concern, other than mythology and questions of cultural change, was the elaboration of theory.

Two years later Florestan Fernandes published his "Tendências teóricas da moderna investigação etnológica no Brasil" ("Theoretical Tendencies of Modern Ethnological Investigation in Brazil"), differentiating three principal "foci of interest in theoretical elaboration." In the order of their importance, these are: reflections on the study of culture change; attention to the investigation of shamanism, magic, religion, and mythology; and reviving interest in problems of social organization. This paper is basic for the study of the history of modern Brazilian ethnology.

Native Peoples of South America, a recent book by Steward and Faron, is a typical North American *textbook* and also, according to its authors, "an interpretative work, written according to a general theoretical point of view" (p. vi). On the subject of Brazilian Indians, and particularly of typology, this theoretical orientation offers the ethnologist no novelties worth mentioning; however, it not infrequently leads the authors to superficial and inexact generalizations.

Fernando de Azevedo's "A antropologia e a sociologia no Brasil" ("Anthropology and Sociology in Brazil"), which covers the major figures from Pero Vaz de Caminha to the moderns, and Estevão Pinto's study of sixteenth century writers may be mentioned as contributions to the study of the history of Brazilian ethnology. The bio-bibliographic essays of Castro Faria on Rodrigues Ferreira and Roquette-Pinto; of Schaden on Karl von den Steinen and Koch-Grünberg; of Darcy Ribeiro on Rondon; and of Baldus on Koch-Grünberg and Rondon are also worth noting.

☐   Moving on to describe recent works on aspects of culture, I wish to start with ergology [study of work—Ed.] and technology. Two works on clothing come to mind: Hans Becher's doctoral thesis on belts and waist strings and Franz Caspar's article on the making and function of the penis sheath *(estôjo peniano).* Ornaments are analyzed by Darcy Ribeiro and Berta G. Ribeiro in their magnificent monograph, *Arte plumária dos índios Kaapor (Feather Art of the Kaapor Indians)*, and by Brigitte Menzel in her thesis on lip, nose, and ear adornments. There is considerable information on body painting, but no systematic study has appeared. Jens Yde indicates that the Waiwai paints his entire body red as a means of protection, "as the evil bush spirits are not able to distinguish red objects," and adds that dogs—especially hunting dogs—are painted completely red for the same reason.

Virginia Watson and Immina Schömig deal with construction. Watson stresses the acculturation manifest in the modification of the structure of Kaiuá houses in southern Mato Grosso. Schömig compares certain special South American Indian structures: those designated exclusively for men and those that serve to isolate the woman during her first menstruation and during childbirth.

Publications on technology proper have been rare in these last seven or eight years. Becher refers to technology in his thesis cited above, and Berta G. Ribeiro analyzes the techniques of fastening and gluing in her interpretative essay "Bases para uma classificação dos adornos plumários dos índios do Brasil" ("Bases for a Classification of the Feather Ornaments of the Indians of Brazil"). But almost nothing of note on basketry and weaving has appeared, and the publications on ceramics are, in general, archaeological. There is, however, one aspect of technology in which great interest has been manifested recently: the study of the preparation of venoms for arrowtips. Field researchers like Frikel, Biocca, and Vellard have written on this topic; a great many of the 2,956 titles in the "curare" bibliography of the Brazilian Institute of Bibliography and Documentation refer to important ethnographic studies of arrowtip venoms of our Indians.

Among the studies of weapons, those of Frederico Lane and Horst Hartmann on bows and arrows, and of Bodo Spranz on spear-throwers are worth noting.

☐ In the area of tribal economy, one of the least developed in the field of Brazilian ethnology, Darcy Ribeiro pioneered with his systematic study of the distribution of collections, hunting, fishing, and cultivation among the Urubu-Kaapor during the four periods of the year characterized by rains, floods, summer, and drought respectively. Observations on the economic activities of the Kamayurá are, in my opinion, the most valuable section of Kalervo Oberg's paper "Indian Tribes of Northern Mato Grosso." In the context of aspects of culture change in the acquisition of subsistence, Otto Zerries studied the measure to which the Waiká can come to be classified as prehorticultural hunters and gatherers or as horticulturists.

Fishing is discussed by Harald Schultz and Johannes Wilbert; the former deals with pirarucu fishing among the Karajá, and the latter with the use of the instrument called *socó* in Maranhão.

Indigenous South American horticulture is classified by Gudmund Hatt in two types: "Semi-Agriculture," in which the men do the clearing and burning and leave all other work to the women; and "Full-Agriculture," in which the men perform almost all tasks, although they occasionally may be aided by the women. Jens Yde discusses these categories and elaborates a list of South American tribes, including those of Brazil, in which the man takes an active part in cultivation. In his article on "Slash-and-Burn Agriculture," Robert L. Carneiro opposes the generalized assumption that moves by settlements of horticultural tribes are necessarily a consequence of the exhaustion of the soil by slash-burn cultivation. To show that this type of cultivation can be compatible with permanent residence, he cites the Kuikúro who subsist largely on manioc cultivation linked to clearing and burning and yet have maintained their settlement in the same location for ninety years, and the Waurá who practice horticulture in the Upper Xingu region and have maintained a relatively fixed settlement. In order to facilitate proper evaluation of possible factors in moves, the author translates them into a mathematical formulation. On the basis of the formulation he makes the following suggestion: "If the ethnographic or archeological record reveals periodic relocations of villages of 500 persons or less, causes *other than soil depletion* should be assumed to have been responsible unless there is clear and conclusive evidence to the contrary." The same author, in collaboration with Gertrude E. Dole, also gives data on "A Mechanism for Mobilizing Labor Among the Kuikuro." Cultivation among the Munduruku was studied by Father Protásio Frikel.

The products of indigenous horticulture are discussed in the work of Brieger and collaborators on the varieties of maize in Brazil; the article of Hans Becher, "A importância da banana entre os índios Surára e Pakidái" ("The Importance of the Banana among the Surára and Pakidái Indians"); that of Dole on the geographic distribution of the various techniques of preparing manioc flour; and the doctoral thesis of Günther Hartmann on alcoholic drinks among the South American Indians, with special reference to the raw materials for their preparation.

An outstanding contribution to the study of problems of commerce in a Brazilian tribe is made by Dole's article "Ownership and Exchange among the Kuikuro Indians of Mato Grosso."

☐   Among the publications of this period which deal with the religion of our Indians, the first to come to mind is Egon Schaden's *Aspectos fundamentais da cultura guaraní (Fundamental Aspects of Guaraní Culture)*, in which he presents an excellent analysis of the eminently religious character of that culture. In the same field, Darcy Ribeiro's paper for the II Reunião Brasileira de Antropologia, which describes the experiences of a Kaapor Indian who went in search of God, merits attention. *Mundurucú Religion* is another important publication; author Robert F. Murphy concluded that, until a few years ago, the essential element in the religous beliefs of the Munduruku was the relation between the world of men and the world of animals of the hunt. According to Murphy, the disappearance of this facet of beliefs is one of the most momentous culture changes. There was a symbiotic relationship between Munduruku society and the animal kingdom: the Indians were dependent upon the animals for their subsistence and, in return, the animals depended upon the Indians for their well-being and proliferation, which was promoted by the celebration of rituals. There is every indication that the Munduruku were hunters rather than horticulturists. In this respect they differ from the typical Tupi tribes in whose linguistic stock they are customarily incorporated. However, supernatural relations with animals also manifest themselves in the custom that the hunter does not eat the animal which he himself has killed. This is a custom common to several tribes of eastern and southern Brazil, as I have shown in a paper read at the XXX Congress of Americanists. Otto Zerries coordinates considerable South American ethnological data on the lord of the animals, the auxiliary spirits of the hunter, the lords of animal species, the ritual of the hunt, and the souls of animals in his book on spirits of the hunt and of the forest.

Concepts of the human soul are discussed by Zerries in his article on the Waiká and by Father Anton Lukesch in his study of the Kayapó of the Rio Fresco. Josef Haekel studies the sacred post as a cult object among several Brazilian tribes. Under the title "The Birth of a Religion," Audrey J. Butt analyzes a semi-Christian religious movement which first arose among the Makuxí and diffused among the Karib tribes of the British Guiana [now Guyana] frontier region with Brazil and with Venezuela. Conceptions of a supreme entity or hero-civilizer were examined by Haekel and by Fathers Kruse, Lukesch, and Saake.

Moreover, myths of the following tribes have been published: Kayapó by Horace Banner, Surára by Hans Becher, Guaraní by León Cadogan and Egon Schaden, Tukáno by Marcos Fulop, Fulniô by Estevão Pinto, Urubu-Kaapor by Francis Huxley and Darcy Ribeiro, Baníwa by Wilhelm Saake, Waiká by Otto Zerries. Heinz Kühne completed a comparative study, with numerous references to the tribes of Brazil, on the role of the jaguar in the mythology of twins in the Americas. The Franciscan Mariano Izquierdo Gallo wrote the voluminous *Mitologia america (American Mythology)* which includes a section titled "Myths of Brazil." The absence of scientific criteria in this work is, at times, shocking. The series *Antologia Ilustrada do Folclore Brasileiro (Illustrated Anthology of Brazilian Folklore),* of which the first volume is "Stories and Legends of the Indians," is destined for the general public; the selection criterion was the provision of a sampling of the most different indigenous cultures distributed in the most diverse regions of the north, south, east, west, and center of Brazil. The contribution of the editor was limited to an indication of sources; the 72 texts, collected and published by various authors, were adapted by the Paulista novelist Afonso Schmidt, literary editor of the series.

Among studies of the shaman, we call attention to a recently published Spanish translation of the basic work by Mircea Eliade on shamanism and archaic techniques of ecstasy. Zerries studied the several types of amiable or hostile demons and spirits with which the South American Indian shaman must enter into relations. Father Saake reproduces the report in which a Baníwa Indian tells how he became a shaman.

☐   Passing from research on relations with the supernatural to research on relations with relatives and members of the tribe itself, we enter the field which has been most neglected in the past, and which is being cultivated today with ever increasing ardor. Even the Russians have been interested in this aspect of our Indian cultures, as the articles by L. A. Fainberg, which appeared in 1954 and 1958 in Soviet publications, although general in nature, bear witness. A work which, despite its reduced size, is one of the best of the last decade is "Cultura e sistema de parentesco das tribos do alto rio Xingu," ("Culture and the Kinship System of the Tribes of the Upper Xingu"). Author Eduardo Galvão concludes that ". . . we believe it possible to prove that, as with other significant aspects of the Xingu culture in the culture area of *'uluri,'* as we call it, kinship systems also reflect the distribution of a uniform type which is characterized by the presence of bilaterality, extension of terms; bilocal and patrilocal residence; avoidance among father-in-law: son-in-law, mother-in-law: daughter-in-law, and brothers-in-law; relations of approximation among cross cousins; simple and sororal polygyny; and the levirate; and the absence of moieties, sibs, or other social subgroups, localized or not. The socio-econòmic unit is the extended family."

The sociological value of the study by Oberg, cited above, in which he presents the kinship nomenclature of 14 tribes, is quite a different matter. One is brought up short by the reflection that the author has had only very brief contacts with the greater number of the tribes he mentions. Oberg himself calls attention to the mutual difficulties of communication between the field researcher and the Indians. He writes, for example: "The language difficulty which we encountered throughout our stay prevented us from gathering much information. We were, however, able to get the kinship terminology . . ." (p. 11). Every researcher with some field experience knows that one of the most arduous tasks in the study of Brazilian Indians is that of getting their kinship terminology.

David Maybury-Lewis ultimately achieved extraordinary mastery of this subject matter. In a study entitled "Kinship and Social Organization in Central Brazil," Maybury-Lewis comments on studies by Nimuendajú and Lévi-Strauss in the light of the results of his own field research among the Xerénte. He presents the kinship terms which he had gathered during the long months of his residence among these Jê. Analyzing data relevant to the matrimonial system as described in Nimuendajú's monograph on the Apinayé, Maybury-Lewis shows in his "Parallel Descent and the Apinayé Anomaly" that for demographic reasons this system could not have functioned at the time of Nimuendajú's field research and is incompatible with the structure of kinship nomenclature. Referring to Nimuendajú's publications on the Jê, Maybury-Lewis laments that "such a gifted observer should have lacked·the acquaintance with social anthropological theory which would have enabled him to make satisfactory analyses of the complex systems he studied. As a result he did not understand the structure of these systems; thus we can never be wholly certain that he is correct in his reports of marriage prohibitions, of kinship terminology, and especially of the crucial cousin-terms" (p. 203).

In "Les organisations dualistes existent-elles?," Claude Lévi-Strauss analyzes the social organization of the Borôro and the Eastern Timbira in particular. He concludes that "Je me suis efforcé de montrer, dans cet article, que l'étude des organisations dites dualistes révélait tant d'anomalies et de contradictions, par rapport à la théorie en vigueur, que l'on aurait intérêt à renoncer à cette dernière et à traiter les formes apparentes de dualisme comme des distortions superficielles de structures dont la nature réelle est autre, et beau-coup plus compliquée" (p. 127). The work has produced an interest-ing controversy between the author and Maybury-Lewis.

In an article entitled "Umwelt, Bevölkerungsdichte und Gesell-schaftsform im Amazonasgebiet," Hans Dietschy proves that tribal moieties attributed to the Karajá by certain North American authors are nonexistent (p. 13) and calls attention to the organization of men into three patrilinear and "at least in theory, endogamous groups."

Tribal moieties in other tribes were also studied: moieties of the Terêna by Roberto Cardoso de Oliveira, the Mundurukú by Robert F. Murphy, and the Kaingáng by the author of the present paper.

The following studies of political organization are worth men-tioning: an article by Dole on the Kuikúro; a chapter on "A chefia da comunidade," ("The Chieftaincy of the Community"), in Schaden's "tese de livre-docência" cited earlier; and Dietschy's study of the chieftaincy among the Karajá. In an essay entitled "Os Tupi e a reação tribal à Conquista," ("The Tupi and the Tribal Reaction to Conquest"), Florestan Fernandes analyzes the functioning of the tribal system of actions and social relations with reference to the organization of the local group and to kinship. In "Intergroup Hos-tility and Social Cohesion," Murphy studies the social function of war in Mundurukú society and concludes that "the institution operated to preserve the integration and solidarity. . . ."

Some studies of phenomena linked to the life cycle of the individual merit attention. There is the posthumous book of Father Wilhelm Schmidt on behavior before and on the occasion of child-birth; the article by María Angélica Carluci, "La couvade en Sudamér-ica," ("The Couvade in South America"), which complements that basic study; the work of Niels Fock, who discusses the theories of Schmidt and others in the light of material he collected among the Waiwai; Dietschy's study of customs related to childbirth among the Karajá; and the report of Métraux and Dreyfus-Roche on their ob-servations among the Kayapó. Becher published data collected among the Surára and Pakidái on the defloration of the girl child before the end of the first year of life. Anderson and Caspar describe the rites of puberty for the girls among the Tukuna and Tuparí, respectively. The latter author, moreover, in another article published in the *Revista do Museu Paulista*, treats the sexual life of the Tuparí in detail. In a paper titled "Extramarital Sex Freedom among the Kuikuru Indians of Mato Grosso," Robert Carneiro shows that almost all the adults of this tribe, young or old, male or female, have one or more extramatrimonial sex partners. Hans Dietschy reports on the problem of incest to discuss the possibility of linking its prohibition with the fundamental myths of the dances and masks in pairs among the Karajá.

☐   In his contribution to the *Encyclopedia of Morals*, Murphy shows how Mundurukú ethics prescribe two mutually contradictory standards of behavior which simultaneously produce harmony within the group and hostility toward everything that is outside the group. The two standards do not conflict; rather, they reinforce each other. In the terminology of Ruth Benedict, the Mundurukú may be called "Dionysian" for their warlike comportment and "Apollonian" for their cooperative and nonaggressive intratribal spirit which, to a certain point, makes them comparable to the Zuni. According to Murphy, the apparent disparity between these two conceptions of desirable behavior indicates the weakness of the configurative interpretations of Benedict and others.

At the III Reunião Brasileira de Antropologia, I discussed another pattern of tribal behavior in my description of the externalization of fear among the Tapirapé. Data on the tribal psyche of the Kaapor is found in the work of Darcy Ribeiro and of Huxley. Dietschy, who views culture as a psycho-hygienic system, demonstrated the connection among the Karajá between the externalization of certain psychic crises and the activities of daily life as, for example, the dance and swimming. Aspects of the behavior of an asocial individual among the Tuparí are analyzed by Caspar in his case study of abnormal personality development. A further contribution to psychology is made by Charles Wagley who describes his relations and experiences with his principal informant among the Tapirapé.

The results of several psycho-diagnostic tests have been interpreted. Thus, Cinira Miranda de Menezes and Cícero Christiano de Sousa studied the material I obtained from the application of the methods of Rorschach and Mira y Lopes among the Kaingáng Indians of Ivaí. Maria Júlia Pourchet administered the tree test and Goodenough's test (drawing a human figure) to the children of the Kaingáng of Palmas. Hans and Nelly Dietschy told us of their experiences in the application of Lüscher's test (selection of eight colors) among the Karajá.

☐   Gene Weltfish's book, *The Origins of Art,* includes two chapters on the plastic arts of our Indians. In the article "Desenho e arte ornamental dos índios brasileiros" ("Design and Ornamental Art of the Brazilian Indians"), Schaden expresses some general ideas regarding these artistic products and stresses the impossibility of understanding them "without a reasonable knowledge of the dominant character of the cultural configuration." In his doctoral thesis on "art as a culture element," A. A. Gerbrands criticizes Max Schmidt's well-known hypothesis that woven patterns of fan-shaped palm leaves gave rise to pyrography and carved geometric painted ornaments. The *Revista do Arquivo Municipal de S. Paulo (Journal of the Municipal Archives of São Paulo),* formerly a good journal, published a worthless 200 page article under the ambitious title "Arte primitiva brasileira" ("Primitive Brazilian Art"). The author, Odorico Pires Pinto, exposed his lack not only of originality but also of the scientific spirit; nonetheless, he was awarded the "João Ribeiro Award" (1951) of the Brazilian Academy of Letters.

The transformation of the Karajá doll from its ancient to its current form attracted the attention of Luís de Castro Faria and Maria Heloisa Fénelon Costa. Body painting among the Kadiuéu, studied earlier by Boggiani, Lévi-Strauss, and Darcy Ribeiro, was the subject of a Russian publication by E. V. Zibert, who used material collected by Fielstrup, a companion of Manizer during the latter's voyages in 1914 and 1915.

The monograph on feather art by Darcy Ribeiro and Berta G. Ribeiro, cited above, refutes all commentators who have used invalid comparisons with the arts of ancient Peru as the basis of their denial that the Brazilian Indian has had any creative force in the plastic arts. Of its kind, the monograph represents a contribution that will be difficult to surpass.

The music of our Indians becomes increasingly better known, thanks to the ethnographers' use of tape recorders. A "longplay" put out by the Musée de l'Homme in Paris under the direction of Simone Dreyfus-Roche, who also wrote the respective commentaries, has made the music of several tribes accessible to the general public. José Geraldo de Souza's article "Contribuição rítmico-modal do canto gregoriano para a música popular brasileira," ("Rhythmic-modal Contribution of the Gregorian Chant to Brazilian Popular Music"), also affords some interesting comments on the music of Brazilian Indians.

There is little worthwhile material on the dance. In my study of "As danças dos Tapirapé," ("Tapirapé Dances"), I refer to functions, form, steps, and musical beat, and add comparative data concerning other Tupi tribes and neighbors. Among the latter are the Karajá: Dietschy has an article on their masked dances. Father Alcionilio Brüzzi Alves da Silva has written on the funeral dances of the Tukáno and Tariâna. It is lamentable that so worthy an entity as the Instituto Indigenista Interamericano (Interamerican Indigenist Institute) has published—and what is more, in a luxury edition—the production of a Mrs. Felícitas Barreto entitled *Danzas indígenas del Brasil (Indigenous Dances of Brazil)*, a book so elementary in conception that one hesitates to mention dishonesty in connection with it. Without a doubt, however, the bibliography, prepared at random, was meant to mislead the reader who is unacquainted with this field by giving him the impression that this is a scientific study. The sources of the data that are used in such confused fashion in the text are not indicated. The names of the photographers of the beautiful illustrative materials are also shrouded in silence.

In a study of the "dance as a social function among the Timbira," Käthe Hye-Kerkdal proves the importance of collective dances in various opportunities of the social life among these Jê. She bases her analysis principally on the results of Nimuendajú's research. In another paper the same author analyzes the relationship between the log races and the social organization of these Indians.

☐ Until a few years ago, interest in the demography of our Indians took a back seat to all the facets of Indian culture mentioned above. This disadvantaged position of demography persisted in spite of earlier contributions made to demographic literature by the renowned Karl von den Steinen after his first expedition on the Xingu River in 1884; by Karl E. Ranke, in 1896; and by Pedro E. de Lima, who visited the upper basin of the Xingu in 1947 and 1952. Consequently, Darcy Ribeiro's presentation at the II Reunião Brasileira de Antropologia of his comparison of demographic data for thirteen tribes which are characterized by different degrees of contact with representatives of our civilization, and by different forms of ecological adaptation, is a landmark in the history of our Indian studies. Ribeiro's paper "Culturas e línguas indígenas do Brasil" ("Indigenous Cultures and Languages of Brazil"), distributed at the III Reunião, contains two tables systematically comparing 230 cases classified by degree of integration into neo-Brazilian society at the beginning and end of the period under consideration, i.e., in 1900 and in 1957.

The various consequences of the contacts of the indigenous population with the three forms of our economic expansion—agricultural, pastoral, and extractive—are studied. Grouping these same cases by linguistic family, Ribeiro establishes the fact that ". . . Tupi groups are more susceptible to the dissociative factors generated in the process of integration, for they have lost 50 percent of their representatives, a far higher proportion than the others" (p. 31). Analysis of the demographic data leads to the conclusion that "There are between 68,100 and 99,700 Indians in contemporary Brazil; even if we accept the most optimistic hypothesis, indigenous Brazilians constitute less than 0.2 percent of the national population" (p. 47). In the "List of Brazilian Indigenous Groups," which is the third section of the publication cited, tribal names are followed by synonyms, current population figures, linguistic classification, geographic location, and category appropriate to describe current stage of integration. With the publication of Darcy Ribeiro's paper, a manual for those interested in knowing the Brazilian Indian problem, mere conjecture about essential topics of Brazilian ethnology has been replaced by exact, well coordinated data.

Roberto Cardoso de Oliveira also presented a demographic study at the III Reunião Brasileira de Antropologia—reporting on the Terêna settlement of Cachoeirinha. Etta Becker-Donner, observing the ill consequences suffered by the Indians as a result of contacts with the white men in the Territory of Rondônia, collected demographic materials.

Rosa Scolnik also dealt with the health of the tribes of the Guaporé basin. Pia Maybury-Lewis studied the same subject among the Xerénte and concluded that this highly acculturated tribe suffered neither nutritional deficiencies nor ill health, but that its problems were social and psychiatric. In this field, attention is called to the research of the following medical doctors: Ataliba Macieira Bellizzi, Noel Nutels, João Leão da Mota, and Amaury Sadock de F. Filho.

There has been a relatively high number of recent publications on the relations between the Indian and the white man, the treatment of the former by the latter, and the consequences of different types of contacts in different epochs. Anchieta's *Poesias,* published in 1954, evidences the attitude of the sixteenth-century Jesuit toward indigenous culture. Florestan Fernandes' substantial contribution to the *História Geral da Civilização Brasileira (General History of Brazilian Civilization),* deals with the incapacity of the Tupinambá "tribal organizational system" to adjust to the new situation created by contact with the white invaders. In his doctoral thesis *The Indian Policy of Portugal in the Amazon Region, 1614-1693,* Mathias C. Kiemen uses documents from the Portuguese, Spanish, and Vatican archives to demonstrate that the Portuguese Crown always sought to protect the Indians, even though it permitted their enslavement in the exceptional circumstances of any "just war." Under the title *Desbravadores (Pioneers),* Father Vitor Hugo wrote a two-volume history of the penetration of the Madeira River basin by Catholic missionaries. Albert Schmid treats of the relations between the Indians and the German colonists in Rio Grande do Sul and Santa Catarina. Father Johann Dornstauder describes the first friendly meeting he had in 1957 with the so-called "Canoeiros" of the Rio Juruena region. In a report dated December 1958, Carlos de Araújo Moreira Neto describes the tragic situation in which he found the Kayapó. Roberto Cardoso de Oliveira shows how anti-assimilationism may be fostered by the presence of the Serviço de Proteção aos Índios among tribes already integrated into the neo-Brazilian economic life of their respective regions. Egon Schaden stresses the necessity of creating among our Indians "an economic mentality" that is indispensable for life in the civilized world, and of gradually modifying behavior patterns and the cultural ideal itself until both are compatible with this mentality. In a contribution to the Seminar in Applied Anthropology at the IV Reunião Brasileira de Antropologia, I tried to indicate ways in which we might collaborate in establishing our Indian cultures as Brazilian subcultures. Thereafter I had the satisfaction of seeing that my ideas coincided with the conception of social integration elaborated by Darcy Ribeiro and others at the IV Congresso Indigenista Interamericano and published in *América Indígena,* Number 1 of 1960.

Culture change in certain tribes has been one of the favorite topics of numerous excellent authors in recent years. At the III Reunião Brasileira de Antropologia, Thales de Azevedo presented an analysis of "Aculturação dirigida" ("Planned Acculturation"), led by the catechists of colonial Brazil. Religious acculturation among the Guaraní was studied by Egon Schaden. William D. Hohenthal concluded that the survival of the Fulniô of Águas Belas as a cultural group is a result of their ethnocentric attachment to the values of their own culture and their consequent contempt for neo-Brazilian culture. Another northeastern tribe, the Canela, was studied by another North American ethnologist, William H. Crocker; since the now less rigidly upheld socio-cultural patterns seem to Crocker to be fundamentally the same as those of Nimuendajú's time, he speaks of cultural stability. "Aculturação indígena no Rio Negro" ("Indian Acculturation on the Rio Negro"), by Eduardo Galvão, and O processo da assimilação dos Terêna (The Process of Assimilation among the Terêna), by Roberto Cardoso de Oliveira, are basic studies. In "Tapirapé Social and Culture Change," Charles Wagley shows how, under the impact of an attack by neighbors, the Tapirapé "society" temporarily ceased to exist while the "culture" continued. Wagley sees this as "a striking example of the difference between a society and its culture." Acculturative phenomena were also studied by Franz Caspar among the Tuparí, by Father Saake among the Borôro, by Harald Schultz and Vilma Chiara among the Tukurina, by Robert Murphy among the Mundurukú, and by Alfonso Trujillo Ferrari among the Kariri.

Problems of culture history, so-called, have been of concern not only to Claude Lévi-Strauss, who based his analysis of the notion of archaism in ethnology upon Brazilian materials, but also to such students of specific culture elements as Zerries, whose work on the bull-roarer and the spirits of the hunt is indicative of this interest. Boglár's article on burial forms and Becher's thesis on belts and waist strings also are based on Brazilian materials.

Several authors have contributed to the classification of Brazilian tribes: Hans Becher, with regard to the inhabitants of the region bounded by the Rio Branco, the Rio Uraricuera, the Parima Mountain, and the Rio Negro; Father Protásio Frikel with reference to the Indians of northern Pará and the frontier regions; Darcy Ribeiro by establishing four categories of contact with our civilization; Crestmír Loukotka, in grouping by linguistic family the northeastern tribes that are not considered Tupi; J. Mattoso Câmara, Jr., in discussing various types of classification of Brazilian Indian languages; Joseph H. Greenberg, with his study, The General Classification of Central and South American Languages; and José Imbelloni, in defending his proposed taxonomy in the light of new contributions toward the racial classification of South American Indians. In "Culture Areas in South America: An Archeological Point of View," Betty J. Meggers and Clifford Evans defend the utility of the culture-area classification established by Steward in the Handbook of South American Indians. In another study published under the title "Identificação das áreas culturais e dos tipos de cultura na base da cerâmica das jazidas arqueológicas" ("Identification of Culture Areas and Types of Culture on the Basis of the Ceramics in Archeological Deposits"),

Meggers and Evans establish "three distinct levels of ceramic development" in South America: Simple, Regular, and Advanced (p. 30). The following conclusion to this attempt at classification is worth noting: "The theoretical conception that all cultural phenomena are functionally interrelated leads us to conclude that differences in ceramic technology can be used to infer the general characteristics of socio-political and religious organization associated with the different ceramic technologies and, therefore, to secure a base for rating the general level of complexity attained by an extinct culture." (ibidem)

The classificatory essay of maximum importance to us is the paper Eduardo Galvão presented at the IV Reunião Brasileira de Antropologia and later published under the title "Areas culturais indígenas do Brasil; 1900-1959," ("Indigenous Culture Areas of Brazil: 1900-1959"). Having reviewed earlier attempts to classify South American Indians by culture area, the author divides Brazil into eleven culture areas: "North Amazon, Juruá-Purus, Guaporé, Tapajós-Madeira, the Upper Xingu, Tocantins-Xingu, Pindaré-Gurupi, Paraguai, Paraná, Tietê-Uruguai, the Northeast." He observes: "We have emphasized the contiguous spatial distribution of both material and socio-cultural culture elements as the decisive criteria. Although specific details of the geographic environment of each area are not covered in this summary description, they were taken into consideration. Definition of the contact situation and of the culture context of the pioneering national frontiers is equally important. We consider the occurrence of intertribal acculturation to be of major significance" (p. 15).

What particularly distinguishes this classification from earlier attempts is its limitation to a specific epoch, that is, to tribes still extant during the first six decades of the twentieth century.

Four of the eleven areas are subdivided into nuclei. Each area synopsis is accompanied by a bibliography; a general bibliography is provided at the close of the paper.

Before adding new items to the bibliography of each of these culture areas, let us complete the panorama of scientific publications on the Brazilian Indian for the years 1953 to 1960 with the citation of those authors who contributed to this literature in disciplines other than ethnology. These are, in Linguistics: Albisetti, Baldus, Barbosa, Boglár, Cadogan, Mattoso Câmara, Faria, Giacone, Greenberg, Guérios, Hanke, Kietzman, Loukotka, Meyer, Nimuendajú, Rodrigues, Schultz, and Swadesh; in Archaeology and Prehistory:

Barata, Becker-Donner, Bigarella, Blasi, Boglár, Borba, Bosch-Gimpera, Cruxent, Emperaire, Evans, Faria, Loureiro Fernandes, Figueiredo, Fuchs, Hanke, Hilbert, Hurt, Laming, Meggers, Ott, Palmatary, Pereira Jr., Putzer, Schmitz, Altenfelder Silva, Tiburtius, and Walter; in Physical Anthropology: Ávila, Bellizzi, Campos, Díaz-Ungría, Loureiro Fernandes, Fortuyn, Imbelloni, Mattos, Ottensooser, Pourchet, Salzano, Walter Silva, and Zerries.

If we list authors of recent publications on specific tribes by name, using the culture area scheme proposed by Galvão, the following picture emerges:

I—NORTH AMAZON, nucleus A:

Oaiana (Wayâna):	Ahlbrinck, Fortuyn.
Tiriyó:	Frikel.
Urukuyana and Aparai:	Melo Carvalho.
Kaxuiâna:	Frikel, Polykrates, Haekel.
West: Makuxí:	Butt, Alcuino Meyer, Nimuendajú.
North: Waiwai:	Evans and Meggers, Fock, Guppy, Yde.

nucleus B:

Waika:	Finney, M. Schuster, Zerries.
Xiriana:	Díaz-Ungría, Zerries.
Pakidái:	Becher.

nucleus C:

Baníwa:	Saake.
Tariâna:	Alves da Silva.
Tukáno:	Fulop, Alves da Silva.
Maku:	Giacone, Schultz, Zerries (Puinave).
Tukuna:	Anderson, Melo Carvalho, Schultz, Roberto Cardoso de Oliveira.
Rio Negro in general:	Galvão.

II—JURUÁ-PURUS:.
Schultz and Chiara, Castelo Branco.

III—GUAPORÉ, nucleus A:

Txapakúra groups:	Pakaanovas: Becker-Donner.

nucleus B:

Tupí: Makuráp:	Becker-Donner.
Huari:	Hanke, Becker-Donner.
Tuparí:	Caspar, Scolnik.
Kanoé:	Hanke.

	nucleus C:
Nambikuára:	Boglár, Lévi-Strauss.
Guaporé in general:	Hugo.

IV—TAPAJÓS-MADEIRA, nucleus A:

Munduruků:	Burks, Frikel, Robert and Yolanda Murphy.
Maué:	Bellizzi, Nunes Pereira.

nucleus B:

Kawahib groups (Tupí):	Lévi-Strauss.

V—UPPER XINGU:

Kamayurá:	Cowell, Oberg, Teves, Weyer, Wustmann.
Yawalapití:	Lhullier dos Santos.
Kalapálo:	Cunha, Saake.
Kuikúro:	Carneiro and Dole.
Trumaí:	Murphy and Quain.
Upper Xingu in general:	Cowell, Dreyfus-Roche, Galvão, Lima, Oberg.

VI—TOCANTINS-XINGU, nucleus A:

Canela:	Crocker, Dietschy, Izikowitz, Vanzolini.
Apinayé:	David Maybury-Lewis.
Krahó:	Schultz, Wustmann.
Eastern Timbira in general:	Hye-Kerkdal, Lévi-Strauss.

nucleus B:

Xerénte:	David and Pia Maybury-Lewis, Baldus.
Akwê-Xavante:	Arnau, Borra, Halik, Weyer.

nucleus C:

Kayapó:	Banner, Bellizzi, Lukesch, Métraux and Dreyfus-Roche, Moreira Neto. Txukahamai: Cowell.
Gaviões:	Carron, Vilar de Carvalho, Moreira Neto.
Mudjetíre:	Vilar de Carvalho.

Tapirapé:	Baldus, Wagley, Cardoso de Oliveira.
Karajá:	Bellizzi, Caldas, Costa, Dietschy, Faria, Schultz, Vásquez, Wustmann.
Borôro:	Albisetti, Baldi, Lévi-Strauss, Saake.

VII—PINDARÉ-GURUPI:

Urubus-Kaapor:	Darcy and Berta G. Ribeiro, Huxley.
Guajá:	Beghin.

VIII—PARAGUAI:

Kadiwéu:	Lévi-Strauss, Susnik, Zibert.
Terêna:	Cardoso de Oliveira, Kietzman.

IX—PARANÁ:

Kayová:	Boglár, Hanke, Philipson, V. Watson.
Mbyá:	Cadogan.
Guaraní in general:	Cadogan, Lane, Nimuendajú, Schaden.
Guaraní of the Paulista Coast:	Goldman.
Guaraní archaeology:	Altenfelder Silva, Schmitz.

X—TIETÊ-URUGUAI:

Kaingáng of São Paulo:	Baldus, Horta Barboza, Lane, Magalhães.
Kaingáng of Paraná and Santa Catarina:	Loureiro Fernandes, Lacerda, Menezes, Pourchet, C. C. de Souza, Dreyfus-Roche.
Kaingáng of Rio Grande do Sul:	Baldus, Fischer.
Kaingáng in general:	Baldus, Paterniani, F. S. G. Schaden.
Xetá:	Loureiro Fernandes, Guérios, Loukotka.

XI—NORTHEAST:

Fulniô:	Hohenthal, E. Pinto.
Karirí:	Trujillo Ferrari.
Xukurú:	Hohenthal.
Northeast in general:	Loukotka.

CONCLUSIONS

The listing above indicates that new studies were made in each of the eleven culture areas during the last seven years. It also shows clearly how much still remains to be done. The area least visited by researchers is Juruá-Purus.

Summarizing the other data presented here, we may make the following statements:

Among the materials published since the appearance of my *Bibliografia Crítica (Critical Bibliography)*, in 1954, the most important for the study of the modern history of Brazilian ethnology is the monograph by Florestan Fernandes which was cited above.

The materials published in ergology and technology largely represent museum and library research. It is devoutly to be hoped that the need for field research will be increasingly recognized by those disciplines which now can benefit from the efficient use of cinematography.

Relatively little has been written about economic activities. What there is almost always consists of brief descriptions of activities of specific tribes. One of our needs is for a systematic inventory of knowledge in this field of Brazilian ethnology to point up the gaps in our present data.

Among the studies of indigenous religion, Schaden's and Murphy's are outstanding for their concern with the religious motif as it is interwoven with the total culture. The myths of a great many tribes have been published.

In ethno-sociology, the analysis of the kinship system has been stressed. Studies of the couvade are outstanding in the group of publications concerned with the life cycle of the individual.

Increasing interest in psychology is evident not only in articles on patterns of tribal behavior, but also in the analysis of individuals and in the application of several modern tests in the tribal setting.

In the Arts in addition to some essays there is a unique monograph, "Arte plumária Kaapor" ("Feather Art of the Kaapor"), by Darcy Ribeiro and Berta G. Ribeiro. Few authors deal with the dance; one, however, has "mistreated" it. Almost nothing has been published on games.

While all the aspects of culture mentioned were studied more or less intensively, the problem of the numbers of culture bearers (Indians) and their decline attracted little attention from researchers until Darcy Ribeiro's demographic study appeared. Now studies of the state of health of the Indians and of relations between Indians and Whites in general are multiplying.

Good studies of acculturation problems are legion. Some European researchers have been interested in questions of Culture History. Ethnologists, linguists, archaeologists, and physical anthropologists have contributed to the classification of Brazilian tribes.

At the I Reunião Brasileira de Antropologia in 1953, I presented a balance sheet of what had been done to advance knowledge of the Brazilian Indian. I concluded that "The best representatives of Brazilian ethnology understand that the moment to produce *multum, non multa* has arrived." In my exposition today I have already mentioned studies that are "multum," that is, basic works, rather than "multa," that is, superficial notes and little articles. Brazilian ethnology has made great progress since that first meeting.

APPENDICES

Appendix I

INDEX OF INDIAN GROUPS IN CONTEMPORARY BRAZIL*

Agavotokúeng
Aiwatéri (Aiwaterí)
Akuěn (Xavante) (Akwě-Xavante)
    (Shavante)
Akwê-Xavante (Akuên) (Xavante)
    (Shavante)
Amahuáka
Amanayé
Amnlapé
Andirá (Arepium) (Maué) (Mawé)
    (Sataré)
Apalaí (Aparaí)
Aparaí (Apalaí)
Apiaká
Apinayé
Apopokúva (Nandéva)
Apurinã (Ipurinân) (Ipuriná) (Kangite)
Arapium (Andirá) (Maué) (Mawé)
    (Sataré)
Arara (Araras) (Kayapó)
Arara (Araras) [non-Kayapó]
Aré (Xetá)
Arecuna (Taulipáng) (Jaricunas)
Arikapú (Maxukí) (Maxubi)
Arikiéna (Waríkyana) (Warikyána)
Aripaktsá (Erigbaagtsa) (Erigpatsa)
Asuriní
Aticum (Atikum) (Uamué)
Atikum (Aticum) (Uamué)
Atruahí (Waimirí) (Yawaperí) (Krixaná)
Aueti (Awéti) (Awetí)
Avá (Canoeiros)
Aweikoma (Bugre) (Botocudos)
    (Kaingáng) (Xokléng) (Shokléng)
    (Caingang)
Awéti (Awetí) (Aueti)

Bakairí
Baníwa (Baniua do Içana)

Baniua do Içana (Baníwa)
Bará (Pokangá) (Pokangá-Tapuya)
Barawâna
Beiço de Pau
Bôca Negra
Bôca Preta (Tenharím)
Borôro
Botocudos (Xokléng) (Aweikoma)
    (Bugre) (Kaingáng) (Shokléng)
    (Caingang)
Bugre (Xokléng) (Aweikoma)
    (Botocudos) (Kaingáng) (Shokléng)
    (Caingang)

Caduveo (Kaduveo) (Kadiwéu)
Caingang (Kaingáng) (Xokléng)
    (Aweikoma) (Bugre) (Botocudos)
    (Shokléng)
Camáyura (Kamayurá) (Kamaiurá)
Campa (Kámpa)
Canela (Canella) (Ramkókamekra)
    (Ramcócamecra)
Canoeiros (Avá)
Capanahua (Kapanáwa)
Caposho (Cumanasho, Macuni, Monaxó)
    (Maxakalí) (Mashacali)
Carajá (Karajá)
Cashinahua (Kaxináua) (Kaxanáwa)
Cayapó (Kaiapó)
Cavuá (Kaiová) (Kaiwá)
Cinta Larga
Cubeu (Kobéwa) (Kobewa)
Cumanasho (Maxakalí) (Caposho,
    Macuni, Monaxó) (Mashacali)

Daní
Desâna
Diarrói
Dioré

---

* List includes names of some tribes now extinct as tribes: i.e., individual survivors of these groups have lost their tribal languages and cultures.

Emerion (Emerilon) (Emerillon)
Emerilon (Emerion) (Emerillon)
Erigbaagtsa (Erigpatsa) (Aripaktsá)
Erigpatsa (Erigbaagtsa) (Aripaktsá)

Fulniô (Carnijó)

Galera
Galibí
Galibí-Marwôrno
Gavião
Gorotíre
Guaharíbo (Waharibo) (Xamatari)
Guaiana (Guayana) (Wayâna) (Oyana)
    (Rucuyenne)
Guajá
Guajajára
Guaraní
Guató
Guayana (Guaiana) (Wayâna) (Oyana)
    (Rucuyenne)
Gueren

Hixkaryána
Hohodene
Huanyam (Urupá) (Kotemoka)
    (Rokorona) (Jaru) (Pakaas Novas)
    (Pakaanovas) (Uómo)

Iamamadi (Jamamadí) (Yamamadi)
Iamináwa (Jamináwa)
Iawalapití (Yawalapití) (Yaulapití)
Iawano (Iawavo)
Iekuana (Mayongóng)
Ingarikó
Ipewí
Ipuriná (Ipurinân) (Kangite) (Apurinã)
Itogapúk (Ntogapig)

Jaboti
Jamamadí (Yamamadi) (Yamamadí)
    (Iamamadí)
Jamináwa (Iaminawa)
Jaricunas (Taulipáng) (Arecuna)
Jaru (Pakaas Novas) (Pakaanovas)
    (Uómo) (Urupá) (Kotemoka)
    (Rokorona) (Huanyam)
Jaruára

Javaé (Javahé) (Karajá) (Xambioá)
    (Carajá)
Júma
Jurúna

Kabixí (Kavixí) (Sararé)
Kadiwéu (Kaduveo) (Caduveo)
Kaduveo (Kadiwéu) (Caduveo) (Mbuá)
    (Mbaye) (Mbyá)
Kaiabí (Kajabí) (Kayabí)
Kaiapó (Cayapó) (Kayapó)
Kaimbé
Kaingáng (Caingang) (Xokléng)
    (Aweikoma) (Bugre) (Botocudos)
    (Shokléng)
Kainguá (Mbuá)
Kaiová (Kaiwá) (Cayuá)
Kaiwá (Kaiová) (Cayuá)
Kajabí (Kayabí) (Kaiabí)
Kalapálo
Kalina
Kamaiurá (Kamayurá) (Camáyura)
Kambiwá
Kámpa (Campa)
Kanamarí
Kangite (Apurinã) (Ipurinân) (Ipuriná)
Kapanáwa (Capanahua)
Karajá (Carajá) (Javaé, Javahé,
    Xambioá)
Karipúna
Kariri
Karitiâna
Káru
Karupáka
Katawiân
Katukína
Kavixi (Kabixi)
Kawahib (Kawahyb)
Kaxanáwa (Kaxanawa) (Kaxináua)
    (Cashinahua)
Kaxararí
Kaxináua (Kaxanáwa) (Kaxanawa)
    (Cashinahua)
Kayabí (Kajabí) (Kaiabí)
Kayapó (Kaiapó) (Cayapó)
Kinikinão
Kirirí
Kobéwa (Kobewa) (Cubeu)

Koripako
Kotemoka (Rokorona) (Huanyam) (Jaru)
(Urupá) (Pakaas Novas)
Krahó
Krem-yê
Kréen-Akaróre
Krikatí
Krixaná (Waimirí) (Yawaperí) (Atruahí)
Kubén-Kragnotíre
Kubén-Kran-Kegn (Kubenkrankegn)
Kuikúro (Kuikuru)
Kulína
Kuruáya

Layâna

Macuni (Maxakalí) (Mashacalí)
(Caposho) (Cumanasho) (Monaxó)
Majubim (Paranawát) (Pawaté)
Makú (Makunabödö)
Makunabödö (Makú)
Makuxí
Mamaindé
Manairisú
Mandawáka
Manitenéri (Manitenerí)
Maopityan (Mapidian) (Wapidian)
(Wapishana) (Wapitxana) (Vapidiana)
Marinahua (Marináwa)
Marúbo
Mashacalí (Maxakalí) (Macuni)
(Monaxó) (Caposho) (Cumanasho)
Matipú (Matipuhy)
Maué (Mawé) (Andirá) (Arapium)
(Sataré)
Maxakalí (Macuni) (Monaxó)
(Mashacalí) (Caposho) (Cumanasho)
Maxukí (Maxubi) (Arikapú)
Máya (Mayu) (Mayoruna)
Mayongóng (Iekuana)
Mayoruna (Máya) (Mayu)
Mbaye (Mbuá or Kainguá) (Mbyá)
(Kaduveo) (Kaiwá)
Mehináku
Menkranotire
Mentuktíre (Meto[c]tire)
Monaxó (Maxakalí) (Maxakali)
(Mashacalí) (Macuni) (Caposho)
(Cumanasho)

Morerébi
Mudjetíre
Mundurucú (Mundurukú)
Mundurukú (Mundurucú)
Mura-Pirahã

Nafuguá (Nahúkua) (Nahukuá)
(Nahukwá)
Nambicuara (Nambikuára)
(Nambikwara)
Nandéva (Apopokúva)
Natú
Ntogapig (Itogapúk)
Nukuiní
Numbiaí (Orelha de Pau)

Oiampik (Oyampi)
Orelha de Pau (Numbiaí)
Oyampi (Oiampik)
Oyana (Wayâna) (Rucuyenne)
(Guayana) (Guaniana)

Pacanahua (Pakanáwa)
Pakaanovas (Pakaas Novas) (Jaru)
(Uómo)
Pakanáwa (Pacanahua)
Pakarará
Pakidái
Palikúr
Pancararú (Pankararú) (Pancaré)
(Pankarú) (Pankarará)
Parahúris
Parakanã (Parakanân)
Paranawát (Pawaté) (Majubim)
Parecí-Kozarini
Paresí (Paressí)
Parikotó (Purukotó)
Parintintín
Parukotó-Charúma (Parukoto-Xarúma)
Patashó (Patoxo)
Pataxó-Hahahãi (Patashó) (Patoxo)
Paumarí (Purupurú)
Pawaté (Majubim) (Paranawát)
Pianokotó-Tiriyó
Pirá-Tapuya (Waikíno) (Piratapuio)
Pokangá (Pokangá-Tapuya) (Bará)
Potiguára
Poyanáwa (Puinahua)
Puinahua (Poyanáwa)

Puruborá
Purukotó (Parikotó)
Purupurú (Paumarí)

Ramcócamecra (Ramkókamekra)
   (Canela) (Canella)
Rodela (Tuxá)
Rokorona (Urupá) (Kotemoka)
   (Huanyam) (Jaru) (Pakaas Novas)
Rucuyenne (Wayâna) (Guayana)
   (Guaiana) (Oyana)

Sabones
Salumá
Sararé (Kabixí)
Sataré (Mawé) (Maué) (Andirá)
   (Arapium)
Shavante (Xavante) (Akuên)
   (Akwê-Xavante)
Sherente (Xerénte)
Shipinahua (Xipináwa)
Shiriâna (Xiriâna)
Shirianá (Xirianá)
Shocú (?) (Xokó) (Shocó)
Shokléng (Xokléng) (Aweikoma) (Bugre)
   (Botocudos) (Kaingáng) (Caingang)
Sikiâna
Suiá (Suyá)
Suruí
Suyá (Suiá)

Tapayúna
Tapirapé
Tariána (Tariâna)
Taulipáng (Jaricunas) (Arecuna)
Tchikão (Txikão) (Tunuli) (Tonore)
Tchukarramẽi (Txukahamẽi)
   (Txukahamãi)
Tembé
Tenetehara
Tenharím (Bôca Preta)
Terêna
Ticúna (Tukúna)
Timbíra
Tirío (Tiriyo) (Trio)
Tonore (Txikão) (Tchikão) (Tunuli)
Trio (Tirió)
Trumái
Tukána (Tukano)

Tukano (Tukána)
Tukumanféd (Tukunaféd)
Tukúna (Ticúna)
Tunuli (Txikão) (Tchikão) (Tonore)
Tuparí
Tupinaki
Turiwára
Tuxá (Rodela)
Tuxináwa
Tuyúca
Txikão (Tchikão) (Tunuli) (Tonore)
Txukahamẽi (Txukahamãi)
   (Tchukarramẽi)

Uamué (Aticum) (Atikum)
Umotína (Umutina)
Uómo (Pakaas Novas) (Pakaanovas)
   (Jaru)
Urubús-Kaapor
Urukuiâna (Urukuyána) (Wayana)
Urupá (Kotemoka) (Rokorona)
   (Huanyam) (Jaru)

Vapidiana (Maopityan) (Mapidian)
   (Wapidian) (Wapishana) (Wapitxana)

Waharibo (Guaharíbo)
Waiká (Wayká)
Waikíno (Pirá-Tapuya)
Waimirí (Yawaperí) (Atruahí)
   (Krixaná)
Waiwai
Wakona
Wapichiyana (See: Wapishana)
Wapishana (Maopityan) (Mapidian)
   (Wapidian) (Wapitxana) (Vapidiana)
Waríkyana (Arikiéna) (Warikyána)
Waurá
Wayká (Waiká)
Wayâna (Oyana) (Rucuyenne)
   (Guayana) (Guaiana)
Wiraféd
Witóto

Xamatari (Guaharíbo)
Xambioá (Javaé) (Javahé) (Karajá)
Xavante (Akuên) (Akwê-Xavante)
   (Shavante)
Xerénte (Sherente)

Xetá (Aré)
Xikrín
Xikrin-Dioré
Xipináwa (Shipinahua)
Xirâna (Shiriâna)
Xiri-aná (Shirianá)
Xogléng (Aweikoma) (Bugre)
 (Botocudos) (Kaingáng) (Shokléng)
 (Caingang)

Xokó (Shocú ?) (Shocó)
Xukurú
Xukurú-Karirí

Yabaâna (Yabarana)
Yamamadí (Iamamadí) (Jamamadí)
Yamináwa (Yaminawa) (Yaminahua)
Yawalapití (Iawalapití) (Yaulapití)
Yawaperí (Atruahí) (Krixaná) (Waimirí)

Appendix II

INDIAN GROUPS OF CONTEMPORARY BRAZIL BY CULTURE AREA

CULTURE AREA I
 Aiwaterí
 Apalaí (Aparaí)
 Aparaí (Apalaí)
 Arikiéna (Waríkyana) (Arikén)
 Baníwa (Baníwa do Içana)
 Desana (Wanána)
 Galibí
 Galibi-Maraworno
 Guaharíbo
 Hixkaryána (Parukotó-Charúma)
 Karipúna
 Káru (Karutãna) (Baníwa)
 Karupáka (Baníwa)
 Kobéwa
 Máku
 Makunabödö (Maku)
 Makuxí (See Parukotó-Charúma)
 Mandawáka
 Mayongóng
 Pakidái
 Palikúr
 Parukotó-Charúma (Parikotó)
 Pianokotó-Tiriyó (Pianokotó)
 Pokango (Tukána)
  (Pokangá-Tapuya) (Bará)
 Tariana
 Taulipang (Jaricunas)
 Ticuna (Tukúna) (Tikuna)
 Tukána
 Tukúna (Ticuna)
 Tuyuca (Tukána)

Urukuyánya
Waiká
Waikíno (Wanâna)
Waiwai (Parukotó-Charúma)
Wanâna (Kótedia)
Wapitxâna (Vapidiana)
Waríkyana (Arikiéna)
Wayana (Urukuyána) (Urukuiâna)
Xirianá

CULTURE AREA II
 Amahuáka
 Apurinã (Ipurinãn) (Kangite)
 Daní
 Jamanadí (Yamamadí) (Iamanedi)
 Jamináwa (Yamináwa)
 Jaruára
 Júma (Yumá)
 Kampa
 Kanamarí (Tamanáua)
 Kapanáwa
 Katukina
 Kaxararí
 Kaxináua (Kaximáwa)
 Kulína (Culino)
 Maniterí (the Peruvian *Piro*)
 Marubo (Marúbo)
 Maya
 Mayorúna (Maya)
 Paumarí (Purupurú)
 Poyanáwa
 Tamanáua (Kanamarí)

CULTURE AREA III

Arara (Araras)
Arikapú (Maxuki) (Maxubi)
Beiço de Pau
Cinta Larga
Galera
Irántxe
Kabixi (Sararê)
Karipúna
Karitiâna
Mamaidé
Manairisú
Maxuki (Arikapú)
Nambikuára
Pakaas Novas (Pakaánovas) (Jaru)
    (Uómo)
Paresí
Puruborá (Aruá)
Sabones
Sarare (Kabixí)
Tuparí
Urupá

CULTURE AREA IV

Apiaká
Aripaktsá
Boca Negra
Boca Preta (Tenharim)
Diarroi (Morerebi) (Diarroi)
Gavião (Gaviões)
    (Surui and Gavião)
Ipewí
Itogapúk (Ntogapig)
Kayabí (Kawahib)
Kuruáya (Mundurukú)?
Mawé (Sataré) (Maré) (Andirá)
    (Arapium)
Morerebi and Diarroi
Mundurukú
Mura-Pirahã (Mura)
Numbiai (Orelha de Pau)
Orelha de Pau (Numbiai)
Parintintín
Sataré (Mawé)
Surui and Gavião
Tapayúna
Tenharim (Boca Preta)

CULTURE AREA V

Agavotokueng
Awéti (Awetí)
Bakairí
Juruna (Jurúna)
Kalapalo (Kalapálo)
Kamayurá
Kayabí
Kuikúro
Matipuhy (Nahukua)
Mehináku
Nahukua (Matipuhy) (Nahukuá)
Suyá
Trumai (Trumái) (Suyá)
Txição (Txikão)
Txukahamẽi (Kaiapó)
Uaiarú (Agavotokueng)
Waurá
Yawalapití

CULTURE AREA VI

Apinayé
Arara (Araras)
Asuriní
Borôno
Canela (Ramkókamekra)
Dióre
Gavião (Gaviões)
Gorotire (Gorotíre)
Javaé (Karajá)
Karajá
Krahó
Kreen-Akarore
Krem-yê
Krikatí
Kubén-Kragnotíre
Kubén-Kran-Kegn
Mentuktire (Txukahamẽi)
Mudjetíre
Parakanân
Tapirapé
Txukahamẽi (Mentuktire)
Xambioá (Karajá) (Javaé)
Xavante
Xerénte
Xikrin

CULTURE AREA VII
Amanayé
Guajá
Guajajára (Tenetehara)
Tembé
Turiwára
Urubús-Kaapor

CULTURE AREA VIII
Guató
Kadiwéu (Édiu-Adig)
Kinikinão (Terêna)
Layâna (Terêna)
Terêna (Kinikinão) (Layâna)

CULTURE AREA IX
Apopokúva (Nandéva)
Kaiwá
Mbuá (Kainguá)
Nandéva (Apopokúva)
Xetá

CULTURE AREA X
Kaingáng (Jê) (Coroado) (Guaianá)
Xokleng (Aweikoma) (Bugre)
  (Botocudos) (Kaingáng)

CULTURE AREA XI
Aticum (Uamué)
Fulniô (Carnijô)
Gueren
Kaimbé
Kambiwá
Kirirí
Maxakalí (Caposho) (Cumanasho)
  (Macuni) (Monaxó)
Pankarará
Pankararú
Pataxó-Hahahãi
Potiguára
Rodela (Tuxá)
Tuxá (Rodela)
Uamué (Aticum)
Xukurú
Xukuru-Kariri

Appendix III
GLOSSARY

ABÓBORA — pumpkin

AGRESTE — term used in northeast Brazil for the rocky timber zone between the coastal plain and the dry sertão (badlands)

ALICIAR — to enlist, to recruit: implies the use of compulsion; to press into service

AMENDOIM — peanut

ARAUCÁRIA — a species of pine tree

ARTE PLUMÁRIA — feather art

ATLATL — spear thrower

BABASSÚ (BABAÇU) — a species of palm tree, valuable as a source of vegetable oils

BALATA — the balata or bully tree, source of balata gum (rubber)

BEIJÚ — tapioca cake

BODOQUES — pellet-bows; a combination of a sling and a bow

BORDUNA — cylindrical club

BORRACHA — rubber (latex of the Hevea)

BRABO — wild, savage

BROCAR — to clear the land of undergrowth, small trees and vines in the preparation of a roça

CABECEIRAS — headwaters

CACAU — cocoa

CACETES DE GUERRA — war clubs

CACHOEIRA — waterfall, rapids

CAMPANHA — open field country, open plains

CAMPESTRE — a small, high campo surrounded by forest

CAMPINA — prairie, a treeless plain, a natural pasture

CAMPO CERRADO — scrub woodland, savannah

CAMPOS — prairie-like pasture lands on the high plateaus and mountain tops

CASA DE DUAS AGUAS — double lean-to

CASA DE UMA AGUA — single lean-to

CASAS DE FORMA COLMEIA — "beehive" houses

CASAS DISPOSTAS EM FERRADURA — houses in a horseshoe shaped arrangement

CASTANHEIRO — nut gatherer

CAUCHO — a gum tree [Avore Moráceas]; castilla rubber; panama rubber

CAUIN (CAUIM, KAWIN, KAWIM) — fermented alcoholic beverage made from manioc mixed with other fruits

CHEFES-PAJÉS — chief medicine men

CHICHA — alcoholic beverage made of fermented fruit or vegetable; referred to as native beer

CONVIVER — to coexist

CORRIDAS DE TORAS	—	log races, i.e., relay races in which male adolescents and adults carry sections of tree trunks
CRESCIMENTO VEGETATIVO	—	natural growth
DESBRAVADOR	—	pioneering
DESCARACTERIZAÇÃO	—	deculturation, detribalization, i.e., loss of language and culture: see Gould, Julius and William L. Kolb, eds. *A Dictionary of the Social Sciences*, N.Y., The Free Press of Glencoe, 1964, p. 195, particularly "2.", for American usage.
ENTERRAMENTO DIRETO	—	primary burial
ERGOLOGIA	—	study of work
ERVA-MATE	—	mate (Ilex paraguaiensis), a holly
ESTEIRA	—	coarse grass mat
ESTÔJO PENIAMO	—	penis sheath
FAIXA CAMPESTRE	—	prairie belt
FARINHA DE MANDIOCA	—	manioc flour
FLAUTA	—	flute
FLEXA	—	arrow tip
GRAUS DE IDADE	—	age groups
GRUPOS DE PRAÇA	—	plaza groups
HILÉIA	—	tropical rain forest
IGARAPÉ (Ig.)	—	small stream between two islands or between an island and a mainland [Amazonas usage: creek]
INHAME	—	yam (also cará)
IPADU	—	coca
JANGADA	—	raft
JIRAUS	—	crude beds made from wooden rods
KAAPI	—	(ayahuasca) a narcotic
LINGUA GERAL	—	European missionary script form of Tupi-Guarani
MACAXEIRA	—	sweet manioc (Manihot aipi)
MACHADOS	—	axes
MALOCA	—	large house, Indian communal dwelling
MANDIOCA	—	the tuber of manioc (Manihot utilissima)
MÁSCARA	—	mask
MATA	—	forest
MATA CILIAR	—	gallery forest
METADE	—	moiety
MILHO	—	maize
MUNICIPIO	—	municipality
NÚCLEO	—	"nucleus", used in this volume to denote a locality whose inhabitants are grouped together under a special regime but not an administrative seat; e.g., an agricultural colony

ONÇA	— jaguar
PAGÉ	— shaman, medicine man
PALHOÇA	— building or shed covered with a thatched roof
PANTANAL	— low-lying swamp area
PARANÁ	— a bayou or distributary of a river
PARDO	— mulatto
PARICÁ	— (Piptadenia) snuff
PAU-ROSA	— rose-wood, tulip-wood
PIAÇABA (PIASSAVA)	— species of palm that produces fibers used in the manufacture of brooms
PINHÃO DE ARAUCÁRIA	— pine nuts
PÔSTO SAGRADO	— sacred post
PRAÇA	— plaza or square
PROPULSOR DE DARDOS	— spearthrower
RANCHO	— a rude hut, open air shed
REMO	— oar
ROÇA	— small subsistence plot in the gallery forests cultivated by slash/burn method
SARABATANA	— blow tube
SARARACA	— fishing arrow
SERINGAL	— a rubber stand
SERINGUEIRO	— rubber collector
TACAPE	— Indian club, cudgel; traditionally used for human sacrifices
TATUAGEM	— tattooing
TECELAGEM	— loom weaving
TECELÃO	— weaver
TERRA FIRME	— forest on land above the flood plains— terra firma
TESE DE LIVRE-DOCÊNCIA	— book written in fulfillment of the requirements of the competition for appointment to a University chair in Brazil
TIMBÓ	— vine from which insecticides are produced
TIMBORANA	— a vine similar to timbó but of no commercial value
TIPITÍ	— tubular basketry press for squeezing manioc
TÔLDO	— shelter
TRANÇADO	— basket weaving
UBÁ	— a fire-hollowed wood canoe (dugout)
URUCCARÍ	— species of palm tree
XINGUANOS	— term used to refer to members of the nine tribes of the upper Xingu region
ZUNIDOR	— bull-roarer

Appendix IV

BIBLIOGRAPHY

The following bibliography has been prepared by ICR for the convenience of students. The intent is to call attention to interesting materials, largely those published during the last decade, and to provide leads to additional references. There has been no attempt to provide an exhaustive bibliography.

The editor acknowledges with gratitude the contributions to this bibliography made by the authors of the papers in this volume. We note particularly our indebtedness to Herbert Baldus. Errors and omissions are, however, our responsibility.

Bibliographies

BALDUS, Herbert
1954a   *Bibliografia comentada de etnologia brasileira.* Rio de Janeiro: Sousa.
1954b   *Bibliografia crítica da etnologia Brasileira.* São Paulo, Brasil: Comissão do IV Centenário da Cidade de São Paulo.

O'LEARY, Timothy
1963   *Ethnographic Bibliography of South America.* New Haven: Human Relations Area Files.

PARISEAU, Earl J., Ed.
1965   *Handbook of Latin American Studies.* No. 27. Social Sciences. Gainesville: University of Florida Press for the Hispanic Foundation, Library of Congress.
         See also volumes issued over the past decade.

Books and Articles

ADAMS, Richard N.
1964   "Rural Labor." John Johnson, Ed. *Continuity and Change in Latin America.* Stanford: Stanford University Press.

ANDERSON, L.
1955/7   "Los Ritos de Pubertad de los Ticuna." *Tradicion* VII, 83-91. Lima.

ARNAUD, Expedito
1961   "Breve informação os índios asuriní e parakanan, Rio Tocanti-

nis, Pará." *Boletim do Museu Paraense Emílio Goeldi,* Nova Série [Antropologia] n.º 11, 22 pp. Belém.

1963*   "A terminiologia de parentesco dos índios Asuriní." *Revista do Museu Paulista,* Nova Série 9, 105-119. São Paulo.

AZEVEDO, Thales de

1959   "Aculturação dirigida." *Trabalhos de Antropologia e Etnologia* XVII, 491-512. Oporto.

BALDUS, Herbert

1931   *Indianerstudien im nordöstlichen Chaco.* Leipzig.

1955   "As danças dos Tapirapé." *Proceedings of the International Congress of Americanists* XXXI(1), 89-96.

1955   "O estudo etnográficio do índio no Brasil." *Revista do Museu Paulista,* Nova Série 9, 247-59. São Paulo.

1956/58   "Cândido Mariano da Silva Rondon, 1865-1958." *Revista do Museu Paulista,* Nova Série 10, 283-93. São Paulo.

1958   *Die Jaguarzwillinge.* Eisenach/Kassel.

1960   *Estórias e lendas dos índios. Seleção e introdução de H. Baldus.* São Paulo: Literart. 303 pp.

1962   "Métodos e resultados da ação indigenista no Brasil." *Revista de Antropologia* X: 1/2, 27-42.

1963*a   "Discurso presidencial na VI Reunião Brasileira de Antropologia." *Revista do Museu Paulista,* Nova Série 9, 11-16. São Paulo.

1963*b   "Métraux e a Etnologia Brasileira." *Revista do Museu Paulista,* Nova Série 9, 45-59. São Paulo.

1964   "Sinopse da bibliografia crítica da etnologia Brasileira, 1953-1960." *Arquivo do Instituto de Antropologia,* Vol. I, n.º 2; 5-22. Natal. (Paper read at the V Reunião Brasileira de Antropologia in Belo Horizonte, June 26, 1961.)

BANNER, Horace

1957   "Mitos dos índios Kayapo." *Revista de Antropologia* V, 37-66. São Paulo.

1961   "O índio Kayapó em seu acampento." *Boletim do Museu Paraense Emílio Goeldi,* Nova Série 13, 51 pages. Belem.

---

* The date on the cover is 1963, but the *Revista* actually appeared in 1965.

BARRETO, Felícitas
1960   *Danzas indígenas del Brasil.* Special Edition Series No. 42. Mexico, D. F.: Instituto Indigenista Interamericano. 138 pp.

BARROS LARAIA, Roque de
1963*   "Arranjos poliandricos na sociedade surui." *Revista do Museu Paulista,* Nova Série 9, 71-75. São Paulo.

BECHER, Hans
1957   "A importância da banana entre os índios Surara e Paikidai." *Revista de Antropologia* V, 192-94. São Paulo.
1959   "Die Stellung des Kindes bei den Surara und Pakadia Indianern." *Ärztliche Jugendkunde* LII, 104-12.
1960   *Die Surára und Pakidái: Yanonámi-Stämme in Nordwestbrasilien.* Hamburg: Museum für Völkerkunde.

BECKER-DONNER, Etta
1960   "Die Wirkung der Zivilisation auf einige Indianerstämme an den Zuflüssen des Guaporé." *Tribus. Veroffentlichungen des Linden-museums,* 197-204. Stuttgart: Museum für Länder und Völkerkunde.

BIOCCA, Ettore
1963*   "A penetração branca e a diffusão da tuberculose entre os índios do rio Negro." *Revista do Museu Paulista,* Nova Série 9, 203-212. São Paulo.

BLOMBERG, Rolf
1960   *Chavante: An Expedition to the Tribes of the Mato Grosso.* London: Allen and Unwin. 119 pp.

BOGLAR, L.
1959   "Some Notes to the Burial Forms of Brazilian Indians." In *Opuscula Ethnologica Memorial Lastovici Biro ' Sacra.* T. Bodrogi, Ed. 159-63. Budapest.

BOTELHO DE MAGALHOES, Amilcar Armando
1947   *Indios do Brasil.* Mexico: Instituto Indigenista Interamericano. 96 pp.

BUTT, Audrey J.
1960   "The Birth of a Religion." *Journal of the [Royal] Anthropological Institute of Great Britain and Ireland* XC, 66-106. London.

* The date on the cover is 1963, but the *Revista* actually appeared in 1965.

CADOGAN, L.
1952   "El concepto guarani de 'alma'." *Folia Linguistica Americana* I(1), 31-34. Buenos Aires.
1955   "Aves y almas de difuntos en la mitologia Guarani y Guajaki." *Anthropos* L, 149-54. Wien.

CARDOSO de OLIVEIRA, Roberto de
1958   "Aspectos demograficos e ecologicas de uma communidade Terena." *Boletim do Museu Nacional* [Antropologia] XVIII (Sept.), 1-17. Rio de Janeiro.
1959   "A situação atual dos Tapirapé." *Boletim do Museu Paraense Emílio Goeldi* [Antropologia] 3 (July). 11 pp. Bélem.
1960a   *O processo da assimilação dos Terêna.* Rio de Janeiro. 160 pp.
1960b   "The Role of Indian Posts in the Process of Assimilation: Two Case Studies." *América Indígena* 20: 2, 89-95.
1964a   *O índio e o mundo dos brancos: a situação dos túkana do alto Solimões.* Corpo e alma do Brasil, 12. São Paulo: Difusão Européia do Livro. 143 pp.
1964b   "Totemismo Tukúna?" In *Beiträge zur Völkerkunde Südamerikas.* Hans Becher, Ed. Hannover: Munstermann-Druck in Kommission. 231-248.

CARLUCI, María Angélica
1953/4 "La 'Couvade' en Sudamerica." *Runa* VI, 142-74. Buenos Aires.

CARNEIRO, Robert L.
1956/8 "Extra-Marital Sex Freedom among the Kuikuru Indians." *Revista do Museu Paulista,* Nova Série X, 135-42. São Paulo.
1960   "Slash-and-Burn Agriculture." *Acts of the International Congress of Anthropological and Ethnological Sciences* V, 229-34.
1961   "Slash-and-Burn Cultivation among the Kuikuru and its Implication for Cultural Development in the Amazon Basin." *Antropológica* (Supplementary Publication) II (Sept.) 44-67. Caracas: Sociedad de Ciencias Naturales La Salle.

CARVALHO, Bernardino de Waiká
1963*   "Breves anotações informativas." *Revista do Museu Paulista,* Nova Série 9, 159-162. São Paulo.

---

* The date on the cover is 1963, but the *Revista* actually appeared in 1965.

CASPAR, Franz

1953   "Some Sex Beliefs and Practices of the Tupari Indians."
        Revista do Museu Paulista, Nova Série VII, 203-48. São
        Paulo.

1955   "Un Caso de Desenvolvimento Anormal da Personalidade
        Observado entre os Tupari." *Proceedings of the Interna-
        tional Congress of Americanists* XXXI (1), 121-26.

1956/8 "Puberty Rites Among the Tupari Indians." *Revista do
        Museu Paulista*, Nova Série X, 143-54. São Paulo.

CASTRO FARIA, Louis de

1963*   "Dez anos após a I Reunião Brasileira de Antropologia."
        Revista do Museu Paulista, Nova Série 9, 17-37. São Paulo.

CASTRO FARIA, Luis

[N.D.] *A contribuição de E. Roquette-Pinto para a antropologia
        Brasileira.* Publication No. 25. Rio de Janeiro: Museu
        Nacional. 14 pp.

CEZAR MELATTI, Júlio

1963*   "O mito e o Xamã." *Revista do Museu Paulista*, Nova Série
        9, 60-70. São Paulo.

CHIARA, Vilma

1961/62 "Folclore Krahó." *Revista do Museu Paulista* 9 (13), 333-75.
        São Paulo.

CLASTRES, Pierre and Lucien SEBAG

1963*   "Cannibalisme et mort chez les Guayakis." *Revista do Museu
        Paulista*, Nova Série 9, 174-181. São Paulo.

CROCKER, William

1961   "The Canela Since Nimuendajú: A Preliminary Report on
        Cultural Change." *Anthropological Quarterly* 34(2), 69-84.

1963*   "A Preliminary Analysis of Some Canela Religious Aspects."
        Revista do Museu Paulista, Nova Série 9, 163-173. São Paulo.

CUNHA, Mario Wagner Viera da
        See Donald Pierson

DIETSCHY, Hans

1959   "Das Häuplingswesen bei den Karaja." ("Chieftainship
        among the Karaja") *Mitteilungen des Museums für Völker-
        kunde in Hamburg*, 25(59), 168-76. Hamburg.

—————
* The date on the cover is 1963, but the *Revista* actually appeared in 1965.

1960   "Note à propos des danses des Carajá. Pas de deux, anitie
           formelle de prohibition de l'inceste." *Bulletin. Société des
           Américanistes* 19, p. 5. Geneva.

DINIZ, Edson Soares
1962   "Os Kayapó-Gorotire; aspectos sócioculturais do momento
           atual." *Boletim do Museu Paraense Emílio Goeldi,* Nova
           Série [Antropologia] 18. Belém: Instituto Nacional de
           Pesquisas da Amazonia. 40 pp.
1963*   "Convívio internétnico e aglutinação intergrupal." *Revista
           do Museu Paulista,* Nova Série 9, 213-220. São Paulo.

DOLE, Gertrude E.
1956/8   "Ownership and Exchange among the Kuikuru Indians."
           Revista do Museu Paulista, Nova Série X, 125-33. São Paulo.
1958   "A Mechanism for Mobilizing Labor among the Kuikuru of
           Central Brazil." *Transactions of the New York Academy of
           Sciences,* 21 (1): 58-61. (In collaboration with Roberto
           Carneiro.)
1960   "Techniques of Preparing Manioc Flour as a Key to Culture
           History in Tropical America." In *Men and Cultures.* Anthony
           F. C. Wallace, Ed. Selected papers of the Fifth International
           Congress of Anthropological and Ethnological Sciences,
           Philadelphia: Univ. of Pennsylvania Press. 241-248.
1964   "Shamanism and Political Control among the Kuikuru." In
           *Beiträge zur Völkerkunde Südamerikas Festgabe zur Herbert
           Baldus.* Hans Becher, Ed. Hannover: Münstermann. 53-62.

FERNANDES, Florestan
1956/57   "Tendências teóricas da moderna investigação etnológica
           no Brasil." *Anhembi* XXIV-XXV, 18-43, 262-83, 460-79.
           [*Current Theoretical Trends of Ethnological Research in
           Brazil.* Translated by Frank Goldman from the Portuguese
           text. *Revista do Museu Paulista,* Nova Série XI. São Paulo,
           1959. 69 pp.]
1958   *A Etnologia e a Sociologia no Brasil.* São Paulo: Editôra
           Anhembi.

FERREIRA, Inacio
196-   *A religião do índio brasileiro.* São Paulo: Lake. 60 pp.

_____

* The date on the cover is 1963, but the *Revista* actually appeared in 1965.

FERREIRA, Manoel Rodrigues
1951   *Cenas da vida indígena; album dos índios do Xingu.* São Paulo: Ediçoes Melhoramentos. 52 pp.

FOCK, Niels
1960   "South American Birth Customs in Theory and Practice." *Folk: Dansk Etnografisk Forening* 2, 51-69. Copenhagen: Danish Ethnographical Association.

FRIKEL, Protásio
1958   "Classificação Linguístico-Etnologicas das tribos indigenas do Pará Setentrional e zonas adjacentes." *Revista de Antropologia,* VI, 113-88.
1959   "Agricultura dos índios mundurukú." *Boletim do Museu Paraense Emílio Goeldi,* Nova Série [Antropologia] 4. Belém. 35 pp.
1960   "Os Tiriyó." *Boletim do Museu Paraense Emílio Goeldi,* Nova Série [Antropologia] 9. Belém.
1961   "Morí—a festa do rapé; indios Kachúyana: Rio Trombetas." *Boletim do Museu Paraense Emílio Goeldi,* Nova Série [Antropologia] 12. Belém. 34 pp.
1963*   "Notas sobre a situação atual dos índios Xikrin do Rio Caetetê. *Revista do Museu Paulista,* Nova Série 9, 145-158. São Paulo.

GALVÃO, Eduardo Eneas
1952   *The Religion of an Amazon Community: A Study in Culture Change.* Ann Arbor: University Microfilms Publi. No. 3884.
1953   "Cultura e sistema de parentesco das tribos do alto rio Xingu." *Boletim do Museu Nacional,* Nova Série [Antropologia] XIV. Rio de Janeiro.
1955   "Santos e Visagems: um estudo da vida religiosa de Ita, Amazonas." *Brasiliana,* 284. (Bibliotecha pedagogica brasileira, series 5). São Paulo: Compania Editoria Nacional.
1959   "Aculturação indígena no Rio Negro." *Boletim do Museu Paraense Emílio Goeldi,* Nova Série [Antropologia] 7. Belém. 60 pp.
1960   "Áreas culturais indígenas do Brasil: 1900-1959." *Boletim do Museu Paraense Emílio Goeldi,* Nova Série [Antropologia] 8, 1-41. Belém. Conselho Nacional de Pesquisas, Instituto

---

* The date on the cover is 1963, but the *Revista* actually appeared in 1965.

Nacional de Pesquisas da Amazõnia. (Paper presented at IV Reunião Brasileira de Antropologia, Julho de 1959, Curitiba.)

1962   "Encontro de sociedades tribal e nacional no Rio Negro, Amazonas." *Congresso Internacional de Americanistas, Actas y Memorias,* 1964, XXXV (3), 329-340. Mexico, D.F.

1963*a   "A Etnologia Brasileira nos últimas anos." *Revista do Museu Paulista,* Nova Série 9, 38-44. São Paulo.

1963*b   "Elementos básicos da horticultura de subsisténcia indígena." *Revista do Museu Paulista,* Nova Série 9, 120-144. São Paulo.

1963*c   "O cavalo na América indígena." *Revista do Museu Paulista,* Nova Série 9, 221-232. São Paulo.

GALVÃO, Eduardo Eneas and Mário F. SIMOES

1965   "Notícia sobre os índios txikao, Alto Xingu." *Boletim do Museu Paraense Emílio Goeldi,* Nova Série [Antropologia] 24, 23 pp. Belém.

GOLDMAN, I.

1963   *The Cubeo: Indians of the Northwest Amazon.* Urbana: University of Illinois Press. 305 pp.

GREENBERG, Joseph

1960   "The General Classification of Central and South American Languages," *Selected Papers, International Congress of Anthropological and Ethnological Sciences,* Philadelphia. pp. 791-94.

HENFREY, Colin

1964   *The Gentle People. A Journey among the Indian Tribes of Guiana.* London: Hutchinson. 265 pp.

1965   *Through Indian Eyes. A Journey among the Indian Tribes of Guiana.* New York: Holt, Rinehart and Winston. 286 pp. [Same as 1964 edition.]

HENRY, Jules

1941   *Jungle People: A Kaingáng Tribe of the Highlands of Brazil.* New York: J. J. Augustin. 215 pp.

HOHENTHAL, W. D., Jr.

1960   "As tribos indígenas do médio e baixo São Francisco." *Revista do Museu Paulista,* Nova Série XII, 31-71. São Paulo.

_____

* The date on the cover is 1963, but the *Revista* actually appeared in 1965.

HUXLEY, Francis
1957   *Affable Savages: An Anthropologist among the Urubu Indians of Brazil.* New York: Viking Press. 285 pp.

HYE-KERKDAL, Kathe
1958   "Tanz als Soziale Funktion bei den Timbira Brasileira." *Proceedings of the International Congress of Americanists* XXXII, 263-70.

KIEMEN, Mathias C.
1954   *The Indian Policy of Portugal in the Amazon Region, 1614-1693.* Washington: Catholic University of America Press. 228 pp.

LAMBERT, Paul
1964   *Fraternelle Amazonia.* Paris: R. Laffont. 299 pp.

LANE, Frederico
1955   "The Pellet-Bow among South American Indians." *Proceedings of the International Congress of Americanists* XXXI (1), 257-66.

LÉVI-STRAUSS, Claude
1956   "Les organisations dualistes existent-elles?" *Bijdragen tot de Taal-Land-en Volkenkunde van Nederlandsch-Indie.* 101-28. 's Gravenhage.
1961   *Tristes Tropiques.* John Russel, Trans. New York: Criterion Books. 1st American printing. 404 pp.

LOMMEL, A. Heg.
1960   *Indianer vom Amazonas.* Kat. Mchn.: [pub. unknown].

LUKESCH, Anton
1962   "Beiträge zur Weltanschauung der Kayapó." *Internationalen Amerikanisten Kongress* XXXIV, 629-36. Vienna, 1960.
1964   "Religionsbuch der Kayapo-Indianer. Beitrag zur Akkomodation und Akkulturation bei Naturvölkern." In *St. Gabrier Studien* 18. Mödling. 250 pp.

MacDONALD, J. Frederick
1965   "Some Considerations about Tupi-Guarani Kinship Structures." *Boletim do Museu Paraense Emílio Goeldi,* Nova Série [Antropologia] 26. 20 pp. Belém.

MAGALHAES RUBINGER, Marcos
1963* "O desaparecimento das tribos indígenas em Minas Gerais e a sobre-vivencia dos índios Maxakali." *Revista do Museu Paulista,* Nova Série 9, 233-262. São Paulo.

MALCHER, José Maria da Gama
1958 *Tribos da Area Amazónica.* Belém: SPVEA, Sector de Coordinação e Divulgação.
1964 *Indios: Grau de integração na comunidade nacional; groupo linguístico; localização.* Nova Série, Publicação no. 1. Rio de Janeiro: Ministerio da Agricultura Conselho Nacional de Proteção aos Indios.

MAYBURY-LEWIS, David
1956 "Kinship and Social Organization in Central Brazil." *Pro-*
(1958) *ceedings of the Thirty-Second International Congress of Americanists.* 123-35. Copenhagen.
1960 "Parallel Descent and the Apinayé Anomaly." *Southwestern Journal of Anthropology* XVI, 191-216.
1965a "Some Crucial Distinctions in Central Brazilian Ethnology." *Anthropos* 60(1-6), 340-358. Fribourg.
1965b *The Savage and the Innocent.* London: Evans Brothers Ltd. 270 pp.
1967 *Akwē-Shavante Society.* Oxford: Clarendon Press. 356 pp.

MAYBURY-LEWIS, Pia
1956 "Diet and Health in an Acculturated Tribe." *Proceedings of the International Congress of Americanists* XXXII, 190-97.

MENEZES, Cinira Miranda de
1953 "O psico-diagnostico miocinetico aplicado a indios Kaingang." *Revista do Museu Paulista,* Nova Série VII, 343-56. São Paulo.

MÉTRAUX, Alfred
1942 *The Native Tribes of Eastern Bolivia & Western Matto-Grosso.* Washington, D.C.: Smithsonian Institution, Bureau of American Ethnology Bulletin No. 134. 182 pp.
1962 "Disparition des Indiens das le Brésil central." *Bulletin of the International Committee on Urgent Anthropological and Ethnological Research* 5. 126-131.

---

* The date on the cover is 1963, but the *Revista* actually appeared in 1965.

MÉTRAUX, Alfred and Simone DREYFUS-ROCHE
1958   "La Naissance et la Première Enfance chez les Indiens Cayapo du Xingu." *International Congress of Americanists* II, 363-78. México, D.F.

MOREIRA NETO, Carlos de Araújo
1959   "Relatorio sobre a situação atual dos índios kayapo." *Revista de Antropologia* VII, 49-64.

MOURA, José de
1960   "Os Münkü: Contribuição ao estudo da tribo Iranche." *Pesquisas* [Antropologia] 10. Pôrto Alegre: Anuário do Instituto Anchietano de Pesquisas. 59 pp.

MURPHY, Robert Francis
1955   *The Trumaí Indians of Central Brazil.* New York: J. J. Augustin. 108 pp.
1956   "Mundurukú Ethics." *Encyclopedia of Morals.* New York: Philosophical Library, 682.
1957   "Intergroup Hostility and Social Cohesion." *American Anthropologist* LIX, 1018-35. Menasha.
1958   *Mundurucú Religion.* University of California: Publications in American Archaeology and Ethnology. 159 pp.
1960   *Headhunters Heritage.* Berkeley and Los Angeles: University of California Press. 202 pp.

NIMUENDAJÚ, Curt
1962   *The Tukuna.* William D. Hohenthal, Trans. Berkeley and Los Angeles: University of California Press. 167 pp.
1965   "The Serente." In *Publications of the F. Webb Hodge Anniversary Publ. Fund.* IV new edition. Los Angeles. 106 pp.

OBERG, Kalervo
1953   *Indian Tribes of Northern Mato Grosso, Brazil.* Publication No. 15, Social Anthropology. Washington, D.C.: Smithsonian Institution.

PIERSON, Donald and Mario Wagner Viera da CUNHA
1947   "Research and Research Possibilities in Brazil with Particular Reference to Culture and Culture Change." *Acta americana* 5 (1, 2), 19-82. [Interamerican Society for Anthropology and Geography, Washington.] Ceased publication in 1948.

PINTO, Estevão
1957/58 "Introdução á história da antropologia indígena no Brasil, século XVI." *América Indígena,* Part I: 17(4), 341-85; Part II: 18(1), 17-49. Mexico, D.F.: Instituto Indigenista Interamericano.

PIRES PINTO, Odorico
1955   "Arte primitiva brasileira." *Revista do Arquivo Municipal,* CLVIII, 7-248. São Paulo.

POURCHET, Maria Júlia
1960   "Os Kaingáng do Paraná, Brasil." *Bulletin of the International Committee on Urgent Anthropological and Ethnological Research* 3. 78-80.

QUAIN, Buell
        See Robert Francis Murphy

RAMOS, Arthur
1944   *Las poblaciones del Brasil.* Mexico: Fondo de cultura económica.

RIBEIRO, Berta G.
1957   "Bases para uma classificação dos adornos plumarios dos índios do Brasil." *Arquivos do Museu Nacional* XLIII. 59-119. Rio de Janeiro.

RIBEIRO, Darcy
1950   *Religião e Mitologia Kadiuéu.* Serviço de Proteção aos Indios Publição n.° 106. Rio de Janeiro: Ministerio da Agricultura, Conselho Nacional de Proteção dos Indios. 222 pp.
1957a   "The Tasks of the Ethnologist and the Linguist in Brazil." *International Social Science Bulletin* 9, 298-3080.
1957b   "Culturas e Linguas Indigenas do Brasil." *Educação e Ciências Sociais,* Vol. 2, n.° 6, Rio de Janeiro.
1957c   "Uira vai ao encontro de Maira." *Anais II Reunião Brasileira de Antropologia,* 17-28. Salvador.
1958   *O indigenista Rondon.* Rio de Janeiro: Ministério da Educação e Cultura, Serviço de Documentação. 75 pp.
1962   *A Política Indigenista Brasileira.* Rio de Janeiro: Ministerio da Agricultura Serviço de Informação o Agricola (Atualidade Agrâria, 1), 178 pp.

RIBEIRO, José
1963   *O jogo dos Buzios e as grandes ceremonias ocultas da Umbanda.* Rio de Janeiro: [pub. unknown]. 137 pp.

RONDON, Candido Mariano da Silva
1946   *Indios do Brasil.* Rio de Janeiro: Conselho Nacional de Proteção aos Indios, Ministério da Agricultura.

SAAKE, Wilhelm
1959   "Iniciação de um pagé entre os baneiva e a cura do 'maracaimbara'." *Sociologia* (Oct.), 434-42. São Paulo: Fundação Escola de Sociologia e Política de São Paulo.

SCHADEN, Egon
1954   "Aspectos fundamentais da cultura guarani." *Boletim, Etnografia e Tupi-Guarani* IV. São Paulo: Universidade de São Paulo, Faculdade de Filosofia, Ciências e Letras. 216 pp.
1955   "Problemas fundamentais e estado atual das pesquisas sôbre índios do Brasil." *America Indígena* XV, 43-55. Mexico, D.F.: Instituto Indigenista Interamericano.
1958   "Desenho e arte ornamental dos indios brasileiros." *Boletim de Psicologia* X (XXXV-XXXVI), 41-51. São Paulo.
1962   *Aspectos fundamentais da cultura guaraní.* São Paulo: Difusão Européia do Livro. 190 pp.
1963*   "Estudos de acultaração indígena." *Revista do Museu Paulista,* Nova Série 9, 263-268. São Paulo.

SCHÖMIG, Immina
1956   "Sonderbauten Südamerikanischer Naturvölker." *Baessler-Archiv.* Berlin, Leipzig.

SCHULTZ, Harald
1953   "A pesca tradicional do pirarucu entre os índios karaja." *Revista do Museu Paulista,* Nova Série VII, 249-55. São Paulo.
1962   *Hombu: Indian Life in the Brazilian Jungle.* New York: Macmillan. 32 pp.

SEBAG, Lucien
        See Pierre Clastres

SICK, Helmut
1960   *Tukani.* R. H. Stevens, Trans. New York: Eriksson-Taphinger Co. 240 pp. (First published in English in 1959 by Burke Publishing Company, Ltd.)

---

* The date on the cover is 1963, but the *Revista* actually appeared in 1965.

SILVA, P. Alcionilio Bruzzi Alves da
1962   *A Civilização Indígena do Uallpés.* São Paulo: Centro de
         Pesquisas de Lauarete Missão. Salcisiana do Rio Negro,
         Amazonas. Brazil.

SIMOES, Mário F.
1963*   "Os Txikão e outras tribos marginais do Alto Xingu." *Re-
         vista do Museu Paulista,* Nova Série 9, 76-104. São Paulo.
         See also Eduardo Galvão.

SOUSA, Cícero Christiano de
1953   "Ometodo de Rorschach aplicado a um groupo de índios
         Kaingang." *Revista do Museu Paulista,* Nova Série VII, 311-
         41. São Paulo.

STEWARD, Julian H., Ed.
1946-   *Handbook of South American Indians.* Smithsonian Institu-
1963   tion: Bureau of American Ethnology, Bulletin 143. Washing-
         ton, D.C.: U.S. Government Printing Office. Vols. I-VI.

VELLARD, Jehan A.
1941   "Les Poisons de Pêche de l'Amerique du Sud." *Revista del
         Instituto de Antropologia de Tucumán,* 11:5, 81-106.
1942   "Poisons de Pêche e Poisons de Chasse." *Boletim do Museu
         Nacional* [Antropologia], XIV/XVII (1938/1941), 345-62.

WAGLEY, Charles
1955   "Tapirapé Social and Culture Change 1940-1953." *Proceed-
         ings of the International Congress of Americanists* XXXI (i),
         99-106.
1960   "Champukwi of the Village of the Tapirs." In *In the Com-
         pany of Man. Twenty Portraits by Anthropologists.* Joseph
         B. Casagrande, Ed. New York: Harper and Brothers. 397-415.

WAGLEY, Charles and Eduardo Eneas GALVÃO
1949   *The Tenetehara Indians of Brazil.* New York: Columbia Uni-
         versity Contributions to Anthropology No. 35, Columbia
         University Press. 200 pp.
1955   *Os Índios Tenetehara: uma cultura em transição.* Rio de
         Janeiro: Ministerio da Educação e Cultura. 235 pp. [This is
         the Portuguese edition of *The Tenetehara Indians of Brazil*
         (1949). It includes an appendix which systematically de-

---

* The date on the cover is 1963, but the *Revista* actually appeared in 1965.

scribes and details the principal elements of the material culture of the Tenetehara, filling a gap not handled in the English edition.—Ed.]

WASSEN, S. Henry
1965   "The Use of Some Specific Kinds of South American Indian Snuff and Related Paraphanalia." *Ethnological Studies* 28. Göteborg: Etnografiska Museet. 132 pp. With appendix by Georg J. Seitz.

WATSON, Virginia
1955   "An Ethnographic Account of Contemporary Cayua Indian Architecture." *Revista do Museu Paulista,* Nova Série IX, 235-45. São Paulo.

WELTFISH, Gene
1963   *The Origins of Art.* Indianapolis: Bobbs-Merrill.

WIESEMANN, Ursula
1964   "Children of Mixed Marriages in relation to Kaingáng Society." *Revista do Museu Paulista,* Nova Série, XV, 315-318.

ZERRIES, Otto
1951   "Wildgeistvorstellungen in Sudamerika." *Anthropos* XLVI, 140-60. Mödling/Wien.
1955   "Krankenheitsdaemonen und Hilfsgeister des Medizinmannes in Süd-Amerika." *International Congress of Americanists* XXX, 162-78.

Periodicals

América Indígena. 1960 passim. Mexico, D.F.: Instituto Indigenista Interamericano.

Arquivos do Instituto de Antropologia. 1 (2). December 1964. Natal, Univ. do Rio Grande do Norte, Instituto de Antropologia.

Boletim de Antropologia. Ano 1 (1). 1957. Fortaleza.

Latin American Research Review. Austin: The University of Texas. Published in February, June, and October beginning in Fall, 1965.

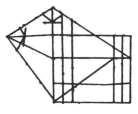
The Symbol is adapted from
the devices used by
Micronesians to teach navigation
in the western Pacific.

The type face used in this book is 10 point Optima
with a 2 point leading and was set by Trade Typographers, Inc.,
of Washington, D. C. It was printed by the offset lithograph process
on Mead Suede Book Substance 70.

E. Smith Associates, Washington, D. C., designed and illustrated the book and
prepared it for printing.

DATE DUE

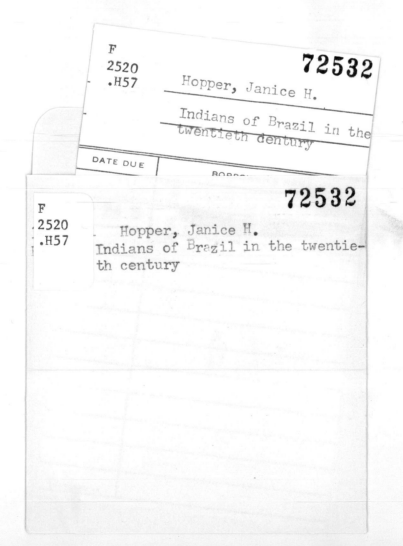

F
2520
.H57   **72532**

　　　　Hopper, Janice H.

　　　　Indians of Brazil in the
　　　　twentieth century

DATE DUE   BORRO

72532

F
.2520
.H57   Hopper, Janice H.
           Indians of Brazil in the twentie-
           th century